# AUSSIE MIGRANT: JOBS

## A Migrant's Essential Guide to Employment in Australia

MIGRANT NINJA
—— MASTERING THE MOVE ——

## THE MIGRANT NINJA SERIES © 2015

All Rights Reserved.

An © Evolving Wordsmith Product

www.aussie-migrant.com.au

# Praise for the Migrant Ninja Series

"Congratulations. We are so fortunate that Jason has shared his considerable experience, deep knowledge and careful research to provide such a comprehensive guide for incoming new Australians. He is gifted with the capacity to write in such a way that it is clear to read and easy to follow. His use of experienced career development practitioners to assist him means that the book addresses all the major issues surrounding career development and employment in a very professional manner. I recommend the book as an extremely useful and valuable resource to those new to Australia and those already in Australia who are finding it difficult to make career progress in a complex and challenging environment." – *COL McCOWAN, OAM is a registered psychologist, teacher and counsellor who worked for State Government for over 20 years in areas related to career guidance. He also led national and international-level career-related activities and was the Manager for over 15 years of the highly successful Careers & Employment service at the Queensland University of Technology.*

"A very well written and comprehensive book for migrant job seekers arriving in Australia. It took me back to my initial days of looking for a job! The information and content are extremely well structured in its flow covering questions that any new migrant may have in relation to securing a job in Australia. I wish I had this kind of information at my disposal when I first migrated to Australia, as it would have made job seeking so much easier. I highly recommend this book to any migrant who wishes to maximise their chances of securing a job in the shortest time possible in OZ" – *PAVITRA RAVISHANKAR. Migrated from India in 2011.*

"I never knew moving to Australia was so challenging. The information and guidance within this book is priceless and so much more than a simple 'How To'. Put together with such love and care by Jason - and it shows throughout. I believe this is a 'must read' for anyone looking to make the journey and I wish you well in your adventure." - *JAMES "The Jobs Guru" INNES is the Founder and Chairman of The CV Centre & The Resume Center - the world's leading CV and Resume consultancies. He is also the author of five best-selling careers books. His current works are: 'The Interview Book', 'The Interview Question & Answer Book', 'The CV Book', 'The Cover Letter Book' and 'Ultimate New Job'.*

"As a recently arrived migrant, I now know first-hand the challenges of getting a job in Australia. This book is the most comprehensive book that is specifically written for migrants. You will be surprised to know the differences of job hunting in Australia and this book will lay a good foundation to begin with. Written in collaboration with experts this book is a must have!" – *SANDESH REGO*. *Migrated from Dubai, 2016.*

## Praise for Aussie Migrant: Money

"Aussie Migrant: Money covers every financial possibility a migrant travelling to Australia will encounter. Insurance, interest, taxation,superannuation, banking, exchange rates, credit cards, debit cards, renting prices, suburb costs, paychecks, income expectancy; a wealth of information obtainable in one place. It's important to familiarise yourself with Australian economic practices and procedures, or you could find yourself in an uncomfortable situation. It's also a good idea to make sure you have plentiful funds on arrival, as it may take a while to find a job if you don't already have one lined up. Are you adequately prepared? In these pages, you will find out." - *FRED SCHEBESTA*. *Director and CoFounder of finder.com.au and credticardfinder.com.au*

'A well researched, comprehensive guide to migration to Australia albeit with an Asian slant. A lot of information provided over a range of topics which will no doubt respond to many unspoken queries . I especially like the Ninja Tips which add to its value." - **PRIA D'SOUZA**, Migrant from Mumbai, India 2002.

"Very precise and detailed information, put together in a way that holds ones interest. Discusses good amount of co-related topics and points revolving around the more crucial and well defined basic topics. Provides great number of resources and links for research. Covers vast amount of info, spread over numerous sources and consolidates into one quick helpful guide for both future migrants as well as migrants already in Australia." - *NIZEL DSOUZA*, Sydney, Class 457 Visa, 2010

"Would recommend to everyone, not just migrants." - **MELISSA**, Senior Amazon Reviewer. 18.May.2016

"I am not a migrant myself, but my wife has migrated to Australia several years ago. The information in this book would have been very helpful to her when she moved. It is very nice to see someone has written a book on migrating to Australia. I would recommend it to anyone who is moving, or thinking about moving to Australia from anywhere in the world. It even helped me understand some things about money that I was unsure about, and I was born here! The

Ninja tips are helpful and point out some practical tips and the Links to the various websites gave me a quick way to read more about a topic." - *AMAZON Customer*. *18.May.2016*

# COPYRIGHT

Published by Evolving Wordsmith 2016

Copyright © 2015 Evolving Wordsmith

A MIGRANT NINJA SERIES

This guide is edited in Australian English.

www.aussie-migrant.com.au

An Evolving Wordsmith Product

ABN – 16289739160

ISBN - 978-0-9945674-1-3 (Print Edition)

ISBN - 978-0-9945674-0-6 (eBook Edition)

## DISCLAIMER

Most of the information provided has been obtained from official sources and from fellow migrants who have shared their own personal experiences. Due to the transient nature of visa procedures and job markets, the information provided may have been affected, therefore, it is highly recommended that you do your own research and follow the links provided wherever possible to obtain latest updates.

For readers who have purchased the physical copy, you can find all the links as an appendix at the back of the book. These links are also available  online - Aussie Migrants/Jobs/Links. These links are arranged chapter-wise just as they appear in the book for ease of reference.

For readers who have opted for the digital version, the links are embedded in the content throughout the book. In case some of the website links do not work (due to updated links or various other reasons) you can get the latest updated links on my website on the same page as mentioned above.

# Aussie Migrant: JOBS

## Table of Contents

# 1. Foreword

Moving to a new country is such a mixture of excited anticipation and nervous apprehension. If you are coming to Australia to live, you are welcome! We have so much to share with you: natural beauty; plenty of space; and a friendly, egalitarian society. Australia is a wonderful place to live, and as a nation, we have a proud history of welcoming migrants to come here and work side-by-side with us.

Some are lured to Australia by the promise of high wages, and it is true that our wages are higher than most. However, this is offset by the cost of living here: Australia is a very expensive place to live. So, you will need to find paid work if you intend to stay. Therefore, getting a job will be a priority for you.

For those lucky enough to be sponsored or supported by local employers, the migration process is as easy as arranging all the logistics of relocation. But others will need to find a job in this country themselves, and job search in a new country can be bewildering and frustrating. In order to be successful, you will need to learn about the Australian workplace culture; the local job market and how it works; and the best ways to market yourself to Australian employers. You can be sure all of these things will be different here from what you are used to in your home country.

What a gem of a book is **Aussie Migrant: JOBS**! It is packed with useful information about visa conditions and working rights, current labour market trends, and recognition of qualifications. It offers practical tips and good advice on job search and self-marketing strategies. And it provides a valuable guide to understanding the workplace culture in this country, as well as your rights as a worker. Jason has partnered with some genuine experts, ranging from professional resume writers to career development practitioners who specialise in working with migrants, to ensure the information and guidance provided here is of a very high standard. I congratulate Jason on producing such a useful resource.

As you read through the book, you will discover there is much for you to learn about your new country. For the past 27 years, I have worked in roles where I have been providing career coaching, advice and guidance to job seekers of all ages; and I have learned about the challenges they face and the best ways to meet those challenges. So, let me offer you some tips of my own, based on what I have learned from the thousands of job seekers I have helped over the years.

## 1. Get connected

Perhaps, the biggest challenge for new migrants who are looking for a job in Australia is the fact that so many of our jobs are obtained through professional and personal connections. For someone new to this country, perhaps, the most valuable thing you can do is work hard to build those connections as quickly as possible. There is a saying here that is very relevant to those who are trying to find a job: "It's not what you know – it's who you know (that matters most)!" In Australia, being connected with people in your profession or industry, and being known by others as someone who is smart, reliable and easy to get along with is almost as important as your formal qualifications. The friends you make here will be a very important part of your job search: they will help you understand Australian culture; they will help you practice your Australian English; and they will connect you with their own networks whenever they can.

## 2. Look for pathways

Migrants are well-placed to take advantage of our increasingly flexible and transient workforce. Project work and temporary roles are available in many fields of work and are a great way for you to demonstrate your value to potential employers while getting some local experience at the same time. Don't be afraid to take on roles like this, if you can get them while you are looking for that big break. They are usually more useful to you in the long run than the kind of interim jobs that many migrants take on, just to get some money coming in. While it's relatively easy to get a job as a cleaner or a taxi driver, it's also easy to get stuck in those jobs. So, look for pathway jobs that are related to your areas of expertise: take on an assistant role if your professional qualifications are not recognised here, or offer to contribute to a project that will give you a chance to show how valuable your knowledge and skills are. Once others see what you can do, they will be able to help you find a more permanent job.

## 3. Focus on outcomes

It will be what you can deliver that will persuade an employer to hire you. Employers want to know what you can do for them, so when you brush up your resume, and when you are talking to potential employers, make sure you highlight the outcomes you have produced in your previous jobs. They may not know your previous employer, and they may not recognise your qualification, but the language of results is universal. If you can tell a potential employer how you have made things better, happier, safer, more profitable or more efficient for your employer or your customers in the past, they will clearly understand the value you offer.

But if I could only give you one tip, it would be to ask for and accept help. It's a big challenge to master a new workplace culture and sell yourself to employers in an entirely new job market. Don't be afraid to seek help. This book is a wonderful start: it truly is a comprehensive guide for new migrants to Australia, and you will find it invaluable, as you navigate the Aussie job market.

I wish you well, as you adjust to life here in Australia. And most of all, I wish you good fortune in your job search!

Mrs Wanda Hayes
National Vice President
Career Development Association of Australia Inc.
Level 1, 18-20 Grenfell Street, Adelaide, 5000
Phone: 08 8211 6961 / Website: www.cdaa.org.au

## 2. Introductory Note

The Great Australian Dream! A large house with a spacious backyard. A modern pool with an impressive Barbeque area. Children playing with a big shaggy-maned dog on the lawn. Smiling neighbours. Gleaming cars. A millionaire lifestyle. Isn't this what comes to mind when you think of migrating to Australia and living this Dream?

Two things stand in your way, though. The first and most obvious one is the very stringent Visa Grant process for skilled migrants. The second step, which is not that obvious and one which is seldom addressed by anyone selling you this Dream, is the ability to be gainfully employed in your own profession at a similar level you have been used to in your home country.

It is said that numbers don't lie. Here are some numbers for you:

- According to a new report by finder.com.au, landing a job is the most difficult part about living in Australia. In fact, almost half (45 percent) of 1000 survey respondents said securing a job was the toughest thing about moving here.
- In one report by Scanlon Found, many migrants arriving on Independent Skilled Visas say they struggle to find work and nearly half indicate they are "just getting along" or struggling to pay bills. Just 36 percent indicated they were employed, while 20 percent were looking for work and the remaining 44 percent were not in the workforce.

- Australian unemployment rate in November 2016 stood at 5.6%.

- For the year 2015-2016, the Permanent Migration Programme and Child outcome visas issued were 189,770. Of this number, 128,550 were from the Skill Stream Visas.

- As at 30 September 2016, the size of the subclass 457 programme has decreased when compared with the same period last programme year. Primary 457 applications granted - 13,239.

- There are presently 103,862 Primary 457 visa holders in Australia and these numbers are predicted to decline as the government puts stricter measures on the grant of this visa.

- Most of the resumes are glanced over within 6 to 10 seconds? Resumes in Australia are markedly different from the one you are probably accustomed to. What do you think your chances are to be noticed?

Lack of Australian experience is actually the biggest barrier any newcomer will face. Poorly written resumes from overseas professionals may fuel employer's doubts about communication. This makes it harder for employers to assess overseas experience. Broadly speaking, Australians are not biased against skilled migrants. When it comes to hiring migrants, Australian employers are just risk-averse.

For the first time ever, you now have a book that addresses all the issues every job-seeking migrant may encounter in Australia. This book is a result of years of research and has the tremendous backing of industry experts, from Resume Writers to Career guidance coaches. This wealth of information located in one convenient location is aimed to put you in the driver's seat as you start your life in Australia.

**How Did the Book Come About?**

A migrant myself, I moved to Australia, along with my wife, on a Permanent Residency visa (Visa Subclass 189) in 2014. During the initial visa application phase, the actual transition to this great country, and during the initial years of settling down, we had our fair share of doubts and queries. As with most migrants, we were excited to make the move as soon as we were granted our visas and to finally live the Big Australian Dream. The one thing we did not factor in was the time it took for us to get our first job in Australia and the insecurity we had to face during that period!

Getting a job is one of the most crucial milestones in every migrant's journey to a new country. A majority of the migrants arriving on a Permanent Resident visa will probably be on the SOL or CSOL and have their skills assessed as a part of their eligibility requirements. One would then safely assume that the relevant industry will have ample job opportunities when the migrant arrives. The ground reality, however, is a lot different.

Unless you are one of the fortunate ones who has got a placement before you have even landed in Australia or if you are in a booming industry which is seeking professionals with niche skill sets, your first big break in Australia may take a while.

It is not all gloom and doom, though. Australian employers are always looking for the best and brightest skilled worker migrants. In 4 years, the prediction is that Australia will need 2.4 million skilled worker immigrants. Why is the demand so great? Australia's workforce is ageing, with over one-quarter of the Australian population aged over 65. By 2020, it is expected that the intake of skilled migrants will rise to 5.2 million. Researchers highlight some of the positives of employing migrants. They are less likely to change jobs as compared to an Australian employee; they have a great work ethic and less baggage from their background. They bring new skills not available in Australia and support Australia's international operations with their knowledge and language skills.

Most migrants in Australia display a positive attitude to life in Australia and high levels of identification with the country. Over 80 percent indicated they are quite satisfied with their lives in Australia. Despite the various challenges faced, Australia remains a good country for immigrants.

The question now remains, how do you get your foot in the door? This book is an attempt to provide the reader with ample tools and resources to help you jump the employment queue and get your dream job in the shortest time possible.

This Book has been created with the help and support of industry experts who are also leaders in their respective field. The chapters on Resume Writing and Selection Process have been written almost exclusively by such experts and I am sure the reader will benefit immensely from their expertise. There is a wealth of information derived as a result of in-depth research online, as well as practical tips gained from fellow migrants who have paved the way for us. Bear in mind though that you may find some minor differences in the formats as far as Resume and Cover Letter layouts are concerned. Just as no two migrants can have the same profile and no two jobs can be the same, similarly, every resume and cover letter will differ based on the specific job requirement. The reader is urged to familiarise himself with all the formats and styles presented in this book and then choose the one that fits him best, based on the industry and position applied for.

**Some of the topics covered in this book are:**

Visa Specific Work Restrictions and Conditions

Overseas Skills Assessment

Average Wages

Contacting Prospective Employers

Golden Rules for Job Hunting

Tapping the Hidden Market

Job Market Demographics

Importance of a Professional Online Profile

Getting the elusive 'Australian' Experience

Writing a winning 'Australia Ready' Resume

Addressing Selection Criteria

Interview Process and tips from Experts

The **STAR** Format of answering Interview Questions

Different types of Employment

Employment Contract

Workplace Etiquettes

Support for Job Seekers

Government Initiatives for Jobseekers

Interview Preparation

Challenging Interview Questions & How to Answer Them

Additionally, there are some Sample Resumes and Cover Letters to help you get started and Chapter 11 has over 180 usable Website Links all in one convenient location. These include state-wise break up of industry related links, government job sites, a list of recruitment companies, information websites and a comprehensive list of the major job portals in Australia.

As Benjamin Franklin once famously said: *"By failing to prepare, you are preparing to fail."*

Be prepared for the job hunt. Be alert for every opportunity. Be ready to face the challenges that come your way. I'm sure in time, like most of the skilled migrant, your very own Australian Dream will someday come true!

**Additional Note**: "Business Card on Steroids". That is how someone recently referred to this book. According to her, the book appears to promote career guidance counsellors, resume writers and the likes. Let me go ahead and address this at the very start of the book. I am a migrant same as you. I am not affiliated with any of the companies mentioned nor do I get any commission for 'promoting' their businesses. Most of the business interests that have been mentioned in the book have either contributed invaluable content freely to this book or I have got their names during the course of my research. Put plainly, my intention here is to provide you, the reader, with as much information as I can so that you may benefit from it.

Additionally, it is noteworthy to mention that investing in a Career guidance counsellor at the onset is one of the wisest investments you can make when you migrate to Australia. The cost of hiring one does seem prohibitive, but so did the visa fees when you put in your migration papers. The boost you may get when you hire one and their guidance at the initial stages of your job hunt may just make the difference in getting a job or going unemployed for a period.

You may want to just hire a resume writer or you may opt to connect only with a language and vocational expert. You may even decide to go ahead on your own steam. This book will surely be able to help you one way or the other.

However, as one of the industry experts rightly mentioned that getting employment in Australia, especially for newly arrived migrants is not based purely on the individual's educational qualifications, his past track records, his resume and cover letter or his performance in the interview. Rather, more often than not, it is the sum total of all these individual factors and therefore it is best to hire professional help who can provide all these services under one umbrella. The choice ultimately is yours!

# 3. The Basics

This Book is aimed at providing in-depth information to migrants who are moving to Australia on a visa which gives them working rights in the country. Hence, it is best to start at the very beginning by giving a summary of the various types of visas that fall under this category.

**Note** - This summary is not exhaustive and only meant to serve as an overview of migration categories with working rights. For more information, research and latest updates, visit the DIBP official website – www.border.gov.au

## General Skilled Migrant (GSM) Stream

For skilled migrants looking to work in Australia, the country offers them a myriad of visa opportunities based on their specific needs. Skilled migration visas offer the best opportunities for workers with specific skills to work and live in Australia. Skilled workers can use their qualifications, work experience and language skills to meet Australian requirements for a visa to work in the country.

MIGRANT NINJA TIP:

**Skill Select aims to ensure that Australia's skilled migration programme efficiently manages the country's specific economic needs at any given point in time.**

In 2012, the immigration authorities in Australia introduced a brand new program for skilled workers, known more commonly as SkillSelect. To apply, every person has to submit an Expression Of Interest (EOI). SkillSelect follows a two-step process to determine the skilled migration application through the online EOI submission. Once complete, an applicant will be invited to submit an application for an Australian visa based on their EOI.

***DID YOU KNOW:***

*Of people migrating to Australia, 68 per cent are skilled migrants and 32 per cent are from family visa streams. This is further broken down to:*

*Skill: 38 per cent employer-sponsored, 34 per cent skilled independent, 22 percent state, territory and regional nominated and 6 per cent business*

*Family: 79 per cent partner, 14 percent parent, 6 percent child and 1 percent other.*

**Different Visas for Living and Working in Australia**

Australia offers different visas for living and working in the country based on fulfilment of certain conditions. Here are some visa options for people looking to live, work and migrate to the country under the skilled migration stream:

## 3.1 Types of Visas – Skilled Migrants

## 3.1.1 Employer Sponsored Categories

### Temporary Work (Skilled) Visa (Subclass 457)

The temporary skilled work visa allows a skilled worker to work in their nominated occupation for an approved sponsor in Australia for up to four years. To be eligible for this visa, you must:

- Be nominated in an occupation on the consolidated skilled occupation list.
- Be sponsored by an approved business.
- Have the skills to fill the position of the approved business.
- Meet licensing and registration requirements.
- Speak vocational English.

The temporary work visa can only be given if the business cannot find an Australian permanent resident or citizen to the skilled job. With a temporary skilled work visa, you can:

- Live and work in Australia for four years.
- Bring your family to study or work.
- Travel to and from Australia without any limitation.

**MIGRANT NINJA TIP:**

**For a 457 Visa:**

- **There is no Medicare cover provided, so, you need private health insurance in Australia.**
- **Children born to you in Australia are entitled to a 457 visa, but they will not get Australian citizenship. If they are born outside Australia, you need to apply for a 457 visa for them.**
- **More details can be obtained from these links: DIBP Information on Temporary visa (subclass 457) and SUBCLASS 457 – A Quick Guide**

## Employer Nomination Scheme (ENS) Visa (Subclass 186)

The Employer Nomination Scheme (ENS) Visa (Subclass 186) is a permanent residency visa for skilled workers under the following streams:

**Direct Entry Stream** – This is for people who have briefly or never worked in Australia, but have been nominated by an approved employer.

**Agreement Stream** – This is for 457 visa holders who are sponsored through a labour agreement by an approved employer.

**Temporary Residence Transition Stream** – This is for 457 visa holders who have completed two years of working with a nominating employer in the same occupation. The employer must want to offer them a permanent job in this occupation to qualify.

This two-step visa requires a nomination from an approved employer in Australia, followed by the nominated stream application. This visa is applied for under the Permanent Employer Sponsored Visa programme and allows you to:

- Live, study and work in Australia.

- Enrol in Medicare.

- Apply for citizenship when eligible.

- Sponsor family members for permanent resident visas.

- Travel to and from Australia.

MIGRANT NINJA TIP:

- **You can apply for this visa from outside Australia. But if you are in the country, you must have a bridging visa A, B or C.**

- Even if you have a 457 visa, you cannot apply on your own. An approved employer must sponsor you to lodge a visa application under this category.
- More details can be obtained from this link: DIBP Information on ENS visa (subclass 186)

# Regional Sponsored Migration Scheme (RSMS) Visa (Subclass 187)

The Regional Sponsored Migration Scheme (RSMS) Visa (Subclass 187) is a permanent residency visa for skilled migrants who are sponsored by regional employers and wish to work in the regional parts of Australia under the following streams:

**Direct Entry Stream** – This is for people who have briefly or never worked in Australia, but have been nominated by an approved regional employer.

**Agreement Stream** – This is for 457 visa holders who are sponsored through a labour agreement by an approved employer.

**Temporary Residence Transition Stream** – This is for 457 visa holders who have completed two years of working with a nominating regional employer in the same occupation. The employer must want to offer them a permanent job in this occupation to qualify.

This two-step visa requires a nomination from an approved regional employer in Australia, followed by the nominated stream application. This visa is applied for under the Permanent Employer Sponsored Visa programme and allows you to:

- Live, study and work in regional Australia.

- Enrol in Medicare.

- Apply for citizenship when eligible.

- Sponsor family members for permanent resident visas.

- Travel to and from Australia.

MIGRANT NINJA TIP:

- **You can apply for this visa from outside Australia. But if you are in the country, you must have a bridging visa A, B or C or a substantive visa.**
- **Regional Australia excludes Brisbane, Sydney, Newcastle, Wollongong, the Gold Coast and Melbourne.**
- **More details can be obtained from the link: DIBP information on RSMS visa (subclass 187)**

## 3.1.2 Tested Skilled Migration

### Skilled Independent Visa (Subclass 189)

The Skilled Independent Visa (Subclass 189) is for skilled workers who aren't sponsored by employers or family members and are not nominated by a territory or state government. You can work in Australia as a permanent resident. To be eligible for this visa, you must:

- Be in a nominated occupation on the skilled occupation list.
- Receive a suitable skills assessment from a relevant Australian body.
- Achieve the minimum requisite points.

- Be under 50 years.
- Be competent in English through the exam.

You will need to submit and expression of interest and must be invited to apply for the visa through Skill Select. The 189 visa allows you to:

- Live, study and work in Australia indefinitely.
- Enrol in Medicare, the healthcare scheme for residents.
- Apply for citizenship when you are eligible.
- Sponsor relatives for permanent residency.
- Travel to and from Australia.

MIGRANT NINJA TIP:

**More details can be obtained from this link:  DIBP Information on visa subclass 189**

**You can apply for Australian residency after spending 4 years living and working in the country, including 1 year as a permanent resident holder.**

**More information is available on the Citizenship web page.**

## Skilled State-Sponsored Visa (Subclass 190)

The skilled state-sponsored visa (subclass 190) is a points-tested visa for skilled workers who are nominated by a territory or state government. This visa allows you to work and live in Australia as a permanent resident. To be eligible for this visa, you must:

- Be invited to apply.
- Be nominated for a job on the consolidated skilled occupation list

- Have received a skills assessment for the occupation.
- Be under 50 years.
- Have the same score as your letter of invitation specification.
- Have competent English skills.

After you submit an expression of interest for this visa, you will then be invited to apply for it through Skill Select. The PR 190 visa allows you to:

- Live, study and work in Australia indefinitely.
- Enrol in Medicare.
- Apply for Australian citizenship when eligible.
- Sponsor relatives for permanent residency.
- Travel to and from Australia.

Before you apply, state and territory government agencies will decide whether to nominate you after checking your expression of interest. Every state or territory has an occupation list to guide the skills they need. In your expression of interest, you can indicate any preferences or you can be available to all. If you accept a state nomination, you must:

- Live in the nominated state or territory for a minimum specified time.
- Inform the state or territory of your address before and after your arrival in Australia.
- Meet any state requirements as specified.

You must comply with Australian laws and your visa conditions specified by the state or territory government.

**For Subclass 190 Visa:**

- **You must spend 2 years in your nominated state within your permanent residency period.**

**More details can be obtained from this link:** <u>DIBP Information on visa subclass 190</u>

# Skilled Regional (Provisional) Visa (Subclass 489), Sponsored

This visa allows skilled workers to work and live in regional parts of Australia for a period up to four years. To be eligible for this visa, you must:

- Be sponsored by a relative lived in a specific designated area.
- Be nominated in an occupation on the skilled occupations list.
- Have had a suitable skills assessment.
- Be under 50 years.
- Achieve the points indicated in your letter of invitation.

This visa allows you to live, study and work in Australia for up to 4 years. You can also travel in and out of the country during the period of your visa. To stay for longer, you will need to apply for a Skilled Regional (Provisional) Renewal (subclass 489) visa.

**For Subclass 489 Visa:**

- Relatives of people holding 475, 489, 487, 496 and 495 visas will need to apply for the Skilled Regional (Provisional) Subsequent Entrant (subclass 489) visa.
- For more information, visit link: DIBP Information on Skilled - Regional (Provisional) visa (subclass 489), Sponsored

## Skilled Regional (Provisional) Visa (Subclass 489), State or Territory Nominated

This visa allows skilled workers to work and live in regional parts of Australia for a period up to four years. To be eligible for this visa, you must:

- Be nominated by an Australian state or territory government agency.
- Be nominated in an occupation on the consolidated skilled occupations list.
- Have had a suitable skills assessment.
- Be under 50 years.
- Achieve the points indicated in your letter of invitation.

This visa allows you to live, study and work in Australia for up to 4 years. You can also travel in and out of the country during the period of your visa. To stay for longer, you will need to apply for a Skilled Regional (Provisional) Renewal (subclass 489) visa.

**For Subclass 489 Visa:**

- Australian Capital Territory does not nominate for the 489 visa.
- Relatives of people holding 475, 489, 487, 496 and 495 visas will need to apply for the Skilled Regional (Provisional) Subsequent Entrant (subclass 489) visa.

You can refer to the following links for specific states if you're interested in applying for a 489 visa.

- VICTORIA
- QUEENSLAND
- NEW SOUTH WALES
- WESTERN AUSTRALIA
- NORTHERN TERRITORY
- TASMANIA
- SOUTH AUSTRALIA
- AUSTRALIAN CAPITAL TERRITORY (Please note the ACT does not have access to nominate subclass 489 visas).

***DID YOU KNOW:***

*At the end of June 2015, the population growth rate of Australia was 1.4%. This rate was based on estimates of one birth every 1 minute and 44 seconds, one death every 3 minutes and 32 seconds, a net gain of one international migrant every 2 minutes and 19 seconds.*

## 3.2 Visa Specific Conditions and Restrictions

The type of visa you have will determine your employment eligibility in Australia. Your visa may come with a certain set of restrictions and conditions that you have to adhere to. Here is an overview:

- You cannot work at all with a visitor visa (Sub-Class 600).
- You can work for only up to 20 hours per week with a student visa (Sub-Class 500).
- You can work for only up to 6 months with one employer on a Working Holiday visa (subclass 417). The visa is valid for up to 1 year. DIBP Information on Subclass 417 Visa This visa is currently available for the following nationals - Belgium, Canada, Cyprus, Denmark, Estonia, Finland, France, Germany, Hong Kong, Republic of Ireland, Italy, Japan, Republic of Korea, Malta, Netherlands, Norway, Sweden, Taiwan, and the United Kingdom.
- You can work with only 1 employer for 6 months on a Work and Holiday visa (subclass 462). The visa is valid for up to 1 year and has an education requirement in comparison to the 417 visa. For more information visit – DIBP Information on Subclass 462 Visa - This visa is currently available for the following nationals only - Argentina, Bangladesh, Chile, China, Indonesia, Israel, Malaysia, Poland, Portugal, Slovak Republic, Slovenia, Spain, Thailand, Turkey, USA and Uruguay
- You will only be able to work for the company who has sponsored you with a Temporary Work (Skilled) visa (subclass 457). If you leave the company for another, the new company has to apply for a fresh 457 visa.
- You will have to work in the state for at least 2 years if you have entered the country on a Skilled Nominated visa (subclass 190). The employee may also be

expected to complete government-conducted surveys and so on.

- Visa entrants on the Skilled Regional (489) visa must only live in the regional parts of the nominated state and cannot live in cities like Melbourne and Sydney.
- Visa entrants on the Skilled Independent visa (subclass 189) cannot access certain social security payments immediately and are subject to a waiting period.

## 457 Work Visa (and how it is different from Permanent Resident visa)

**Note** – There is presently a lot of changes surrounding this sub-class due to the continuing debate about the unusually large number of visas issued in this category in relation to the current unemployment situation in the country. Always check the DIBP Website for latest updates.

- 457 visa holders can only work for sponsoring employers and cannot have secondary employment. If you are let go from your job, you are given a grace period of 90 days to get a new sponsoring employer. If you are unable to do so, you have to leave Australia.
- Certain states like NSW charge school fees even in state run schools if on a 457 Visa. (In NSW, it will cost you approximately $4500 per year for public schooling, whereas Queensland doesn't have these fees). Permanent Residents have free access to state schools.
- Under the rules of citizenship, the first three years of your 457 count towards getting citizenship, but you

must also complete 1 extra year as a permanent resident. (The requirement is 4 years for citizenship, including 1 year as a permanent resident).

- Your children born in Australia will also need to get a 457 visa – they will not get automatic citizenship unless you have a permanent residency visa.

- Your spouse will have unrestricted rights to work in Australia. But this will not be easy in career-oriented organisations because employers prefer to employ PR holders or citizens.

- Your children are treated as overseas students once they attend an Australian university.

- Once your children cross 18, it may be harder for you to get them included in your permanent residency application. In some instances, they may have to go home because they are considered independent even if the whole family gets permanent residency visas.

- As a 457 Visa holder, you may be subject to certain FIRB restrictions when it comes to buying property. If you are looking to buy an established property, you can get approval if you have over 12 months more on your visa.

- You are not eligible for Medicare benefits other than inter-country reciprocal healthcare schemes for certain nationalities. You or your employer must get a private health insurance cover.

- You don't have any entitlement to welfare or social security benefits. This includes benefits paid to new mothers.

- You are not automatically entitled to Permanent Residency. Your employer generally will not sponsor a PR visa. If the family faces divorce, death or illness during the PR visa application process, you may face difficulty. However, this not impossible.
- Some occupations are closed to people without PR visas or citizenship.
- You cannot sponsor PR visas for relatives and cannot sign an Assurance of Support for migration.
- There are no restrictions to obtain credit cards and loans, but you may find it harder to do so.
- In some states like NSW, you have to wait to get your Australian driving licence and you will get restricted validity.
- 457 visa holders can access their superannuation (minus tax) when they leave the country.

Although 457 visa holders pay the same taxes as Australia citizens and PR holders, some tax breaks are available. For example, Living Away from Home Allowance (LAFHA) and Medicare Levy Exemption. Some of these will need negotiation with employers as part of salary packages.

Many 457 holders consider the tax allowances as not enough to compensate for the restricted rights they have when compared to permanent residents. Under Government proposals from 1 July 2006, 457 visa holders are not measured by non-Australian income. This will benefit those who have large overseas investments.

Get further information on the 457 visa through this guide.

## DID YOU KNOW:

- *In the 2016-17 year (to 30 September 2016) - 11,950 subclass 457 visa holders were granted permanent residence or a provisional visa, a decrease of 21.8 per cent from the previous year.*
- *The vast majority of permanent visa grants to subclass 457 visa holders were in the economic migration stream (96.4 per cent), with the remaining permanent visa grants in the family stream (3.6 per cent)*

MIGRANT NINJA TIP:

VEVO - is an online service enabling you to check your visa details and conditions. VEVO can also give details of your visa conditions to prospective employers with your permission.

## 3.3 Averages Wages in Australia

One of the foremost questions on every migrant's mind is what kind of wages one can expect in Australia. Here are a few statistics and comparisons to put things in perspective.

According to ABS (Australian Bureau of Statistics) report, the Full-Time Adult Average Weekly Total Earnings in May 2016 was $1,575.40.

Those employed in the Mining industry had the highest Full-Time Adult Average Weekly Ordinary Time Earnings in Australia at $2,597.30. The industry with the lowest level of Full-Time Adult Average Weekly Ordinary Time Earnings was the Accommodation and food services industry ($1,069.80).

Full-Time Adult Average Weekly Ordinary Time Earnings was highest for the Australian Capital Territory and Western Australia, $1,725.40, and $1,698.60 respectively.

### DID YOU KNOW:

*In Australia, the average household net-adjusted disposable income per capita is US$ 33,138 a year, higher than the OECD average of US$ 29,016.*

With a minimum hourly rate of $17.70 (which works out to $672.70 a week based on a 38 hour work week) Australia has the most generous national minimum wage in the developed world, according to a report from the Organisation for Economic Co-operation and Development. Mentioned below are a few comparisons and statistics that provide an insight into the wage conditions all across Australia.

### DID YOU KNOW:

*Here are the minimum wage rates per hour in some of the countries as a comparison:*

*(For sake of uniformity, all wages converted to AUD based on exchange rate at 31.May.2016)*

*Australia: $17.70 per hour*

*United Kingdom: $14.66 per hour*

*France: $14.98 per hour*

*Germany: $13.17 per hour*

*New Zealand: $14.22 per hour*

*Canada: $10.45 - 13.81 per hour*

*United States: $10.08 per hour (Note - Many US states also have their own minimum wage laws)*

*Japan: $10.01 per hour*

*China: $1.68 - 3.93 per hour*

*India: $3.09 - 7.44 per day*

*Philippines: $13.32 per day*

Full-time earnings in Australia averaged $78,832 a year in the second quarter of 2016. With overtime and bonuses, the average Australian earnings were $81,947 per annum.

The average full-time male salary (excluding overtime) in Australia is $83,902 per annum

The average full-time female salary in Australia (excluding overtime) is $70,392 per annum.

Workers in Capital Territory (ACT) are Australia's highest paid workers, while Tasmania has the lowest average salary.

## Average Full-Time Ordinary Time Earnings 2016

State - Average Annual Wage

Tasmania - $69,477

South Australia - $73,757

Victoria - $75,634

Queensland - $75,936

New South Wales - $80,132

Northern Territory -  $81,624

Western Australia - $88,327

Capital Territory - $89,846

# Industry Averages - Weekly Salary for 2016 (Source ABS)

Mining - $2597.30

Manufacturing - $1363.80

Electricity, Gas, Water and Waste Services - $1734.30

Construction - $1502.90

Wholesale Trade - $1456.90

Retail Trade - $1114.90

Accommodation and Food Services - $1069.80

Transport, Postal and Warehousing - $1549.90

Information Media and Telecommunications - $1806.50

Financial and Insurance Services - $1822.90

Rental, Hiring and Real Estate Services - $1369.40

Professional, Scientific and Technical Services - $1746.20

Administrative and Support Services - $1283.10

Public Administration and Safety - $1571.10

Education and Training - $1640.60

Health Care and Social Assistance - $1440.90

Arts and Recreation Services - $1368.40

Source - www.abs.gov.au

# Average Weekly Cash Earnings in Australia

## (BASED ON ABS DATA – 22.Jan.2015)

| JOB DESCRIPTION | AVERAGE WEEKLY CASH EARNINGS (AUD $) |
|---|---|
| 1112 General managers | 2,573.60 |
| 1311 Advertising and sales managers | 2,153.50 |
| 1322 Finance managers | 2,777.90 |
| 1323 Human resource managers | 2,414.00 |
| 1325 Research and development managers | 2,738.20 |
| 1331 Construction managers | 2,148.90 |
| 1332 Engineering managers | 2,692.20 |
| 1336 Supply and distribution managers | 2,194.30 |
| 1341 Child care centre managers | 1,160.50 |
| 1344 Other education managers | 2,167.60 |
| 1411 Cafe and restaurant managers | 1,035.20 |
| 1421 Retail managers | 1,143.90 |
| 1491 Amusement, fitness and sports centre managers | 1,344.50 |
| 2113 Photographers | 1,335.20 |

| | |
|---|---|
| 2124 Journalists and other writers | 1,344.00 |
| 2211 Accountants | 1,432.40 |
| 2251 Advertising & marketing professionals | 1,504.00 |
| 2253 Public relations professionals | 1,449.20 |
| 2311 Air transport professionals | 2,226.50 |
| 2312 Marine transport professionals | 2,298.90 |
| 2321 Architects and landscape architects | 1,687.20 |
| 2323 Fashion, industrial & jewellery designers | 1,375.70 |
| 2324 Graphic/web designers & illustrator | 1,278.00 |
| 2325 Interior designers | 1,681.90 |
| 2333 Electrical engineers | 2,018.50 |
| 2334 Electronics engineers | 1,691.00 |
| 2336 Mining engineers | 2,666.20 |
| 2347 Veterinarians | 1,177.90 |
| 2411 Early childhood (pre-primary school) teachers | 1,070.20 |
| 2412 Primary school teachers | 1,279.20 |
| 2414 Secondary school teachers | 1,371.70 |
| 2415 Special education teachers | 1,036.80 |
| 2421 University lecturers and tutors | 1,469.70 |
| 2422 Vocational education teachers | 1,263.50 |

| | |
|---|---|
| 2492 Private tutors and teachers | 417.20 |
| 2493 Teachers of English to speakers of other languages | 998.00 |
| 2511 Dieticians | 1,133.20 |
| 2514 Optometrists and orthoptists | 1,203.40 |
| 2515 Pharmacists | 1,211.80 |
| 2523 Dental practitioners | 2,480.60 |
| 2524 Occupational therapists | 1,160.20 |
| 2525 Physiotherapists | 1,134.80 |
| 2527 Speech professionals and audiologists | 1,120.20 |
| 2531 Generalist medical practitioners | 2,618.60 |
| 2532 Anaesthetists | 4,344.90 |
| 2533 Internal medicine specialists | 2,398.20 |
| 2534 Psychiatrists | 3,387.20 |
| 2535 Surgeons | 2,655.70 |
| 2541 Midwives | 1,249.00 |
| 2544 Registered nurses | 1,220.10 |
| 2613 Software applications programmers | 1,825.30 |
| 3211 Automotive electricians | 1,761.60 |
| 3212 Motor mechanics | 1,083.50 |
| 3231 Aircraft maintenance engineers | 2,038.70 |
| 3243 Vehicle painters | 1,172.10 |

| | |
|---|---|
| 3311 Bricklayers and stonemasons | 1,206.10 |
| 3312 Carpenters and joiners | 1,229.90 |
| 3341 Plumbers | 1,293.50 |
| 3411 Electricians | 1,713.70 |
| 3421 Air-conditioning &refrigeration mechanics | 960.60 |
| 3511 Bakers and pastry cooks | 943.70 |
| 3513 Chefs | 973.90 |
| 3514 Cooks | 690.70 |
| 3611 Animal attendants and trainers | 469.20 |
| 3613 Veterinary nurses | 564.70 |
| 3622 Gardeners | 931.80 |
| 3911 Hairdressers | 666.20 |
| 3942 Wood machinists & trade workers | 792.30 |
| 4112 Dental hygienists, technicians and therapists | 1,050.50 |
| 4113 Diversional therapists | 641.20 |
| 4114 Enrolled and mothercraft nurses | 884.10 |
| 4115 Indigenous health workers | 1,421.50 |
| 4116 Massage therapists | 457.00 |
| 4117 Welfare support workers | 1,020.70 |
| 4211 Child carers | 536.90 |
| 4221 Education aides | 641.80 |

| | |
|---|---|
| 4231 Aged and disabled carers | 679.00 |
| 4234 Special care workers | 971.30 |
| 4312 Cafe workers | 422.80 |
| 4315 Waiters | 426.00 |
| 4511 Beauty therapists | 502.20 |
| 4512 Driving instructors | 738.90 |
| 4516 Tourism and travel advisers | 1,206.10 |
| 4517 Travel attendants | 878.20 |
| 4521 Fitness instructors | 381.00 |
| 5511 Accounting clerks | 1,046.70 |
| 5512 Bookkeepers | 643.90 |
| 5997 Library assistants | 683.80 |
| 6113 Sales representatives | 1,372.10 |
| 6121 Real estate sales agents | 1,279.00 |
| 7312 Bus and coach drivers | 903.80 |
| 7321 Delivery drivers | 711.80 |
| 7331 Truck drivers | 1,417.20 |
| 7411 Store persons | 932.20 |
| 8113 Domestic cleaners | 390.50 |
| 8114 Housekeepers | 467.50 |
| 8211 Building and plumbing labourers | 1,501.70 |
| 8511 Fast food cooks | 208.4 |

MIGRANT NINJA TIP:

**If you want to find wages for a specific profession or designation visit – PAYSCALE**

# 3.4 Statistical Data

## Job Statistics by Salaries/Growth/Regions/Industries

The Australian Department of Immigration publishes a list of skills where there is a shortage, known as the Skilled Occupation List or SOL and the Consolidated Skilled Occupation List or CSOL. While this is a good indication of skill shortages, keep in mind that the actual market conditions may differ. There are cases when people come under the skilled occupation list, but still have to wait awhile for a job.

If you are planning to migrate to Australia, it's prudent to conduct your own analysis before making any decisions to enter the country. This level of judiciousness will put you in a better position when it comes to planning your move to Australia.

The Australian job occupation matrix published by the Australian Department of Employment gives a good indication of the jobs, unemployment rate, salary bracket and possible growth. This guide will help you take a look at the job market based on several categories.

*DID YOU KNOW:*

*Three decades ago, the average full-time worker took home just under $19,000 a year in a time when the average house price was less than $150,000. Today annual earnings exceed*

*$73,000 with the average house price in most capital cities exceeding $520,000.*

## Jobs by Salaries

The general rule is that highly skilled or high-risk jobs command a higher salary. If you are in the below professions, you can expect a salary in excess of $1700 per week, which is considered to be excellent to enjoy a high standard of living.

- Actuaries, Mathematicians and Statisticians
- Chemical, Gas, Petroleum & Power Plant Operators
- Civil Engineering Technicians and Draftspersons
- Civil, Mining and Electrical Engineers
- Drillers, Miners and Shot Firers
- Economists
- Education Advisers and Reviewers
- Engineering and Building Technicians
- General Managers, Managing Directors and Chief Executives
- Geologists and Geophysicists
- Land Economists and Valuers
- Managers (Corporate Services, Engineering, Finance, HR, ICT, Policy and Planning)
- Medical Practitioners and Surgeons
- School Principals, University Lecturers and Tutors

If you are qualified but do not come under the top category, you may fall into the second category. These jobs below command a salary between $1,300 to $1,700 per week:

- Accountants

- Air Transport Professionals
- Architects and Landscape Architects
- Architectural, Building and Surveying Technicians
- Archivists, Curators and Records Managers
- Auditors and Company Secretaries
- Barristers
- Chemists and Food and Wine Scientists
- Computer Network Professionals
- Crane, Hoist and Lift Operators
- Construction and Mining Labourers
- Dental Hygienists, Technicians and Therapists
- Directors, Artistic, and Media Producers and Presenters
- Electricians and Electrical Distribution Trades Workers
- Engineering Draftspersons and Technicians (Electrical and Mechanical)
- Engineers (Electronics, ICT Support and Test, Industrial, Mechanical and Production, Telecom, Chemical and Materials )
- Environmental and Occupational Health Professionals
- Financial Dealers, Investment Advisers and Managers
- Fire and Emergency Workers
- Health Diagnostic and Promotion Professionals
- ICT professions including Business and Systems Analysts, Sales Professionals, Security, Database and Systems Administrators, Support and Test Engineers

- ICT Sales Professionals
- Intelligence and Policy Analysts
- Journalists and Other Writers
- Legal Executives and Conveyancers
- Management and Organisation Analysts
- Managers (Advertising and Sales, Construction, Health and Welfare Services, Retail, Hospitality, Production, R&D, Supply and Distribution)
- Manufacturers
- Media Producers and Presenters, and Artistic Directors
- Medical Imaging Professionals
- Nurse Managers, Educators and Researchers
- Optometrists and Orthoptists
- Programme and Project Administrators
- Physiotherapists
- Police
- Policy and Intelligence Analysts
- Prison Officers
- Psychologists
- Scientists,( Agricultural and Forestry, Environmental, Life, Medical Laboratory, Food and Wine, and Chemists)
- Software and Applications Programmers
- Solicitors
- Sportspersons
- Structural Steel Construction Workers
- Teachers, ( Primary, Secondary, Special, Vocational)

- Technicians and Draftspersons, Electrical and Mechanical Engineering
- Technicians, Architectural, Building and Surveying
- Technical Sales Representatives
- Telecommunications Technical Specialists
- Training and Development Professionals
- Train and Tram Drivers
- Veterinarians

## Jobs by Growth in the Next 5 Years

The Australian Department of Employment has predicted more than 100% growth in the below professions over the next 5 years:

- Dental Hygienists, Technicians and Therapists
- Nurse Educators and Researchers
- Optometrists and Orthoptists
- Retail Supervisors
- Early Childhood Teachers (Pre-primary School)

While these are expected to nearly double in the next 5 years, some jobs are expected to grow between 50 and 100 percent over the next few years:

- Anaesthetists
- Barristers
- Clerks
- Farm Workers, Mixed Crop and Livestock
- Gallery, Library and Museum Technicians
- Geologists and Geophysicists

- Greenkeepers
- ICT Managers
- Internal Medicine Specialists
- Legal Executives and Conveyancers
- Mining Engineers
- Occupational Therapists
- Plastics and Rubber Factory Workers
- Pharmacists
- Retail Supervisors
- Actors, Dancers and Other Entertainers

On the other hand, there is expected to be a decline of over 50 percent in some professions, so people engaged in these industries should exercise caution.

- Health Therapists
- Engineering Draftspersons and Technicians, Electronic
- Machine Operators, Clay, Concrete, Glass and Stone
- Photographic Developers and Printers
- Teachers of English to Speakers of Other Languages
- Technicians and Draftspersons, Electronic Engineering
- Upholsterers

**_DID YOU KNOW:_**

**_Bungy Jump Masters ranks as the job which fewest people in Australia can do. In fact, as per one record, there are only 3 Bungy Jump Masters in all of Australia!_**

# Jobs by Regions

Healthcare and social Assistance, retail trade, manufacturing and education industries employ the highest number of people across all states. But some jobs have higher demand in some states than others. The list below refers to popular occupations in each Australian state.

## New South Wales (NSW)

- Financial and Insurance services
- Professional, Scientific and Technical services
- Transport and Warehousing
- Accommodation and food services
- Wholesale Trade

## Victoria (VIC)

- Manufacturing
- Retail trade
- Professional, Scientific and Technical services
- Construction.

## Queensland (QLD)

- Agriculture
- Mining
- Construction
- Retail trade
- Accommodation and food service
- Transport postal and warehousing

## South Australia (SA)

- Agriculture
- Manufacturing
- Retail Trade
- Healthcare

## Western Australia (WA)

- Mining (300% more than the country average)
- Construction

## Tasmania (TAS)

- Agriculture
- Electricity, Water and Gas
- Retail trade
- Food and Accommodation services
- Public administration
- Education and training
- Healthcare

## Northern Territory (NT)

- Public Admin and Safety
- Mining
- Education and Training

## Australian Capital Territory (ACT)

- Public Admin and Safety
- Professional, Scientific and Technical services
- Education and Training

## Jobs by Industry

The Australian Bureau of Statistics (ABS) typically releases data of people employed in Australia by industry.

- Agriculture, fishing and forestry employ 2.8 percent of the population.
- Construction employs 8.8 percent of the population.
- Manufacturing employs 8.1 percent of the population.
- Retail trade employs 10.9 percent of the population.
- Warehousing, transport and postal employs 5.1 percent of the population.
- Healthcare and social assistance employ 12.2 percent of the population.
- Education and training employ 7.8 percent of the population.
- Scientific, professional and technical services employ 7.6 percent of the population.
- Financial and insurance services employ 3.6 percent of the population.
- Information media and telecommunications employ 1.7 percent of the population.

If you're just starting your career in regional or rural areas, you can refer to this web page for more information. You can also get more information about Australian jobs and occupations with the help of this Occupation Matrix. More information and statistics can also be found here.

## DID YOU KNOW:

### Key Facts about Rural Australia

- Rural and regional areas accommodate more than a third of Australia's population and generate two-thirds of its net export.
- Seven million people, or 37 percent of the Australian population, live outside the state and territory capital cities.
- The healthy, friendly and safe environment and community lifestyle of regional Australia attract many people from the cities.
- In 2006, regional Australia contributed around $65 billion, or about 67 percent, of the country's export revenue.
- Major sectors of the Australian economy—resources, energy and primary industries—are located in regional Australia.

# 4. Getting Started

## 4.1 Challenges Faced As a Migrant

Migrating to a new country and starting life all over again is never easy and each migrant will have a unique set of conditions which in turn will create specific challenges. Listed below are some of them.

**Cost of Living**

The biggest challenge most people face when they first arrive in Australia is the cost of living. The cost of living in Sydney is one of the highest in the world. A recent study conducted by UBS ranks Sydney as the ninth most expensive city in the world, which can be tough for migrants coming in from developing countries. When you arrive initially, it is but natural to convert the cost of every item to your home currency and then have a nervous breakdown when you compare the cost of every transaction to the prices back home. It all changes when you start getting a regular income.

Australians, after all, get one of the highest minimum wages in the world.

*DID YOU KNOW:*

*Here are some average living costs in Sydney (Source - Numbeo) (November 2016)*

*1 Pair of Jeans (Levis 501 Or Similar) - $102.92*

*Rent per month for an apartment (1 bedroom) in City Centre - $2,527.31*

*Chicken Breasts (Boneless, Skinless), (1kg) - $11.12*

*Banana (1kg) - $3.02*

*Tomato (1kg) - $4.63*

*Potato (1kg) - $2.73*

*Basic (Electricity, Heating, Water, Garbage) for 85m2 Apartment - $168.67 per month*

*McMeal at McDonalds (or Equivalent Combo Meal) - $10.00*

*Cappuccino (regular) - $3.76*

*Coke/Pepsi (0.33 liter bottle) - $3.21*

*Average Monthly Disposable Salary (Net After Tax) - $4,558.14*

## Language Barriers

A larger part of the migrant population that comes to Australia each year is now predominantly from Asia where English is not necessarily the first language. Hence, one of the major challenges faced is learning effective English speaking.

Being able to communicate (or not) affects every area of life in which we have to interact with others. From jobs to schooling, to simply finding your way around or buying food, learning a native language is essential. Fortunately, Australia offers a lot of support for new arrivals to address this issue (See relevant chapter in this book)

*DID YOU KNOW:*

*Almost 6 million migrants, born in over 200 countries, live in Australia.*

*People born in the United Kingdom continued to be the largest group of overseas-born residents, accounting for 1.2 million people. The next largest group was born in New Zealand with 544,000 people, followed by China (380,000 people), India (341,000) and Italy (216,000).*

## Employment and Lack of Local Experience

Another factor that new immigrants are unaware of is that most organisations want to hire candidates with local experience. This means that migrants will face a tougher time acquiring a job if they go head to head with locally experienced candidates – especially in jobs related to teaching, advertising, communications and banking. In most cases, migrants will eventually get a job, but they will have to take up interim jobs in the meanwhile, to keep up with the cost of living. Don't get disheartened just yet. Read the chapter on myths about getting a job in Australia.

## Possible Loneliness

Loneliness is prevalent among people who come from bustling towns, especially from highly populated countries such as China and India. Australia is a huge country and most of the country is sparsely populated. However, the size of the population and its density is not the actual issue. At its core is the feeling of alienation and having no local friends or support system to reach out to, at least initially. Remember, all migrants start out this way. How quickly you build a network and build a friend circle will all depend on your initiative and how much you socialise. You better learn to fire up the BBQ Grill quickly!

MIGRANT NINJA TIP: **Accept your new situation and find a way to integrate into your new 'local' conditions by absorbing ways that things are done here. Join local community groups and**

**clubs to overcome feelings of loneliness when you first enter Australia.**

## No official recognition of overseas qualifications

A very common challenge faced by migrants is that their overseas qualifications are not recognised in Australia unless authenticated by an Australian organisation. Most local employers may have never heard of the relevant Indian or Chinese university, for example, and this is quite understandable.

## Cultural differences

This is not necessarily the first on the list of practical considerations for immigrants. However, many immigrants report that on arrival, it is the cultural differences that really make a big impression. This can range from social customs to more significant issues such as attitudes towards gender, religious diversity, ethnicity and sexuality, which can all be vastly different in a new country. This can raise a host of problems for both immigrants and the people they interact with. It can also lead to a sense of isolation for immigrants. It is important to accept that values will be different and that this is something that you cannot control. Accepting different values doesn't mean you have to take them on as your own but you may need to learn to respect them in others.

Subtle discrimination sometimes occurs in the job market. Recruitment officers spot "ethnic applicants" by their names, photos or accents. Chinese try to get around this by adopting a Western name, a ploy which is anathema to Indians who are deeply attached to their own name. One again, read the chapter on myths about getting a job in Australia to get the full picture.

***DID YOU KNOW:***

***Australia is a religiously diverse country and it has no official religion.***

***Christianity is the predominant faith of Australia. In the 2011 census, 61.1% of the population classified themselves as being affiliated with the Christian faith.***

***The second-largest group and the one which had grown the fastest was the 22.3% who claimed to have no religion.***

***Minority religions practised in Australia include Buddhism (2.5% of the population), Islam (2.2%), Hinduism (1.3%) and Judaism (0.5%).***

## Moving with Children

Parents may experience certain challenges when bringing their children to a new country. Children may either quickly immerse in the new culture or take a long time to integrate with the local community.

Parents will also face the challenge of looking for schools, dealing with the new education systems, the differences in style of teaching and the apprehension of making friends with the local children and their parents.

With regards to school, parents often feel disappointed to see their children struggling to keep up in class, and many parents report bullying and discrimination as a result of cultural differences. Kids are often placed by their age rather than by their ability, and for those who are unable to speak English, it's virtually impossible to keep up. To add further insult to injury, parents may not have the education or language skills to assist their children, and they may not be able to communicate with faculty to address the problem.

## Transportation

Access to transportation can be essential, in that, it will make access to education and employment far easier. Immigrants face particular problems in this respect on two levels. Firstly, your driver's licence may not be recognised in your new country, which means there may be costs associated with becoming qualified. Secondly, that language barrier can, again, make understanding or even finding useful local public transit services a hard task. Initially, it is normally possible to drive using your home-country licence, but eventually, you will need to change it to the national licence. Public transit timetables can be challenging as well, at least for the first few months until you settle down.

**DID YOU KNOW:**

*Australia is a Car Nation with 13.3m passenger vehicles. Almost 2 in 3 Australian commuters get to work by private car (65.5%) with just 1 in 10 relying on public transport.*

## 4.2 Creating a Professional Online Profile

*Guest Article by* ___The Resume Centre___

Social media sites such as LinkedIn, Facebook, Twitter, and the creation of blogs or your own website can be a great networking tool and way of promoting your own personal brand online. LinkedIn, for example, now has 467 million members worldwide, and has become one of the premier sites for finding a job and reaching out to other professionals.

So how do you start?

As it is so important now when it comes to job search, join LinkedIn and create your profile. Decide what name to use. If you are known by a nickname personally, but use a different version of your name professionally, choose which version you will use and stick to it.

Choose an appropriate photo. Make sure it has a high pixel count and that you are professionally dressed. This is for public consumption, so remember to strike the right image. Your photo will often be the first impression you make on somebody.

Define who you are. Write a personal headline that is concise, clear and memorable.

Highlight your skills and achievements. For example, LinkedIn's Skills section gives you the opportunity to highlight your skills. Although you can list up to 50 skills, it is recommended you focus on those you feel are a personal strength and would help further your career goals.

Introduce yourself. LinkedIn provides users with the opportunity to create a 2,000-word character summary. This is your chance to introduce yourself, your background, experience and interests.

Many of the rules that apply to LinkedIn can also be applied to Facebook, although, you may need to check your privacy settings, to differentiate your public professional persona from your private individual activities. Set up friends' lists to filter friends and work colleagues into relevant groups, and make sure that certain settings are not available to your professional network. That drunken birthday bash last month may have been a lot of fun and yielded some great photos, but would you really want a potential employer to see them?

Having created your profile, now is the time to make use of it. Connect to family and friends, and begin to build your networks. Don't only reach out to people you know, but look for people who have a job similar to yours or want to do, and try and make contact with them.

Join industry, alumni and personal interest groups and take an active role in online discussions. This is a great way of meeting others and expanding your networks.

Request recommendations and endorsements from previous employers and colleagues. This is another means of building a strong network.

You might also consider creating your own blog or website. If you do, make sure that you create content that is professional and meaningful, post new material regularly and reference, where possible, your online profiles.

Whatever social media you use or online profile you develop, there are some general rules you need to observe. Make sure that your personal life remains private, and only what you want others to see is visible. Use privacy settings to make sure you know what information you are sharing with the public, and, where necessary, adjust them. Google yourself. You might be surprised at what you find and, remember, employers will often use search engines to find out more about potential employees. If there is something online that you would rather be deleted, you may want to contact Google, Yahoo or one of the other search engines to see if it can be removed.

Be careful of what you post. If in doubt, leave it out, is always the golden rule! If you have posted something controversial, negative or derogatory, it could leave a bad impression on a potential recruiter.

Place URLs (Uniform Resource Locators) on resumes, cover letters and on email signatures which link to your online profile.

Building an effective online professional profile takes time, but it is something that is increasingly important. As so much recruitment is now done online, you cannot afford not to have an effective presence out there.

## 4.3 Skills Assessment

Australia is regarded as a skill-based job market, in comparison to the qualification-based job market found in most Asian countries. With this in mind, migrants should be in a position to demonstrate the necessary skills for the applied position. This effectively means that you need to present your skills in a manner that emphasises a direct benefit to the company you are applying to. For instance, if you hold a technology business analysis degree, you must demonstrate how your degree has taught you intricate analytical and well-rounded communication skills – factors that are integral to succeeding in a role as a business analyst for any company.

## Getting Overseas Qualifications Assessed By Australian Organisations

If you and/or your partner haven't already done so as a part of the visa process, you may need to get your skills assessed by an Australian organisation after you arrive and before securing a job.

*Example 1* - The main applicant's skills may have been assessed as part of the *SkillSelect* migration process, but the partner (whose skills were not assessed as the secondary applicant) may need an assessment.

*Example 2* – You had moved to Australia after having you skills assessed as a management accountant (because it was on the SOL) and you are now looking for a job as a social worker, an alternate career you were employed in your home country. To get employed as a social worker in Australia, you will need to get your skills assessed.

Every state has a governing body that can provide skills assessment for permanent residents or citizens for the relevant state you are living in.

## Who Assesses Overseas Qualifications?

Overseas qualifications are assessed by several different organisations in Australia. Your overseas qualification may need to be assessed for working, studying or migration to Australia.

**_Note_** - If you would like to migrate to Australia, contact the Department of Immigration and Border Protection. During the points-based migration process, relevant assessing authorities based on your occupation check your skills. You may contact the individual assessing authority if you are looking for a valid skills assessment.

## How Does Qualification Assessment work?

The qualification and skills to work in Australia depend entirely on the occupation. Some occupations require professional qualifications from recognised bodies before you commence work. Meeting these qualification requirements is different from applying for a job. All employers will eventually decide on who to employ based on a combination of factors – from experience and qualification to skill and capability.

Many new migrants to Australia possess a range of qualifications and skills that they've gained in their home country. However, as a general rule, most Australian employers will value local experience above overseas experience. As a result, you'll need to ascertain whether or not those qualifications will be recognised in Australia.

There are a number of ways you can go about getting your overseas professional qualifications recognised in Australia. This stage is referred to as Recognition of Prior Learning (RPL). Major professional industry associations are a good place to start looking for details on industry requirements for the assessment of your professional qualifications. In fact, many of these organisations are in charge of assessing those qualifications.

The National Office of Overseas Skills Recognition (NOOSR) - can assess your overseas qualifications in terms of how they fit into the Australian Qualifications Framework.

**Specialised Occupations**

For occupations where specialised knowledge and skills are required in Australia, you may need to get licensed, registered, professional memberships and fulfil other specialised requirements before you begin work. Special bodies are available to assess existing and recommend new qualifications across different states in Australia. You can get more information about responsible authorities on the Immigration Department's Australian Skills Recognition Information page.

**General Occupations**

If you are a permanent resident or an Australian citizen looking for a job without any specialised qualifications needed, then you can get in touch with an Overseas Qualifications Unit (OQU) of a relevant Australian state or territory government to see whether your overseas qualification is recognised in the country. The OQU will assess your qualification and provide you with advice on getting it recognised. If you're looking for state organisation OQU's, check out National Office of Overseas Skills Recognition (NOOSR) as mentioned above.

## Skills Assessment by VETASSESS

VETASSESS is another organisation who can assess your skills, if you are already in Australia, and have them formally recognised to improve your chances of finding employment. You can apply for their service if you're an Australian skilled worker or migrant with recent work experience.

# Overseas Qualifications Unit (OQU)

The Overseas Qualifications Unit (OQU) assesses eligible qualifications gained overseas to determine their comparability with Australian standards. The OQU can assess post-secondary qualifications including:

formal technical and vocational qualifications (Certificate IV and above); and

formal higher education qualifications (bachelor degree and above).

Following are the statewide websites Links:

Main Website - Department of Education and Training / Qualification Recognition

Western Australia

Australian Capital Territory

Queensland

South Australia

Victoria

Northern Territory

**New South Wales -** There is no Overseas Qualification Unit in NSW. However, trade qualifications can be assessed. - www.training.nsw.gov.au

**Tasmania** - No website. Overseas Qualifications Unit, Tasmanian Qualifications Authority. Phone: (03)61656000 / Email: enquiries@tqa.tas.gov.au

**NOTE -** If your overseas degree is not equivalent to an Australian qualification, you may be able to seek employment in your chosen occupation, but at a lower entry level. However, remember that certain occupations in Australia, such as those in the healthcare sector, require you to pass certain industry specific examinations first.

## Recognition of Prior Learning (RPL)

Registered Training Organisations (RTOs) can also help out when it comes to recognition of prior learning (RPL). These organisations can determine whether there are any gaps in the knowledge you've acquired overseas and the knowledge you'd acquire if you obtain a similar qualification in Australia.

If your qualifications aren't recognised, or if there are gaps in the knowledge you've acquired overseas, you might like to seek further study to fill these gaps and obtain relevant qualifications to meet Australian standards. Referred to as 'gap training' or 'up-skilling', this training can be undertaken at relevant universities or higher education institutions.

## Recognition of prior learning (RPL) and credit transfer

## What is Skills Recognition?

Skills Recognition, sometimes called Recognition of Prior Learning (RPL) or recognition of current competencies (RCC) is the process of gaining formal recognition – a national qualification - for the skills and knowledge that you have obtained through your work history, previous study and life experience

**I have no qualifications from my industry but I have skills, knowledge and experience gained from working in that industry. What can I do to have these skills recognised?**

The RPL process takes into account all relevant skills, knowledge and experience that you have, regardless of the way you got them. This includes experience and training you have gained through paid work, volunteer work or just life in general.

Through the RPL process, you may be able to gain a complete qualification or, if you have gaps in your knowledge, parts of a qualification. If you need to, you can complete the rest of the qualification through training.

### Why would I bother with RPL?

RPL is generally faster than completing a qualification from scratch and provides you with the opportunity to get:

- a promotion or more money;

- entry into a different career or job;

- entry to or credit in another course; and

- satisfaction from having your skills formally recognised.

The qualification you get is the same that you would get if you completed a full training qualification, but with the added bonus that you won't spend time in the classroom going over things you already know, making it faster. Education and training providers are responsible for decisions regarding recognition of prior learning (RPL) and credit transfer.

Students will usually need to enrol in a course to apply for RPL or credit transfer, and education and training providers often charge fees for these services. RPL and credit transfer processes match what students can demonstrate they already know against the learning outcomes of a course. The AQF(Australian Qualifications Framework) pathways policy and explanations on RPL and credit transfer provide more information for students and education and training providers.For further information, contact your education and training provider directly. Following are the statewide RPL website Links:

Western Australia

Australian Capital Territory

Queensland

South Australia

Victoria

Northern Territory

New South Wales

Tasmania

## What is a registered training organisation (RTO)?

Registered training organisations (RTOs) are those training providers registered by ASQA (or, in some cases, a state regulator) to deliver vocational education and training (VET) services.

There are currently around 5000 RTOs in Australia. A complete list of RTOs is maintained at training.gov.au, the authoritative national register of the VET sector in Australia

**ASQA (Australian Skills Quality Authority)** is the regulatory body for - Registered Training Organisations (RTOs) in the Australian Capital Territory, New South Wales, the Northern Territory, Queensland, South Australia and Tasmania.

ASQA also regulates providers in Victoria and/or Western Australia that:

- offer courses in any of the following states (including by offering courses online): the Australian Capital Territory, New South Wales, the Northern Territory, Queensland, South Australia and Tasmania, or
- offer courses to overseas students studying in Australia on student visas.

For more information, visit: Australian Skills Quality Authority / About RTO's

Links to other VET sector websites: LINK

## 4.4 Contacting Prospective Employers

Australia is always on the lookout for migrants with high-value skills and qualifications, but it can be challenging to land a job when you first come here. It's vital that you are realistic enough to understand that your dream job may take some time. Prospective employers usually always ask about residency status. Keep in mind that searching for a job and landing one from overseas may not be possible, however, it is recommended that you start applying a couple of months before you plan to arrive in Australia. Here are some tips when it comes to contacting prospective employers:

- Visit Australian job sites before migrating, so that you can familiarise yourself with the jobs available. Apart from looking for jobs, invest time in reading the blogs associated with these portals as they provide tonnes of invaluable advice and help you get a feel for what sort of salary and working conditions you can expect with your skills, qualifications and experience.
- Most jobs in Australia are not advertised. Most are found through personal and professional networks. Join your industry association before you leave your home country and use your own networks to contact people in Australia and start networking now to tap into this hidden job market.
- Approach companies and exporters in your own country who have offices in Australia.
- Research the kinds of networks that will be available in the area where you plan to live. Networks may include

groups such as volunteer groups, sports clubs, professional bodies and community groups. Join online Forums, Facebook groups and community websites to get a head start even before you arrive.

- Apply for job vacancies just a few weeks before your intended travel to Australia, mentioning your tentative availability date, because prospective employers are unlikely to wait for too long.

- Don't hesitate to send an application letter with your Resume to as many potential employers and recruitment agents in Australia to let them know you're available.

- Provide an Australian mobile number and address as soon as you arrive and provide updated Resumes to the prospective employers.

- Don't expect to land a job at the same or higher level than when you were home because you don't have 'local' Australian knowledge. This, of course, does not apply to niche industries, professions or top management level jobs. See Chapter on **Myths about Employment**

- Be flexible with your first employer and don't try to over negotiate because you can lose out on the opportunity.

- Learn how to prepare an 'Australian Ready' Resume and Cover Letter and learn how to address Selection Criteria. This will take some effort, dedication and time so start practising as early as you can.

MIGRANT NINJA TIP:

**ExpatForum and Australia Forum - have designated posts created by members who target to arrive in a target city within a certain time frame and stay connected from the time they have applied for their visas. It is a great social platform for connecting with fellow migrants.**

Keep in mind that migrants can take quite a while to find a job, so don't feel dejected when you don't score a job on your first interview. Some of the top job sites worth looking at are (A more comprehensive list is provided in the subsequent chapters):

- www.careerone.com.au
- www.seek.com.au
- www.careerjet.com.au
- www.jobs.com.au
- www.jobisjob.com.au
- www.mycareer.com.au

There are a number of different ways to find jobs in Australia, apart from going online. You can visit government departments, industry associations, educational institutions, professional forums and other employment networks to help you find a job.

Even whilst you are preparing for your move to Australia, you can undertake some concrete steps to be successful. Contacting prospective employers before you arrive in the country will help set up some potential appointments once you arrive. You should be prepared to do some unpaid voluntary work if you're looking for a specific job because this can provide you with the valuable Australian experience you need for the future and more importantly help you network.

**According to one research, only 30-40% of jobs are actually advertised, which includes recruitment agencies. If you aren't having any luck with agencies, it may be that you need to revise your job hunt strategy to include the hidden job market and at the same time look for ways to improve your skills and experience.**

When you contact recruiters and employers, always keep a record of them, so that you know who you have contacted to avoid overwhelming them with too many emails. Even though you have many skills already, you must be prepared to learn new skills. You must be ready to meet new people in person or online when you're in the process of contacting prospective employers for a job. It is essential for you to research the industry and profession you would like to work in Australia. You need to know the major organisations in the industry, the associations representing professionals in that profession, the various online and printed publications available and key individuals in both the industry and the profession. The good thing is that Australia is blessed with a lot of quality resources, written in English and produced by government, private and non-government organisations. Whilst you may be familiar with your industry and profession in your current location, you need to learn how it is regulated in Australia, what qualifications are required and where you can go to source new mentors and professional development opportunities. The job hunting process may also be different from your past experience. Most new arrivals in Australia find their first job through networking (not applying for jobs via websites or through recruitment agencies).

You will also need to understand how the market is different in Australia, what the typical workplace culture is like and how people manage their careers. This information is not automatically available, so finding some people to talk to before you arrive in Australia will give you some good clues before you start applying for jobs.

Most importantly, be consistent in your efforts and flexible in your approach. Life in Australia will naturally be different from what you have experienced so far in your original country of residence. Although, you may be very familiar with how things work in your home town, there is every chance, even if English is your first language, that there will be many differences in work culture and the job hunt process. It is important to be open to new ways of doing things, self-learn and continually strive to improve your understanding the 'Australian' way of doing things.

## 4.5 Golden Rules for Job Hunting

*Reproduced with permission of <u>Successful Resume</u>s Australia*

### RULES OF JOB HUNTING

Hunting for a new job is a complex, time-consuming process. It is important to organise yourself and to try to adopt a disciplined approach to job hunting. Here are some tips to help you plan out a job search strategy and find your next job.

### KNOW YOURSELF AND WHAT YOU'RE LOOKING FOR

1. Understand your personal qualities   your strengths and weaknesses – what roles, work environments and management styles best suit you. These attributes should be highlighted and addressed in your resume, application letter and any other documentation sent through as part of your application. Remember that consistency is key – your personal brand should be reflected in all your communications with a prospective employer.

2. Decide what you want, and find out about it. Dedicate at least 20 minutes a day to researching current jobs and advertised positions.

### GET YOUR DOCUMENTS IN ORDER AND UP TO DATE

3. Make sure you have an intelligent, persuasive resume to give to recruiters and to use for job applications online. Your resume should profile you accurately, highlight your expertise and achievements in measurable terms, and ensure you stand out from the crowd. Your resume should also form the basis for developing your online brand presence, via LinkedIn.

## USE SOCIAL MEDIA TO YOUR ADVANTAGE

Hirers, employers and recruiters are using social media in all forms to identify, source and verify applicants. Social media can make or break your ability to secure your next role, so it's important to get this right.

4. Manage your personal branding online.

Quite simply, make yourself "Google" worthy. Check what comes up on Google if you do a search on yourself. What will a recruiter or HR manager find when they search for your name online? First and foremost, you need to make sure your social media profiles are updated with the latest privacy settings, so your first impression isn't one of a drunken night of partying, inappropriate language, complaining about a job you hate or even using poor vocabulary. Regardless of your security settings, it is always best to only post material on any social media site that you would be happy for a current or prospective employer to see.

5. Create a professional LinkedIn page that reflects your resume, and take the time to build your professional network via LinkedIn groups and online forums.

If you create a professional LinkedIn Profile and smart Facebook profile with appropriate security settings, these are the results that will appear when HR departments and recruiters do a brief background check. Your Successful Resumes consultant can help you to set up a professional LinkedIn profile.

6. Use your online brand to demonstrate who you are and your attributes:

Talk about your volunteer work. Even when your volunteer work is completely unrelated to the type of paid work you're looking for, make sure it's listed on social media profiles. Your ability to engage with your local community will help you stand out from the crowd, and most importantly, it tells your next employer about who you are as a person.

Include professional affiliations and memberships. Let your next employer know that you're well connected, committed to the ongoing professional development and just plain interested in what you do. An employee who proactively investigates and stays up to date with their industry is more likely to be engaged by their job and motivated by factors beyond salary.

Celebrate sport, dance, drama and any other extracurricular activities. Do you like to cook? Create craft and handiwork? Act? Stroll your local marketplace hunting for treasures? Whatever you're interested in, let your next employer know. They may be surprised to find you have a creative flair, and they're likely to be intrigued by unusual hobbies.

Support your friends' endeavours, post newsworthy events and share relevant information. Comment on blogs, articles and posts that interest you. Demonstrate that you are engaged in the world around you, both locally and internationally. Sharing information on social networks is a fantastic way to show that you are capable of knowledge sharing and developing positive networks.

7. Build up your online networks. Networking, online and offline, is a key part of the job search process. There is a certain percentage of jobs that aren't advertised, and the only way to access these opportunities is to network.

## TAKE THE TIME TO SET UP SYSTEMS THAT WILL WORK FOR YOU

8. Set up an email account dedicated to your job search. Keep it professional, simple and straightforward, ideally including your name. Avoid using slang, inappropriate language or too many numbers in your email address.

9. Dedicate time to set up accounts and register your details with careers websites, online job boards, and recruitment company websites. This is repetitive and may be boring, but it's quicker and easier to register your details in multiple places at once. Keep your requirements consistent, make sure your details such as phone number and email address are accurate, and sign up to receive job opportunities sent to your inbox.

## CONNECT WITH RECRUITERS

10. Research and identify recruitment companies, especially those who specialise in your field or industry. Break this process down into small daily activities - during your lunch break or morning coffee break, call one company and ask to speak to a recruiter who specialises in your area. Set up a time to meet with them.

11. Making time to meet with recruiters is important. If you work full time, you may want to consider taking a day off from

your work commitments. Alternately, many recruiters will meet clients after hours.

## INCORPORATE INFORMATIONAL INTERVIEWS INTO YOUR SEARCH

12. Informational interviews provide a valuable technique for tapping into the hidden job market. We know that many jobs are not advertised and you are likely to find your perfect job by networking and informal channels. Done properly, an information interview can help to identify opportunities and help to firm up what you really want out of your next role

## IDENTIFY AND PREPARE YOUR REFEREES

13. Your referees are a vital element of your job application, so select them carefully and make sure they are appropriately briefed and prepared to attest to your career history, achievements, role within a team, work ethic and overall character. Choose your referees to complement the position that you are applying for. You may select a previous employer, colleague, client, supplier or stakeholder. Make sure that they are comfortable with being your referee, and if they aren't, select an alternative.

Your referees must be reasonably familiar with your employment history, so you should send them a copy of your resume, so that they can back up the claims documented in your written application.

Ensure you have their contact details and know of any plans they may have to be overseas or away in the near future. When you are ready to start applying for roles, thoroughly brief your referees – tell them about the role you have applied for, and send them a copy of the advertisement/position description.

## BE DISCIPLINED AND PERSISTENT

14. Always follow-up with companies when you have sent in your resume in response to a job advertisement. Within a week of submitting your document, call them to make sure they have received it. Then ask when you can expect a response, or what the next step in the process may be.

15. Practice makes perfect – so start preparing for your interview as early as possible. Ask your Successful Resumes consultant for interview tips and resources, then supplement these with an online or in-person coaching session. A two-hour intensive session - delivered via phone, Skype or face-to-face – can teach you how to prepare and structure your responses to common interview questions.

A more in-depth interview coaching package may also provide customised support to help you prepare for specific interviews, taking you through the research you need to undertake, providing mock interviews and assisting you in refining your body language.

*Contact the resume writers at Successful Resumes for more information. The company provides a range of services to help further your career including resumes, cover letters, selection criteria responses, LinkedIn profiles, interview coaching and career advice. Their expertise spans all industry sectors and positions - from CEO's and managers to graduates or trade apprentices.*

## 4.6 Networking: Tapping the Hidden Job Market

**By Terry O'Reilly, OBP Australia**

Most jobs are not advertised. That's a common understanding, although it's impossible to put an exact percentage on just how many constitute the hidden job market. The point is, you need to do more than merely apply for advertised positions and send your resume to recruiters.

### Internal referrals

My first question to job seekers is, '*Do you know anybody in the company who would be willing to refer you?*' Preferably, this would be an ex-colleague, but even a friend can be useful if they are prepared to vouch for your professional skills and experience. Increasingly, companies are offering bonuses to employees who can refer a suitable candidate for a position before it is advertised publicly, potentially saving thousands of dollars on external recruitment costs. Most migrants will know of compatriots who have made the transition to employment in Australia; it's just a matter of tracking them down and re-establishing contact.

### Industry knowledge

Those who find work quickly are generally those who have good knowledge of the players in their industry. By doing your company research before you emigrate, you can minimise your period of unemployment in Australia. Once you have identified the relevant companies, through a combination of LinkedIn, company websites and even the Yellow Pages directory, your next step is to draft an expression of interest (EOI) email to key personnel in your target companies. Of course, your approach needs to be professional and culturally appropriate, so it's best to seek guidance on the wording of your message. A poor email message could kill any chance of obtaining work with the company. Keep it concise and personalised – address people by their first name.

The purpose of an unsolicited approach is to contact a hiring manager prior to a job being advertised; timing and luck are critical, as you will not know when a company will be in the position to hire. Even if you don't secure employment via direct contact, in the process, you will develop a deeper understanding of your industry in Australia which is beneficial in the long run.

**Insider knowledge**

Networking widely with your professional peers will give you access to insider knowledge – Who's hiring and when? Start building your network through Linkedin, professional forums, MeetUps, etc. Join Linkedin Groups relevant to your profession, post comments and get active. Message people via your common Linkedin group membership to avoid being reported as spam by InMail recipients whom you do not know. The last thing you want is to be blocked from using LinkedIn because you have been reported as a pest. There are also online industry forums, such as Whirlpool for IT professionals, which can be a great way to establish new and useful connections.

**Networking Services**

Organisations such as OBP Australia have acquired connections across all industries and professions, so use their services to get introduced to your professional peers. Targeted approaches can save you time in the long run.

MIGRANT NINJA TIP:

**Success in the hidden job market is all about networking. For example, a good networker may hear from a business owner that he is on the lookout for a manager for one of his new branch office. The networker helps connect this businessman with his colleague who has the skills to take up that particular position.**

**Here is how networking provides access to the hidden job market:**

Apart from networking online, one of the most effective ways of networking is by volunteering in your local community. It helps integrate faster into the Australian way of life, meet new people and make friends.

It is also a great way of getting local references when the job comes along. Your potential employers will want to talk about you with someone who knows you and how you work and behave in a work environment.

If English is not your first language, volunteering will provide you with opportunities to practice your English. Apart from boosting your confidence, volunteering can also help you acquire new skills that you can include on your resume.

And it speaks volumes about you to potential employers.

Networking is not just about getting that elusive job; it is about broadening your social and professional circles. All these connections will help you in the long run well after you have got your first job.

Get people to know you through constant association - Word of mouth (Who do you know.....and who knows you?), by being proactive (getting to know people in your industry and helping others on every opportunity) and reputation (Your personal skills and branding)

## 4.7 How to Get the Elusive 'Australian' Experience
### By Terry O'Reilly, OBP Australia

For many jobs, contrary to popular conception, you do not necessarily need local experience to secure employment in Australia, particularly for highly technical roles. For example, if you're a software developer with hardcore programming skills, or have experience with a specific technology for which there is high demand, chances are you will be able to find work without having local experience, possibly while still offshore. For others, unfortunately, it's not so easy.

Having local experience reassures recruiters that you are familiar with the Australian culture, industry standards and work practices. Recruiters, who may be lacking subject area expertise, can verify the claims in your resume by contacting a local referee, thereby minimising the risk of forwarding an unsuitable candidate to their 'client' (employer). You may find that 'no local experience' is less of an issue when dealing directly with technical hiring managers inside companies.

Many companies and organisations have their own internship programs or are open to hosting a supported unpaid work placement, best organised through a company that facilitates work placements. Independent approaches to companies for a work placement are generally poorly received, as there are factors such as insurance, etc. which must be considered, and companies need to feel reassured that due process is being followed. If you do engage the services of a work placement facilitation organisation, make sure the placement is relevant to your skills and experience. For example, there is little value in a mechanical engineer undertaking a placement where the duties are purely administrative. Seek advice from an organisation such as OBP Australia, which is experienced in placement arrangements for overseas born professionals.

MIGRANT NINJA TIP:

**Well, if you did not live in Australia at all, you possibly could not have any 'local' experience. So how do you overcome this?**

**In some cases, especially for highly skilled jobs, if your skills and experience are what an employer needs, lacking Australian experience may never be an issue.**

**The more you understand the Australian work culture, the more you will be able to adapt your job search techniques to be successful. Never underestimate the value of a part-time job or volunteering.**

**Australian employers value all local experience, however, if you are doing one of the 'survival' jobs, for example, working**

in a supermarket, do not include this experience as your latest experience on the front page of your CV, especially if you are looking for a highly skilled or professional job placement. You can include this in the 'Other Experience' section towards the end of the CV.

Also, it does not count for work experience if, for example, you are working in a gas station as a temporary employee, but looking for placement in the hospitality industry. What it does do, however, is provide the employer with evidence of your ability to work and interact with your colleagues in an Australian workplace. Additionally, you now have a local referee whom your prospective employer can contact to get a character and work reference.

To summarise some of the main factors, which will give you the edge when seeking the first break, are:

- A Winning Resume
- Strong verbal and non-verbal communication skills
- Seeking Professional help from career guidance experts and Resume Writers
- Networking
- Volunteering

## 4.8 How to become 'Employable' in Australia

*By Pria D'souza, Principal Consultant, STRYD **Consulting***

Australia has many career opportunities for migrants. The challenge is to find the right one for you. Whilst there may be jobs in the fruit picking or meat packing industry, is this what you want to do?

To become employable, you need to research and explore the market for industries that are hiring, refer to information earlier in this document, but also look up newspaper career sections to monitor trends in your local area. For example: if you have chosen to enter the country via Brisbane, what are the local industries in search of talent. If you are an ICT specialist, are there companies looking for this special expertise in Brisbane. Is this the hub for that particular industry?

Head offices are generally based in Sydney or Melbourne, for multinationals. Certainly, most blue chip Australian companies like the BHP Billiton, Commonwealth Bank, Telstra etc. run from these 2 major cities, therefore finding work in the Capital cities have more scope. However, regional areas might have certain opportunities that are willing to give you that first break! My advice to all migrants is: take the first job you are offered, then you are able to say "I have Australian experience".

The main checklist to become employable is:

**Resume**: ensure you have a good and up to date Resume, this is your first introduction to employers, and this is what documents all your achievements, starting with the most recent.

**Certificates/Cards**: research the prerequisites for a particular industry, which may be certificates or industry-specific cards .e.g. white card (construction) or blue card (working with Children). It could mean a Driver's licence, Fork Lift Licence or other necessary documents you will need to have to do a particular job. Most times you are able to do these courses or apply for licences online but they have fees attached.

**Networking**: This is a term you will hear often, earlier, we have alluded to the hidden job market.

These are jobs advertised through word of mouth. A small business will say I need some kitchen hands or a part/ time admin assistant. By law, every vacancy has to be advertised, however, the law does not say where you have to advertise. It suffices to say if you put up a poster outside your office to say you are looking for workers and that meets the requirements. So, if I put up a job ad on the company website, I can say I advertised a vacancy. Then I can call up a few friends and direct them to the website and that could lead to the position being filled. So get the word out to as many people you can.

**Community engagement:** The Australian Community is a rich and diverse commodity for a migrant. It is a palpable force that can support, guide and direct you towards a satisfying career. It plays a big part in creating and moulding a culture of a city, town or region. To understand this, a migrant must look for and get involved in some volunteering in the community. Choose an industry you have an interest in, whether it is Social work, like working with the disadvantaged or fundraising if you are business minded. Look for a not for profit organisation like The Salvation Army, St Vincent de Paul, which is affectionately referred to as Vinnies, Brotherhood of St Laurence etc.

**Recruitment Agencies**: If by now you are not engaged in some kind of work, whether paid or unpaid, search for a local recruitment company. The yellow pages or local newspaper will give you some tips, otherwise just Google recruitment agencies. There are targeted companies that look after white collar or blue collar vacancies. Call them or walk into their local office and arrange a meeting with a consultant. The opportunity to actually speak with a real person is by far the best experience.

Remember, go prepared with questions about the industry you are looking to be employed in. Have a relaxed chat and you will find, not only are you more confident, but you have more information that you could ever find online.

Being a Careers Counsellor my self, I have worked with a diverse range of people looking for work. New migrants, established personnel that are looking to transfer their skills to a new career, people made redundant (lost their job) due to company restructures etc. The latter being quite common in the last six months.

I am more than happy to set up a chat with you in any shape or form (in this age of Skype anything is possible!) to help you on your journey. It is a journey that you are about to embark on, let the opportunities widen your scope for a rewarding career.

I wish you all the best.


Pria D'Souza
Principal Consultant
STRYD Consulting (**S**triving **T**owards **R**eaching **Y**our **D**reams)
Tel: +61(0)403 557 972
Email: 2priadsouza@gmail.com

## 4.9 Some myths about getting a job in Australia

Although, this book addresses the need for 'local Australian' experience and 'local qualifications', it would be remiss not to mention that although these factors do play a role when gauging employability in Australia, it is not an absolute prerequisite.

Do not let statistics or hearsay bog you down. There are definitely lots of migrants out there who have landed a job even before they arrived or within a month of settling in Australia. While a lot could be attributed to the industry they are in, their skill set and industry experience, there are many instances where none of this had a part to play.

Remember, Australian employers have different expectations specific to local conditions and requirements as compared to other countries. There will always be a learning curve for a new migrant in his first job in Australia irrespective of his skills or years of experience because the soft skills required will naturally be somewhat different from what he is usually accustomed to.

It is vital that you focus on getting employed, rather than getting demotivated by these myths. You have been invited to Australia based on your qualifications and work experience, so, surely, there is some thought gone behind issuing you the visa. Trust in yourself and stay positive.

Here are six common myths to avoid when looking for a job. These myths are not based on reality and facts, but rather on generalisation and people's interpretation based on their personal circumstances.

## Myth 1 - "I do not have local Australian Experience."

Reality — While some employers do prefer local work experience, it is not an absolute essential. All the employer is interested in is how good is he at his job, how will he blend in with his colleagues at the workplace and how aware is he of local rules, customs and etiquettes. Assure him your understanding of these basic requirements and the job is yours!

Learn to present your skills and experience in a manner that will prove you invaluable to the organisation.

## Myth 2 - "Maybe I should settle for an entry level job instead."

Reality— The mob is always at the bottom rung of every organisation. You have more competition for an entry level position because you will have a lot of people applying for the role. The more niche your skill set, the more leverage you have for getting a suitable position. Identify the unique skills you offer, target jobs that match those skills and market yourself in a way that makes you seem indispensable to the employer. Done right, you can aim higher, reduce your competition and will more likely be considered for the job.

## Myth 3 - "My Overseas qualifications are not recognised."

Reality — It is a fallacy that overseas experience is not accepted in Australia. More often than not, it is the way the candidate has presented the value of that experience. For example, you could have worked in one of the largest firms in your home country and had an excellent track record and industry recognition. How can you expect a prospective employer in Sydney to be interested in this statistic? In all probability, he may not have even heard about the ex-company.

What you can talk about rather, is the challenges you faced and the value you added to the company. Rather than talking about how big the company was, mention how your skill set increased revenues and generated increased sales. If you handled a team of junior employees, emphasise the role you played in mentoring them and talk about your leadership skills.

If you appear to be the right fit for the job and possess the drive and right attitude, the prospective employer may even guide you to get the relevant local equivalent certificate as well as any industry specific training that may be required.

The more you understand the Australian work culture, the more you will be able to adapt your job search techniques to be successful. Remember it is not what you can offer the organisation; it is how you present your skills to them.

**Myth 4 - "My ethnicity and country of origin is the real problem."**

Reality — No it's not. Almost 6 million migrants, born in over 200 countries, live in Australia. With almost a quarter of its population born overseas, Melbourne alone is home to residents from 180 countries, who speak over 233 languages and dialects and follow 116 religious faiths! Do you really think employers can get picky when finding suitable employees?

It is not what they expect, but it is rather how you present yourself. How willing are you to learn new cultures? How eager are you to blend in and embrace the viewpoints of others in the

workplace? How open are you to socialising with other employees? There will definitely be a small percentage of employers who do discriminate when recruiting but this is equally true anywhere else in the world. Focus on selling your talent and soft skills and notice how you become suddenly more attractive to employers.

## Myth 5 - "My profession is in recession."

Reality — Skilled professional visas are allocated based on the skill shortage in a particular occupation or geographical area, which means there will be jobs. There is an ongoing debate which highlights the fact that many Australians with similar skill sets are unemployed, so, why should these professions continue to be on the SOL or CSOL. In the meanwhile, the migration programme does go on, skilled migrants do get employed irrespective of the unemployment rate and success stories abound. It will take time, but your break too will come. As is mentioned elsewhere in this book, not all jobs are advertised on major job sites. You should learn to tap the hidden market, network in a big way and research your industry. Of course, in many a case, it is all about "Being in the right place at the right time." Whilst it is good to be aware of the challenges you may encounter when entering the job markets, do not let them rattle you. Improvise when you talk to your employers, be creative when writing your resumes and cover letters, seek advice from professionals, research your industry thoroughly and Keep Trying!

## Myth 6 - "I've applied for over 100 jobs but not got a call for a single interview"

Reality — When was the last time you did a health check on your Resume and Cover Letter. As this book will show you, resume writing is a skill in itself. Whilst most resumes are merely glanced at in 10 seconds or less, nowadays, most recruitment agencies use online programmes to scan resumes. Chances are that you are still using the resume you used back home, and unfortunately, this puts you at the end of the line, not at the very beginning. All your experience and qualifications are of no use if you cannot even make it to the first round of interviews. Rework your resume in the Australian format or hire a professional to get one done for you.

# 5. Resumes, Cover Letters & Selection Criteria

This chapter has been created with content derived from experts. The field of Resume Writing is as vast and daunting as the prospect of the job hunt itself. As a new arrival to Australia, you must be aware of the fact that this is one of the most crucial skill set that you need to develop. There are two broad choices you can make – Pay a premium and hire an expert to do this for you OR master the skill by learning from online content, fellow migrants and pure trial and error. Although, the cost of hiring a professional seems prohibitive, the benefits far outweigh expenditure.

This book intends to lay the road map for you so that you may get a good head start and learn the basics. Additionally, you will be presented with all the options when you need to seek further information and/or professional help.

There is no 'One Size Fits All' remedy as far as writing resumes and cover letters go. I could provide double the amount of content presently included in this segment, but that will only serve to overwhelm and possibly confuse you. Just be aware that each industry, each department and each job profile will require a tailor made resume and cover letter. Do not make the error of using a single format across all job applications. Invest your time in developing this vital skill. Failure to do so may just be the critical factor that separates you and the next candidate who gets the interview call.

## 5.1 Key Difference in an Australian Resume

Every country has its own recruitment procedure, and more often than not, what works in one country will not work in another. You may have the necessary skill set, but if you are not able to present it in a customary manner in Australia, chances are you will have to wait for a considerable amount of time for the interview call.

A Resume that works in India may not work in China and what works in either country is not likely to work in Australia.

Australian employers are very focused on skills and evidence on how you have used these skills. (You may have noticed most Australian jobs ask for minimum experience)

For example, a Diploma is only of value in Australia if you can provide evidence of how you have put this to use in your career and how you can demonstrate the practical knowledge.

Instead of just listing educational qualifications, consider including projects you were involved in the course of your education and how the employer can benefit from your expertise.

### The Key Differences in an Australian Resume - *Guest Article by* _The Resume Centre_

For people new to Australia, there are some differences to note when preparing their resume for the first time. The nomenclature itself, for example. Whilst people from the US and Canada will have grown-up with the term resume, those from the UK, Europe, South Africa and even New Zealand will be more familiar with the name CV (Curriculum Vitae) to describe the document which summarises their career history, skills and accomplishments.

Before however, explaining the differences, it might be helpful to identify the commonalities between a resume and a CV.

Correct spelling and grammar is critically important in any professional document, yet 60% of all resumes/CV's contain at least one linguistic error. It is astonishing how many candidates fail to use a spell checker or bother to proofread their documents before submitting them. Make sure that you spell the words the Australian way, which is closer to British rather than American English. Colour, rather than colour, for example.

Layout and formatting are important whatever type of document you are preparing. Avoid unusual fonts, colours and typefaces, make sure there are plenty of spaces between sections, and use bullet points where applicable (but not too many!). Nobody can expect their resumes to be read if they are cluttered, messy or misaligned.

Superfluous personal detail should be omitted, wherever you are based. Many countries now have legislation in place aimed at preventing discrimination on the basis of age, ethnic background, sexual orientation, religious or political affiliations. Australia is no exception. Do not mention your age, date of birth, marital status, religious or political beliefs. They are unlikely to have any relevance to your ability to perform a particular role and they take up valuable space on your resume. Including them could also work against you if a recruiter has a bias against one group or another (sadly this happens).

Equally, unless you are an actor or applying for a modelling job, do not include a photo of yourself on your resume/cv. Whilst there are some countries where this is normal practice, Australia, like the US and the UK, is not one. Beauty is in the eye of the beholder, and while you may think you look like George Clooney or Angelina Jolie, a potential recruiter may think you are closer to Quasimodo!

Finally, do not include the names of your references in your document. Again, this takes up valuable space, and the time when they are likely to be needed is when you have been offered the job. Simply state that, references are available on request.

Having dealt with the similarities, now let's look at the differences.

Career history is one key area. Whilst best practice suggests a resume should be no longer than one page in the US/Canada and 2 pages in the UK, there are not the same restrictions on length in Australia. This means that a greater emphasis is placed on the inclusion of all the roles you have worked, not just those relevant to the job on offer. This means that any gaps in your CV will be a red flag for an employer.

Australia puts a lot of emphasis on the description of key skills in a resume, more than many other countries. Candidates should be careful to distinguish between skills – such as knowledge of a particular software or coding language – and competencies, such as being a team player. Avoid emphasising behaviours too much in your resume – they can be discussed at interview.

Equally, Australian resumes tend to steer away from descriptions of an individual's personality – for example, "a committed, pro-active individual". Again, recruiters prefer to draw these facets out during an interview itself.

Finally, there is the cover letter which, in some parts of the world, is seen as a necessary complement to the resume. In Australia, its role is less clear. If you are applying for a senior role, you will definitely need one, but, if you are applying for an IT position, probably not. However, if in doubt, make sure you have a cover letter.

Much of the content of an Australian resume could be found in the equivalent document in the UK, US or Canada. The basic rules of correct spelling and grammar, good layout and formatting, and the omission of superfluous personal details and photographs still apply. Australians do prefer a fuller career history and emphasise skills rather than competencies; however, on balance, the similarities to resumes/CV's in other parts of the world are greater than the differences.

## 5.2 Preparing a Winning Resume

*Reproduced with permission of University of Tasmania, Student Leadership, Career Development and Employment team*

A resume is one of the key components of the job application process. It should paint a picture for the reader of your skills and suitability for the job, and any experiences you have gained that would be beneficial to the position. Your resume is a marketing tool that sells your skills, qualifications and achievements to a prospective employer.

Employers can often receive several hundred resumes and someone inevitably has the task of reading them all. It is highly likely that someone reading your resume will develop an impression of you within the first 20-30 seconds. It, therefore, needs to be informative, succinct and interesting to stand out from the crowd. The best way to do this is to clearly express how your skills and experiences match those that the employer is looking for.

## STARTING THE PROCESS

Take it seriously. Be prepared to spend time drafting and refining your resume so that it clearly demonstrates and markets your skills and suitability for a position. Approach your resume writing by using the following broad process:

Gather information on yourself - use brainstorming, records of achievement or participation, work history, copies of transcripts etc. to generate the raw material.

Think about the audience for your resume and decide what is relevant to them.

Select a format and specific section headings that best categorise you and your information.

Draft the content of the resume and allow time for reflection and review.

Revise again, approach resume writing like writing a university assignment - it takes time to research, write and revise - don't wait until the day the job application is due to write your resume!

## YOUR AUDIENCE

Your resume is not a static document: it should be re-evaluated and updated regularly, in light of a particular audience each time you use it. The emphasis on various skills and experiences will vary according to the job and the employer.

## RESUME FORMAT

All resumes should include core information about personal details, education, work experience and relevant skills/achievements; as well as information about interests (hobbies, sports, community service etc.). However, there are various ways to structure the material in your resume in order to present your 'story' in the most effective way.

**Common resume formats are:**

**Chronological** - is the most common resume format. Emphasises your past experiences from the most recent date and works backwards. Sometimes known as a reverse chronological order, this format is easy for an employer to navigate and clearly identify what you have been doing, and when.

**Functional** - describes functions or areas of skills you hold, with a lesser emphasis on positions previously held. This format may be useful for students with limited or no work experience, or people with significant gaps in career activity due to travel, raising children etc.

**Combination / Hybrid** - includes elements of both the chronological and functional formats.

**SECTION HEADINGS**

Once you have selected your preferred format, you can make some decisions about the information you want to include, and how to present it clearly and powerfully to the employer.

There is no set template or 'one' way to format a resume, but it should be visually clear, concise, and in a style you are comfortable with. Think about how an employer would view your information, and use strong 'active' words to describe tasks and responsibilities.

Employers like to see what experiences you may have aside from studies and paid work, as they want to employ people with diverse abilities and qualities. Your resume should, therefore, be a broad snapshot of you as a person – your education and work experiences, as well as your extracurricular interests and achievements.

For example, to describe contributions you have made in the community, you might choose *'Community Service'*, or *'Voluntary Work'*. If you have exhibited your work, you may choose *'Exhibitions'*, or if you are a member of a society, you may choose *'Professional Memberships'*.

Your resume is individual to you, and so you should include information under headings that reflect this.

**Sample headings you may like to use:**

• Educational Background or Tertiary Education

- Employment or Work Experience

- Key Skills or Skills Summary

- Key Achievements

- Awards or Prizes

- Career Objective, Career Goal or Personal profile

- Voluntary or Community Service

- Computer or IT Skills

- Research

- Professional or Clinical Experience

- Publications or Conferences

- Language Skills

- Professional or Society Memberships

- Qualifications

- Extra-curricular activities or Hobbies & Interests

- Sporting Achievements

- Exhibitions

- Funding Grants

- University Projects

- Career Highlights or Achievements

- Referees (x2 minimum)

## RESUME DO's AND DON'TS

• Do make sure your name and personal details stand out at top of page and keep to 2-4 pages maximum length.

• Don't include personal information – DOB / Marital Status / Health / Photo.

• Do use clean, simple font style and layout, with evenly spaced words and lines – Times New Roman, Arial, and Calibri are good fonts.

• Do not use the same resume for every job application.

• Do proofread – no typos or grammatical errors.

• Don't go back as far as primary school – keep information current & relevant.

• Do use succinct statements and appropriate use of bullet points.

• Don't forget to get permission from your referees.

• Do include page numbers and ensure email and mobile contacts are professional.

• Do put your most powerful, relevant information on the first page.

## THINGS TO REMEMBER

• Understand the purpose and audience of your resume.

• Select a style and format that presents you well.

• Include information that is current and relevant, and exclude information that isn't.

**FURTHER READING**

A simple internet search for 'resumes' will generate a wealth of information and resources. You may also like to look on social media sites like LinkedIn, Facebook, Google Circle and Whirlpool for online web chats and blogs that may help. The following are a few key resources that will help to start your resume research.

*Books*

Bright, J. & Earl, J. 2004, Resumes that Get Shortlisted: proven strategies to get the job you want

Stevens, P. 2000, Win that Job

Villiers, A. 2005, How to Write and Talk to Selection Criteria (Chapter 7)

*Internet*

www.careerone.com.au (click on 'Resume' or 'Career Advice')

www.seek.com.au (click on 'Salary, Advice & Tips')

www.dummies.com (click on Business & Careers then Careers)

## 5.3 Preparing a Cover Letter

*Reproduced with permission of University of Tasmania, **Student Leadership, Career Development and Employment team***

A cover letter (sometimes called an application letter) is an important component of your communication with potential employers. It is the first document they will read and first impressions are vital when forming opinions.

In the past, cover letters were used as a covering page for the rest of the job application documents and may have been very brief and uninformative about the candidate.

In today's competitive employment environment, you should use every opportunity to market your skills professionally. A cover letter should demonstrate to the reader that you have read the job advert carefully and you are interested in the position. It should give the employer a 'snapshot' of the reasons why they should employ you.

A good letter will introduce you in a clear and focused way and encourage the employer to read the rest of your application with interest. Do not rewrite your resume in your letter, but do draw attention to your most relevant and important achievements relevant to the position.

Given that your cover letter is designed to summarise the highlights of your resume and statement addressing selection criteria (if required), it should be the final document that is written after you have considered the position and your abilities in relation to it.

## WHAT SHOULD A COVER LETTER COMMUNICATE?

Cover letters should communicate:

• your interest in the position (if advertised position) or potential opportunities

• your understanding and interest in the organisation

• the key skills, qualifications and abilities you have to offer

• what action you want from the organisation

Use positive, confident language throughout – a cover letter is a professional marketing tool and should demonstrate your suitability for the job by communicating to an employer how you will assist the organisation in reaching their goals.

Ensure you have proofread your letter carefully – grammatical or spelling errors will create a negative impression with a potential employer.

**WHEN SHOULD I INCLUDE A COVER LETTER?**

It is always a good practice to write a cover letter when making contact with an employer, whether that is for:

• formal job application process by post

• cold canvassing – contacting an organisation/employer to introduce yourself and see if employment opportunities

• formal job applications online – if requested (at times there will be no place to attach).

It can be unclear at times in formal job applications whether an employer expects a cover letter, so if in doubt, ring the contact person to discuss.

Remember, the cover letter is about marketing you and creating a good first impression – so it is a good practice to write one for every job application/opportunity.

**FORMATTING YOUR COVER LETTER**

Cover letters should be professional and written in business style format – your details on the top right, company details on the left. Given employers will not have time to read lengthy documents during the shortlisting phase, keep your letter to 1 page.

## Paragraph 1

If replying to an advertisement, state the position you are applying for, any reference numbers and where you found the job vacancy. State what interests you about the job and how that links to what you know about the organisation needs.

## OR

If cold canvassing, state the reason for writing and describe the type of work you are seeking, then why you are interested in working for the organisation. This sentence/s should combine your knowledge of the organisation with your experience and skills and how that links to what you know about the organisation needs.

## Paragraph 2

A brief overview of what you've done in your life and your qualifications (a snapshot of your resume). This can include examples of your academic, employment and voluntary experiences, as well as extracurricular interests.

## Paragraph 3

Your three main selling points – what can you contribute to the organisation? Give an example of each in a brief way (Bullet points work well for this).

*Hint – ensure here that your key skills/strengths link to the position available and / or what the company may be looking for, as well as personal attributes highly regarded by employers – e.g. teamwork, communication, planning skills.

**Paragraph 4**

Reiterate your interest in the position/company. Explain what you have enclosed (resume, selection criteria, academic transcript) and ask for something – an opportunity to discuss your application in more detail, or to discuss what opportunity may exist in their organisation in the future. Reiterate how they can contact you.

Finish the letter with:

Yours sincerely,


Signature

Your Name

## WHAT IF I AM APPLYING ONLINE?

More and more job applications are now being sent to employers online, either by a web portal system or via email. So should you still write a cover letter? Any opportunity to market your skills and knowledge to an employer should be taken up – so it is good practice to write a cover letter for each online application.

## ONLINE APPLICATIONS

Read the instructions carefully for online applications, as many have word limits or no text box to include information you would normally put in a cover letter. If there is space to include a cover letter or attach it, do so. If there is only space to attach your resume, consider putting the cover letter and resume together and attach as one document.

## EMAIL

There are 2 ways to send a cover letter via email:

• in a separate document attached to the email

• within the body of the email – using the same format suggestions as the previous page

Whichever way you choose to send it, cover letters completed online should maintain a professional and business-like approach. Ensure you have the correct email address for the application to be sent to.

* Hint – think about sending attachments to an online application as a PDF to ensure they cannot be corrupted/changed. However, read instructions carefully as many organisations ask for documents to be sent in Word format.

## DO'S AND DON'T'S

**The cover letter should:**

• be to the point – clearly linking your experience to the role being advertised

• be positive and upbeat – make the employer interested in reading your resume

• be personal – where possible, find out who you should address the letter to

- be tailored – for each position you apply for

**The application letter should NOT:**

- be a summary or repeat of your resume

- be a uniform letter you send with all job applications

- be more than 1 page in length

- be unprofessional – use positive professional language throughout

## 5.4 Eight Amazing Tips on Writing a Cover Letter!

*As posted on www.resumecentre.com.au. Reproduced with permission of The Resume Centre*

A well-written cover letter can often be the difference between an interviewer reading your Resume or rejecting it out of hand. Nearly 50% of all recruiters, according to a survey cited by **James Innes** in **The Cover Letter Book**, regard the cover letter as important as the Resume. Yet, they are often neglected or receive far less attention by candidates.

A cover letter is the ideal opportunity to succinctly summarise the skills and experience highlighted in your Resume, whilst also giving you more freedom to express your personality. It can emphasise your strengths and downplay any weaknesses or gaps in experience you may have. In effect, a good cover letter is an invitation to read your Resume and find out more about you; a bad one can stop the hiring process dead in its tracks.

Whilst cover letters fall into two broad categories – speculative and advert-response – there are common features that make for a successful letter.

### 1)    Make sure you reach the Right Person

While it can take some research, especially in the case of a speculative letter, the best person to address the letter to is the person who will decide whether to interview you or not.

### 2)    Establish your Audience

Determine your audience so that you can phrase your letter appropriately. There are three main categories of readers for a job application: HR personnel, managers/directors and specialist external recruiters. Each type of reader has different motivations when reading a cover letter. An HR professional will be trained to select best matches between the candidate and the profile established for the vacant role. A manager or director will be looking for somebody they want to work with – somebody who can make a contribution to their team. And an external recruitment consultant will be looking for somebody they can sell to their client.

### 3)    Include your Personal Details

A proper cover letter begins with a letterhead which includes all your relevant details – name, address, telephone number and email address.

### 4)    Pay Attention to the Basics

As with any professional document, make sure the basics are addressed. Pay attention to spelling, typos and punctuation as these can be your undoing. Never send any document until you have run a spell checker first. Pay attention to spacing and layout and ensure an appropriate typeface is used, perhaps one that is consistent with your Resume. The cover letter should be dated, with your name should be clearly stated at the end.

### 5) Grab Their Attention Immediately

Cut to the chase! Your opening paragraph should tell them what you want, what you are offering and why that should be of interest to them.

### 6) Maintain the Reader's Interest

The central paragraphs of your letter should be used to explain what you have to offer, giving concrete examples where possible, and referencing your Resume. This should include your key selling points, and how these meet their needs. If at all possible, indicate you have an understanding of their particular company or organisation, and the challenges they face.

### 7) Sign-Off: Your Call to Action

The final paragraph should be upbeat and positive, and whilst not being too pushy or arrogant, suggest why arranging a meeting with you would be in their interest, as well as yours!

### 8) Keep it Brief

A cover letter should be no more than one page long. Any longer and it just won't get read. So make it short, punchy and to the point.

A good cover letter can be the difference between getting an interview or being relegated to the 'also rans'. Yet, it seldom gets the time or attention devoted to a Resume. Candidates uncertain about their ability to craft a suitably powerful cover letter should follow the tips above. Alternatively, they could use the services of a CV writing service such as **The Resume Centre** who employ professional writers skilled at writing powerful and effective cover letters

## 5.5 Addressing Selection Criteria

This is generally required for most Commonwealth and State Government positions in Australia, where all details of the position are listed and the prospective candidate has to demonstrate knowledge of the skills and knowledge required. Selection Criteria may sometimes also be required in some non-government and private organisations.

There are two types of criterion: **essential and desirable**. As an applicant, you must address each criterion.

### SAMPLE SELECTION CRITIERIA

*Note - Along with a list of Key duties that every job description will list, usually there is also a document attached which provides a detailed role description. This will state the Key attributes that you need to address in the selection criteria.*

*The following is an example of the Key Attributes as mentioned in the Role Description for Manager, Financial Management in one of the Queensland Government's Departments as advertised on the Smartjobs website.*

*Job details*

*Job type: Permanent Full-time*

*Occupational group: Accounting and Finance*

*Workplace Location: Brisbane Inner City*

*Key Attributes*

*To be successful in this role you will be able to demonstrate the following capabilities as they apply to the role:*

*Shapes strategic thinking - Inspires a sense of purpose and direction in the leadership and development of the team to enable the delivery of strategic and operational priorities to achieve the goals of the CAA and client agencies.*

*Achieves results – Demonstrates thorough knowledge of contemporary financial management and whole of government initiatives and issues relevant to the organisation and client operations. Uses superior analytical and problem solving skills to identify opportunities for continuous improvement. Anticipates change and builds contingencies into plans to ensure tasks are completed.*

*Cultivates productive working relationships - Establishes strategic and collaborative relationships with stakeholders, peers and colleagues across the organisation and client agencies. Consults and shares information within own team and upwards to ensure all parties are kept informed of progress and issues.*

*Exemplifies personal drive and integrity - Demonstrates professionalism and can focus on achieving objectives even under difficult circumstances. Remains positive and responds to pressure in a controlled manner. Treats people fairly and equitably and is transparent in dealings with others.*

*Communicates with influence - Focuses on key points and uses appropriate, unambiguous language. Anticipates the position of other parties in advance and frames own case accordingly. Listens carefully to others and checks to ensure their views have been understood.*

*Note – See below section for tips on how to address Selection Criteria*

## Working with selection criteria

*The following is reproduced with permission of University of Tasmania, Student Leadership, Career Development and Employment team*

Selection criteria are the key competencies required for a position; they include the skills, knowledge, experience, values and personal attributes required.

Some common examples of selection criteria include:

• Well-developed communication skills

• Ability to work as part of a team

• Ability to work under pressure

• Ability to prioritise tasks

• Administrative and financial experience

### When selection criteria are provided

Commonwealth and state government departments throughout Australia have a system whereby all the details of a position are available for applicants to help them prepare their application. This includes a position description and the skills and knowledge required (often referred to as the Selection Criteria or Knowledge and Skills Required). Non-government and many industry employers also produce formal selection criteria for applicants to address.

There are two types of criterion: **essential and desirable**. As an applicant, you must address each criterion.

### When selection criteria are not provided

If the organisation does not have any formal selection criteria for you to address, you must still tailor your application to their needs. You can do this by using some of the keywords in the advertisement and attaching a supporting statement which is prepared in the same way as formal selection criteria.

**When minimal information is provided**

In very rare circumstances, you will be provided with little or no information about the knowledge and skills that are required. In this case, all you can do is prepare a very strong cover letter, setting out your particular claims to the position.

## Basic guidelines for addressing selection criteria

The basic guidelines for addressing selection criteria are as follows:

**Collect the information**

Ensure you gather all necessary material from the employer:

• get the position description;

• find out the knowledge and skills required;

• ask further questions to clarify issues by contacting personnel (indicated in the advertisement or position description); and

• don't assume any details without checking.

**Identify each criterion**

Write down each criterion and break it up into distinct, workable parts. For example, if one of the criterion statements reads "must have strong written and oral communication skills, the ability to work well in a team as well as high-level

121

negotiation and liaison skills", you need to divide the statement up as follows:

• strong written and oral communication skills;

• the ability to work well in a team;

• High-level negotiation skills; and

• high-level liaison skills.

**Brainstorm your examples**

You must address each part of all of the criteria listed, giving fairly equal attention to each. For each part, brainstorm as many examples as possible of your background in this area. Don't be too selective at this stage about what to include.

**Revise and refine**

When you have completed the brainstorm for each criterion, go back and select the examples that you think best addresses each one. You'll find you'll do a bit of 'cutting and pasting' before you end up with the most appropriate and powerful examples under each heading.

Make sure that you use a variety of experiences throughout your statement. Be careful not to use your involvement in a particular activity (no matter how significant) as the only evidence for every criterion.

## Writing up the selection criteria

When addressing selection criteria, it is useful to apply the **STAR** model. Placing examples of how you have demonstrated your skills into the STAR model is critical for developing an effective statement.

The **STAR** acronym stands for:

• **S** ituation (briefly describe the context)

• **T** ask (what were your responsibilities or initiatives?)

• **A** ction (what did you do?)

• **R** esult (what were the outcomes?)

For each criterion:

• write the name of each criterion exactly as it is worded in the application package;

• start with a positive claim;

• give a specific example;

• describe how you acted; and

• describe the result.

For example:

### Excellent verbal communication skills

*"I have highly-developed verbal communication skills, which have been enhanced through a number of experiences. [POSITIVE CLAIM]*

*In my role as Vice-President of the Seacliff Tennis Club during 2005 [SITUATION], I was asked to speak to the local Rotary club in support of an application for sponsorship [TASK].*

*I gave a 20-minute presentation outlining the Club's aims and responded to questions from Rotary members [ACTION].*

*The tennis club's application was successful and we received a $5000 sponsorship from Rotary [RESULT]".*

## Other tips to keep in mind when addressing selection criteria

• Dot point form and/or concise sentences make your application easier to read.

• Use examples to back up every statement you make (use examples that can be visualised).

• Don't just feed their words back to them – make every sentence count by focusing on what you have to offer.

• For a listing of words you can use in your statements, see the list of buzz words at the end of this article.

• Each criterion should be approximately half a page.

• When each criterion is given a weighting of importance you should dedicate a proportionate amount of detail to each part.

• When a statement asks for qualifications or some other information that is finite, the length can be shorter.

## Editing checklist

Before submitting your application you should check your selection criteria against the following checklist:

• responses sound professional and active

• information is logical and consistent

• checked for grammatical errors

• verb tenses are accurate and consistent

- sentences are concise

- avoid abbreviations or unexplained acronyms

- avoid weakening qualifiers

- put most important information first

## A final note

Once you have addressed the selection criteria you will be well prepared for the next stage of the job search process – the interview. This is because selection criteria usually form the basis of interview questions.

At interviews, candidates are usually asked questions that are directly related to the selection criteria. This allows you to prepare responses that are an extension of what you have written in your Statement Addressing Selection Criteria.

## Buzz words for job applications

The following vocabulary is a useful reference list of 'active' language:

**A** – accelerated, accomplished, accounted for, achieved, acquired, acted, adapted, addressed, administered, adopted, advanced, advised, aided, allocated, allowed, analysed, applied, appointed, appraised, approved, arranged, assembled, assessed, assigned, assisted, assured, attained, attuned to, audited, authored, automated, avoided, awarded

**B** – balanced, began, believed, broadened, brought in/about, budgeted

**C** - calculated, catalogued, characterised, clarified, collaborated, competent with, compiled, concentrated, conceptualised, conducted, configured, consolidated, constructed, consulted, contacted, contained, contemplated, continued, contracted, contributed, coordinated, critiqued, curtailed

**D** – delegated, demonstrated, designed, despatched, determined, developed, devised, diagnosed, differentiated, directed, disseminated, distinguished, diversified, diverted, documented

**E** – edited, eliminated, employed, empowered, enabled, enacted, encouraged, engaged, engineered, enhanced, enlisted, enrolled, ensured, equated, established, evaluated, examined, executed, exhibited, expedited, experienced, experimented, extracted

**F** – facilitated, familiarised, fashioned, financed, fine-tuned, focused, forecast, formulated, founded

**G** – gained, generated, grouped, guided

**H** – handled, harmonised, headed, held, hosted

**I** – identified, illustrated, implemented, indexed, influenced, initiated, instigated, integrated, interpreted, introduced, investigated, issued

**J** – joined, judged

**K** - kept

**L** – launched, lectured, led, liaised, lowered

**M** – made, maintained, managed, manipulated, manufactured, mapped, marketed, master-minded, measured, mediated, mentored, modelled, moderated, modified, monitored, motivated

**N** - named, navigated, negotiated, networked, nominated, noted

**O** – obtained, opened, operated, organised, originated, overcame, overhauled, oversaw

**P** – packaged, participated, perfected, performed, permitted, persuaded, pioneered, planned, presided over, processed, produced, programmed, projected, promoted, proposed, provided, publicised, published, purchased

**Q** – qualified, quantified

**R** – ratified, recognised, recommended, reconciled, recruited, rectified, referred, reformed, regulated, rehabilitated, reorganised, represented, researched, restructured, retrieved, reversed, revised

**S** – scheduled, screened, selected, served as, settled, simplified, solved, specified, streamlined, strengthened, structured, succeeded, suggested, summarised, supervised, surpassed, surveyed, systemised

**T** – tabulated, taken part, theorised, trained, transcribed, translated, trimmed, turned around

**U**- undertook, unified, upgraded, used, utilised

**V** – validated, verified, versed, viable, voted

**W** – widened, won, wrote

## 5.6 Application Tracking System (ATS)

**By Terry O'Reilly, OBP Australia**

Wouldn't it be great if your application documents, on which you have spent many hours preparing, were read by another human? Chances are that, instead, they will be 'read' by software. Recruiters and employers simply receive far too many applications for it to be physically possible for a human to read everyone. Applicant Tracking Systems (ATS) are an efficient way of screening out candidates who lack the required skills and experience, albeit, through a crude filtration process of counting keywords which eliminate suitable candidates as well.

Most applications that are submitted by uploading documents to the web (Apply Now, Submit, etc.) pass through an ATS; the URL indicating which HR software (*TALEO, PageUpPeople, etc.*) is being used. So, it is important to understand how ATS work to ensure you are ranked as highly as possible in the application process. An ATS counts the number of keywords used in your application - 'Keywords' are what the employer/recruiter deems essential for the role, and are weighted according to importance. It is wise to seek guidance from an expert on which words in the position description (PD) are important and how to best insert them with high frequency into your documents.

Avoid using tricks to lift your score/candidate ranking, as these are easily identifiable and are likely to backfire when a person reads your documents. For example, keywords in the white text will be counted for each entry, but will not appear to the naked eye. It's best to submit applications that do not bring your integrity into question. Here are a few tips on what to do, and not do, to ensure your documents are ATS compliant and will score as highly as possible:

- Do not use tables
- Upload in the format requested by the advertiser (MS Word is usually a safe option)
- Keep it simple and avoid unnecessary formatting (colours, underlining, alternating alignment, etc.)
- Do not insert images
- Do not use headers & footers
- Avoid dates of employment appearing first on the left side of the page

As with all your documents, have them reviewed by an expert who can advise on ways to improve your formatting and content.

## 5.7 How to get your Resume to pass the 10-second test

Did you know that most employers and hiring agencies typically decide within 10 seconds whether your resume is worth a second glance? Does your resume have an impressive opening that will grab the reader's attention in those crucial 10 seconds? Chances are most probably not! It's not easy to advertise and market ourselves, but it's something you need to master if you want to get your foot in the door.

A resume that launches right into a factual description of your work history and job duties is doomed for failure because everyone who is applying for a particular job will have pretty much the same qualifications. The secret is to differentiate yourself and target your reader's emotions in those first 10 seconds. You need to tell the reader how you will fulfil their organisation's needs and provide solutions to their issues.

Do a role reversal and start thinking like the hiring manager. Read the job posting thoroughly. Visit the employer's website, and familiarise yourself with current issues and come up with possible solutions. Then brainstorm your key strengths, and what special skills or accomplishments you currently have that align with the companies requirements. Some ideas might be:

Saving money or time,

Improving morale,

Customer satisfaction,

Identifying unsafe practices,

Increasing sales,

Budget control,

Working with tight deadlines

Next, take it one step further by using numbers or percentages wherever possible, or describing any special circumstances surrounding the accomplishments.

For example:

*Developed and implemented a flexible roster for shift workers at XYZ with an algorithm check to work out optimum rest hours. This resulted in increased productivity by 11% in a* *matter of six months and drop in injury rates by 5%. This resulted in gross annual savings of $9,000 for the company.*

Make your starting pitch jump off the page in the first 10 seconds and make you stand out among other applicants.

Put these highlights at the top of the resume, under a heading such as Summary of Qualifications or Major Achievements.

If you are successful in grabbing their attention, the next steps become easier. The potential recruiter will re-read your resume, take note of your qualifications and relevant work experience and before you know it, you will be in front of the interview panel.

Remember, the purpose of a Resume is not to sell yourself, but to get you that interview!

**The Resume Checklist:**

- Two pages or less.

- Formatting is standard and easily readable. Uses only standard fonts (Times New Roman, Ariel, etc.) No coloured text, graphics or other non-professional flourishes.

- Is saved in the standard Microsoft Word format – .doc (not .docx or .pdf.)

- Contact information is up front and easy to spot. Email address that sounds professional.

- Contains no typos, spelling mistakes or grammatical errors.

- Chronological format (as opposed to "Functional.") Lists the most recent and relevant companies you've worked for, what positions you held and the dates you worked at each place. Has brief one-line descriptions of the companies. Has bullets that show what skills were used and what you accomplished at each place.

- Answers the question: "Why should someone hire you?"

- Contains quantifiable results, accomplishments and achievements using numbers, dollars, percentages, names of any awards you've won, etc. Provides concrete, measurable data whenever possible.

- Highlight important background, experience, and skills relevant to the post applied for.

- Highlights your most marketable skills.

- Contains all the various keywords common in your industry, and typically found on job descriptions for positions you match. (Do not generalise and use one Resume for every job application)

- Makes use of "actionable" words (e.g. "created," "completed," "built," "developed," etc.) to highlight your accomplishments.

- Avoids using the "I" word.

-Avoids personal details that have no connection to your professional profile (e.g. hobbies, family information, non-work related activities, etc.)

## 5.8 Resume Do's and Don'ts – Employers Perspective

*As posted on www.resumecentre.com.au. Reproduced with permission of The Resume Centre*

Think it's unfair that your carefully crafted Resume gets only a few seconds' attention from a prospective employer? Try and understand it from their viewpoint.

For any but the largest companies, which may have a separate HR or personnel department to screen initial candidates, in most cases, it is the potential future boss who has to view candidate Resumes. This is on top of the normal day job. They may have meetings to attend, reports to write, phone calls to make, deadlines to meet, perhaps, a business trip to prepare for, and all the other myriad things that make up a working day. Recruitment is another task to add to an already full "to do" list.

With the best will in the world, they just do not have time to read every Resume they receive in detail, especially as for some positions, the number of applications received can run into the hundreds. Time to them is usually the resource they lack most. So your Resume literally needs to stand out when they scan it for the first time, so that it can be transferred to the "worth a further look" pile.

You owe it to them, and yourself, to make sure the time they invest on your Resume is worth the effort. So ensure there are no spelling or grammar errors, the layout is clear and logical, your accomplishments are well highlighted, and a proper professional profile is included.

Getting a professional Resume done by a company such as The Resume Centre can help you get past these initial barriers, and earn that all-important interview. For a busy employer with such limited time, you need to make it easier for them to give you a chance.

### Following Article also provided by The Resume Centre

Here are some Do's and Don'ts to bear in mind if you want your resume read by an employer.

- Do check the spelling and grammar. Statistics show that 60% of all resumes contain at least one linguistic error. So, do use the spellchecker and proofread your resume before submitting it.
- Do pay attention to the formatting and layout of your resume. Use a professional font such as Arial or Times New Roman, make sure there is clear space between

sections, and that indentations and alignments are consistent. Use bullet points where applicable (but not too many).

- Do include your contact details on the resume. After all, how is the recruiter going to reach out to you if they don't know your phone number or email address?

- Do make sure your resume includes a proper professional profile/objective section. This should be a brief opening paragraph which aims to summarise your background, experience and potential value to an employer. This is the written equivalent of an elevator speech.

- Do quantify achievements where possible. Rather than a vague statement such as "increased sales year over year", restate this as "increased sales in the Northern Region by 33% over an 18 month period".

- Don't include superfluous personal details such as age, sex, marital status or religion. Unless this is relevant to the job itself, such data is irrelevant and takes up precious space on your resume. Furthermore, with many countries now having legislation in place outlawing discrimination on the grounds of age, ethnic background, sexual orientation, religious or political beliefs, it is at best inappropriate, and at worst illegal for an employer to ask about such matters. So don't mention them.

- Don't include a photo with your resume. Unless you are an actor or a model, the first time the recruiter should see your face is across the table in the interview room.

You may think you have film star looks, but remember beauty is in the eye of the beholder. A photo could give a recruiter an adverse view of you from the outset.

- Don't make your resume stand out with fancy colours, logos or other gimmicks. Unless you are a graphic designer or applying for a creative position, in media, for example, such a move is likely to irritate a recruiter and will backfire on you.

- Don't include bold sweeping claims with no substantive proof. You may be a "bold, visionary, creative team player with an entrepreneurial spirit", but so are thousands of other candidates. Prove it with real achievements and accomplishments.

- Don't include the names of your referees. First of all, this takes up valuable space on your resume and, except in exceptional circumstances, are only relevant once a job offer has been made. Furthermore, the value of references has diminished as many employers are now reluctant to provide any more information on a past employee than a bland confirmation of dates of employment and job title, because of a fear of subsequent litigation.

# 6. The Selection Process

## By Terry O'Reilly, OBP Australia

## 6.1 The Interview

Your resume has done its job and you've been granted an interview. While the news may fill you with dread or anticipation, you should gain confidence knowing that the employer likes you – at least on paper. Now they just need to like you in person. As with success in most things in life, it's all about preparation and understanding what is required to succeed.

### 6.1.1 Types of Interview Formats

Depending on your profession, the level of responsibility attached to the role and the type of employer, an interview can be conducted in a variety of ways.

**Single Interviewer**

If there is only one person interviewing you, either there is not a lot of responsibility attached to the job, it is a very small company or it is a first round interview conducted by a recruiter or HR. Preliminary interviews are often designed to assess your communication skills, professionalism and general suitability. Questions may not go beyond... *Tell me about yourself. Why have you applied for this job? What value can you add to the organisation?* And perhaps a behavioural question or two to assess how you would react in a typical work situation. Your aim here is to be friendly, confident and have some good, succinct responses about what brings you here today. Usually, technical questions are left to the second round if the interviewer is a generalist HR person.

## Technical Interview

For some purely technical roles such as software tester or developer, there is not much point in assessing your personality and fit if you simply can't do the job. In such situations, candidates may face a test as a prerequisite for proceeding to the next stage of the interview process. Testers may be asked to write a test case, developers may be asked to write code or answer theoretical programming questions and administrative assistants may be required to sit a typing speed test.

## Panel Interview

Probably the most common format is the panel interview consisting of a technical expert, a manager (your prospective boss) and HR. Three is a typical number of interviewers and gender balance is usually a consideration. Such interviews can last up to an hour (sometimes longer) and you are bombarded from all angles – technical, behavioural and open-ended prompts designed to let you speak to see where you go.

## Presentation Interview

Typically used for sales and marketing roles, presentation interviews are demanding, requiring you to present ideas or solutions with minimal preparation time. For example, as a Marketing professional, you may be given a brief to develop a strategy or marketing plan for a new product, and told you have 30 minutes to prepare a presentation to the team. In this scenario, you will be assessed on your marketing knowledge, clear thinking, presentation skills and general professionalism.

## Group Interview

Common for Customer Service jobs and where the employer is trying to assess which role you naturally adopt in a team environment, group interviews usually involve an activity. For example, a group of engineers may be asked to work as a team to solve a design issue. Team members' performance will reveal assertiveness, ability to work together (listening, willingness to share an idea, etc.) technical competence, presentation skills and contribute to that all important decisive factor – gut feeling.

## Café Interview

Architects, graphic designers and other professionals with an artistic bent often find themselves having interviews over coffee. Don't be fooled by the casual atmosphere, you are still being assessed, albeit, in a less structured way. Apart from capability, 'fit' and 'likeability' are key determinants for whether you will be offered the job.

## Incidental interaction

Unscheduled, informal encounters with prospective employers, although not formally interviews, are often just as crucial in establishing a first impression. Whether it is at a conference, industry forum, meet-up or social event, your first interaction may be the decisive factor. Carry a business card (your resume is too large) with you always for that chance encounter, so you can turn any event into a networking opportunity. Networking is a 'slow-burn' strategy, so don't be too direct or pushy; it's best to let relationships evolve naturally and not start talking about employment as your first discussion topic. It may be one or two years down the track before anything comes to fruition.

## 6.1.2 How to Ace a Phone or Video Interview

### Phone interviews

Often, the first phase of the interview process and used as a screening device to weed out those with a level of English not quite adequate for a professional environment, phone interviews have advantages and disadvantages for the candidate.

### Technology

Modern day smartphones offer incredible convenience and diverse functionality, but we seem to have lost out in the quality of audio. I remember several years ago when we had a power outage that rendered our home cordless phone useless, I had to plug in the old wired phone to a connection in the wall that hadn't been used in ages. I wasn't even sure it was going to work. Well, when I made a call and heard the person on the other end, I couldn't believe my ears; it sounded as though they were standing next to me in the same room. We have become desensitised to inferior audio plagued by micro dropouts, unstable connections and limited coverage. Unfortunately, this inevitably detracts from good communication. As if it isn't hard enough speaking in a language other than your first; you must contend with the technology as well. A bad connection could really test the employer's patience.

- Buy a decent phone and subscribe to a quality carrier
- Check to see if you have good coverage prior the interview – call a friend or two.
- If in doubt, and if possible, use a landline (Do they still exist?) if the quality is better.
- Do not use speaker phone – test your headset and speaking directly to the phone mic, experimenting to find the best quality audio you can get.
- Remove as much ambient noise as possible – children, traffic, ceiling fans, hand tools, televisions, etc.

**Unexpected calls** from employers and recruiters put you on the back foot, leaving you vulnerable and unprepared. To ensure you have power in the conversation...

- Never allow yourself to be interviewed while in a noisy or public environment. If you receive a call while shopping or on public transport, explain your situation to the caller and let him/her know that you will call back in 10 minutes. Make sure you get the name of the person, the company they represent and their phone number. Don't be afraid to ask the information gathering questions, – be assertive and polite.
- Always carry a list of the people and organisations you have contacted recently regarding employment, with notes on the correspondence thus far. Refer to the list,

prepare what you are going to say and find a quiet space before returning the call.

- Slow down the tempo of the conversation by asking questions if you are unclear about anything, seeking clarification. *'I'm sorry, I didn't catch your name.' 'And where did you say you were from?'* You need to know if the person is an external recruiter or an employer.

- Speak clearly, slowly - if you tend to race, and with pauses between each of your statements. People will have more respect for you if you speak like someone who commands attention. Rushing just makes you sound unprofessional and flaky.

The same advice applies to **Scheduled calls,** but you have the added advantage of being able to prepare.

- Have your notes in front of you - consisting of prompts, short passages you want to remember, information about the employer and questions you would like to ask. This is certainly something you can't do face-to-face.

## Communication Skills

As with face-to-face interviews, underpinning your performance on the phone will be your ability to communicate.

Do you continually ask people to repeat themselves? Or do you finish the conversation wondering whether you've missed something crucial? Do people have trouble understanding *you* on the phone? If so, you need to practise. The more you talk on the phone, the more comfortable you will become. As fruitless as some of your conversations with recruiters may be, you can still use these opportunities to improve your phone communication. Record yourself and listen to your speech. Only then can you hear how others hear you, and you can adjust accordingly.

## Voicemail message

Does your message sound like this?

5 rings... *You've called the number of* ... [five-second delay] ... *Raj... Please leave a message after the tone*. Using a pre-recorded Telstra message is not very personal, and the gap left for you to record your name sounds clumsy and unprofessional. Or perhaps, you've recorded your own message. Have you listened to it? Is what you would expect from a professional?

Try: '*Hi, you've called Raj Patel. Please leave a message and I'll get back to you.*' – It's simple and brief.

## Live video interviews

Whether they are recorded or live Skype sessions, video interviews can be more difficult than your traditional interview. Here are a few tips to make sure you present yourself in the most professional manner.

- Prepare for the interview as you would for any interview; it's still an interview.
- Your computer should be positioned so the camera is at eye level
- Do **not** sit with a window behind you. If there is natural light in the room, make sure it is on your face.

- Use a high-quality headset with a good microphone – USB only. Audio is everything – interviewers will put up with a few frozen frames and video delay, but if the audio is poor – forget it. You may have just blown your chance.

- Test your internet connection to ensure you have sufficient upload and download speeds for a high-quality video-over-Internet experience. Purchase a USB 4G dongle if you need to a get faster, more reliable Internet connection.

- Find a quiet room with no distractions or ambient noise – children, traffic, television, etc.

- Look into the camera lens when you speak – imagine it is the interviewer. Resist looking at the image of yourself or the interviewer. To fully engage the interviewer, you need to look into his/her eyes, that is – the camera.

- Speak as if the interviewer is in the room. Project your voice – you need good volume to sound confident. Smile and be expressive. This can be hard if it is a recorded interview, but you need to try to make sure your personality comes through.

**Recorded webcam interviews**

As if face-to-face job interviews are not hard enough. Try convincing your webcam that you're the right person for the job.

Several overseas born professionals I've assisted recently have had to submit recorded job interviews, usually with large corporates who must be receiving hundreds of applications and find this screening process of value. It's no use complaining, so let's have a look at why webcam interviews are being used and how you can best prepare.

Just to clarify, we are not talking about real-time interviews conducted over Skype. This is where you are emailed a login link and you get, let's say, 20 minutes to answer half a dozen questions without notice.

For example:

- Tell us about how you prioritise tasks
- Tell us how you dealt with your most difficult client
- Tell us about a successful team you worked in
- Tell us about your leadership qualities
- Tell us about a time when you had to make a difficult decision

## Why are some employers using webcam interviews?

Employers may say that they receive so many applications that they simply don't have time to interview everyone and this is a quick way to see more people. They may be missing talent by assessing someone purely on written applications; it gives them an opportunity to see the 'whole person'. No doubt there is truth in the above explanation, but I'm guessing there are other reasons, ones that employers may feel less comfortable in making explicit.

For some roles, you are judged on how you look, sound and present yourself; none of these qualities can be seen in your CV and cover letter. Client-facing roles require you to be confident, socially adept and possess excellent communication skills. Think – Business Development, Account Manager, Sales & Marketing, Public Accountant, etc.

Will clients warm to you? Are you articulate? Do you know what you're talking about? Are you confident and assertive enough to negotiate strongly? Will you be able to handle the pressure? How will the team feel about you? These concerns are present at face-to-face interviews as well. But, no matter how much they would like to, it's not possible for the interviewer to fast-forward an applicant who is in the room.

A quick look at an applicant on video will help the employer to weed out those who do not portray good cultural fit. A candidate whose values, beliefs, outlook and behaviour are congruent with those existing within the current organisation is likely to be a good cultural fit for the organisation. Surely a real interview would be a better way of ascertaining 'fit', but a recorded interview can still provide some insight. The examples you provide as responses to the questions will shed light on your behaviour in given situations. Your attire, body language and spoken delivery will be used to assess your confidence and professionalism.

Now, what about the other 'culture'? That's right, culture as in the behaviours and beliefs characteristic of a particular ethnic group. For overseas born professionals, you will be facing an additional culture question. A video recording may reveal behaviours that an Australian employer sees as culturally jarring and as a would-be barrier to effective stakeholder engagement should they decide to appoint you. Voice projection, body language, eye contact (even though there is no eye with which to make contact in a video recording), level of formality, appropriateness of expressions and familiarity with idioms, etc. are all aspects of language & culture with which many overseas born professionals struggle. An employer will never cite this as a reason for using recorded video interviews, but you should be aware that they are assessing the 'whole person' and are trying to gauge whether you would be a good fit.

## Preparation

- As with any interview, **prepare examples** from your work experience to demonstrate how you have done what they are looking for. Questions usually revolve around how you handle difficult situations, problems or conflict, as well as positive ones, which ask you to demonstrate achievements, teamwork, leadership, etc. You can find a myriad of examples on the web. Give examples; don't ramble on with motherhood statements.

- **Practice speaking** your responses aloud and preferably record them so you can listen back and reflect, making necessary adjustments to the content and delivery. Practice, practice, practice. Get some feedback on your performance.

- Get the **lighting** right. Nobody looks good on webcam, but you can improve your appearance by having sufficient light on your face. Bring in extra desk lamps pointing to the ceiling, as general room lighting is usually not enough. Check your appearance on Skype or any other software that allows you to see yourself. And the golden rule for lighting – **no windows behind you**, or any source of light directed at the camera.

- Your **background** should be plain with no distractions.
- The **camera** should be at eye level. Raise your laptop on books if need be. Looking down into a camera will distort your face.
- Check your audio. Get familiar with your device and how to adjust audio settings to get the best quality and level.
- Check **specification requirements** for devices. Some sites will ask you to use an iPhone or tablet. If you are using your phone, rest it on something stable at eye level; do not hold it in your hand. If you have a choice of device, check to see which offers the best quality. An iPad is sometimes better than a cheap PC laptop - Mac devices generally have high-quality audio-visual components.
- **Cover your screen image**. It is virtually impossible not to look at yourself if you can see your image while you are speaking. This is a major distraction and will detract from your performance. You may not be able to minimise the image because you'll have to click on to the next question, but you can cover your screen image with a piece of card strategically placed. Make sure you do not cover the camera.
- **Read the instructions** on how to record & submit your video. Getting stressed out because you haven't carefully read the instructions is the last thing you want.

- Most importantly, **look into the camera**. You need to make a connection with the viewer even though they are not in the room. Treat the camera as the interviewer's eyes. Some people suggest having a friend in the room sitting behind the device – not the best idea. It will appear that you are looking into the distance, not at the viewer.

- **Dress appropriately** for the interview. Just because you are recording it in your bedroom, doesn't mean you should wear your pyjamas.

## 6.1.3 Preparation

Know the job. Know the company. Know why you are the right person for the role.

How can you convince an employer that you can do the job, if you are not sure what the job entails? Do your research well in advance by dissecting the position description and company website. Seek out press releases, annual reports or any other sources of information that may be relevant.

If there is a contact person listed in the job ad, ring them. You may be able to elicit more information that could be helpful in your preparation. They may not be forthcoming with information, but it's worth a try. You can ask specific technical questions about the role, or practical questions such as, *'Is it a new position, or is it replacing someone leaving?'* One or two questions will suffice, and hopefully, the contact person will reveal some useful information about the role or current projects.

There are certain parts of an interview where you'll able to recite your prepared responses. Tell me about yourself. Why have you applied for the job? Etc.

## Write, Check, Rehearse

*'She doesn't sound like the person in the CV'.*

*'I'm not convinced he's been a Team Lead'.*

[Frequent comments I've heard from employers over the years after they've met the person in the CV]

You've received professional assistance in creating an impressive CV, but that is all wasted if you can't match it with your communication and interpersonal skills. Your ability to articulate what you have done and to speak with the confidence of a professional is crucial in any interaction you have with your prospective employer. What are you doing in preparation for this inevitable encounter? If the answer is, 'nothing', you need to think again. You may be competing against candidates who were born in Australia, have local experience, speak English as their first language and are adept at weaving humour and cultural references into the conversation.

Let's have a look at a three-step approach to preparation:

- **Write**

  Write down what you want to say to the prompt, '*Tell me about yourself*', for example, or any question you are likely to be asked by an employer. Writing your response allows you to organise your ideas so you are succinct. It also allows you to read your response and identify things you'd like to change – Can you substitute with a better word to express your idea? Are you using appropriate technical language? Do you sound like an expert? Or is the language dumbed-down because of your limited vocabulary? A written response also allows you to pass on the spiel to someone else for feedback – the next step in the preparation process.

*Warning: Written English and spoken English are not the same. One danger of writing it down is that it reads like written English. Avoid markers like, 'Moreover', etc. Some words we use in written English are rarely used in spoken English. Professional advice will be able to iron out any issues you have with your choice of expressions.*

- **Check**

Get someone who has been in Australia for a long time, preferably a speaker of English as their first language, to check your spiel – even better if it is a mentor from your profession. Take advice and make changes.

- **Rehearse**

This is the stage that most people do not bother attempting. It is one thing to have the knowledge in your head; it is another matter altogether to have it come out of your mouth the way you want it to sound. Producing language, like any active skill, requires practice.

Read your spiel aloud, record it (audio/video) & listen to your voice. The simple act of listening to yourself will prompt you to make changes to the content and delivery. Get into the habit of recording yourself and playing it back. Better still, get professional tuition to produce impressive and professional spoken English, along with some tips about local culture to give you that extra edge over other candidates. You can also use those numerous discussions you have with recruiters, over the phone or face-to-face, to practise your speaking skills.

## 6.1.4 Dealing with Anxiety

The most common cause of anxiety in job interviews is fear of the unknown. You should be able to determine most of what an interviewer is going to throw at you, so there is no reason why you can't prepare responses to avoid surprises. Follow the steps above to ensure you are as prepared as possible.

Then there is the weakness that you are hoping nobody will question you on – *'What experience have you had working in a SAP environment?'* Yikes! Well, it was in the position description, so you've had time to think of a response. Avoidance or hoping something won't happen is high octane fuel for anxiety. Prepare your best response, and then you will have peace of mind that at least you know what you are going to say.

Allow yourself plenty of time to arrive at the interview location without fear of delay. I suggest arriving near the office an hour before to minimise causes of delay, travel the route the day before and do anything you can to avoid being late – a stress you do not need.

Take the pressure off yourself. If you don't get the job, yes, it's disappointing but you will wake up the next day – life goes on.

Do whatever you need to be alert and alive – drink your morning coffee, exercise, get some fresh air, etc.

Don't forget to breathe. When we get nervous, we tend to take short, shallow breaths which don't help with voice projection and exuding confidence.

## 6.1.5 What to Wear/ Interview Attire

Know your industry and know the culture of your employer. I once knew an accountant who went to an interview dressed in a standard dark suit and tie. Unfortunately, he didn't do his research on the company - a design studio where the average age of the team was about 26 years old. When he arrived, the interviewers were dressed in shorts and thongs (flip-flops) and the office was a cool converted warehouse. He looked as though he'd lost his way and was asking for directions to a funeral.

For general business attire, go to the city at 8:45 am and watch the passengers get off the train. You'll get a feel for what's standard. Fashions change, so it's important to keep abreast. Ties seem to be less common than they were 10 years ago, but are still essential for some employers. Ask around.

Warning: Any suit is not necessarily appropriate – colour, style and fit are equally important to demonstrate you fit in. It's best to buy a suit in Australia and get advice on style and fit for your age & profession. For women, there is a little more flexibility. Again, use your eyes and ask the opinion of several people.

## 6.2 Psychometric Testing and Aptitude Tests

Psychometric tests are designed to assess your cognitive ability and suitability for particular jobs based on your personality type and preferences. Tests are usually broken up into categories: personality, aptitude, verbal reasoning, numerical reasoning, abstract reasoning, situational judgement, etc. Much effort from psychologists had been devoted to ensuring that the tests work as an accurate measure of the type of person you are, with often up to 100 questions making up the test.

With practice, you can certainly improve (to some degree) your score for tests designed to measure your intelligence. There are plenty of free sample tests available on the web, and it's a good idea to familiarise yourself with the format and type of questions. Preparation for the day of the test is also important:

- Get a good night's sleep - you need to be alert
- Use a calculator for the numerical reasoning if permitted
- Practice doing the test as quickly as you can once you are comfortable with the format

It is a little more difficult to prepare for the personality test component. The idea is that you should answer questions honestly, and your responses will indicate to what degree you are suited to the role. That's fine if your personality is well-aligned to your profession, but problematic if not. I once knew a Business Analyst with 10 years of international experience, who was told repeatedly that his personality test indicated that he was not suited to being a Business Analyst. You can imagine how this was received. I suppose at this point you would need to understand the character traits expected for your profession and answer accordingly. Trying to trick the system is probably not advisable and usually unnecessary anyway.

## 6.3 How to Address Tough Interview Questions

A good interview is a conversation. If it is a series of Q&A exchanges, chances are you will not be successful; the employer will not get a feel of what it would be like to work with you, where conversations are the norm and a means to solve problems. It should be an opportunity for the employer to assess whether you are the right person for the job, but it is also an opportunity for you to decide if the job is right for you. A problem with focusing too much on potential questions is that we forget that it's really a process to assess your 'fit' for the job. So, if the employer is asking all the questions, the onus is on you to turn it into a conversation. You do that by asking questions to create a two-way flow.

Providing suggested answers to tough questions is fraught; what may be appropriate for one situation could be highly inappropriate in another. Instead, let's look at ways to approach interview questions. Ideally, you should be able to predict the vast majority of what is going to be asked in an interview. However, only coaching and practice is going to lift you the heights of an elite performer.

## What is your weakness?

Ask yourself why you do the job you do. My guess is it's because you like it and you are good at it. As a logical extension of this reasoning, you should be residing in your strengths, not weaknesses. Your major weaknesses should be in areas outside your vocational realm. You need to be confident. The employer wants someone who can do the job, not someone who sees themselves as lacking.

The following items are **NOT weaknesses**; they are opportunities. Do NOT 'own' a weakness that will prevent you from being employed.

- No local experience
- Not familiar with a particular software package
- Age

The following items are weaknesses. If you have these weaknesses, fix them. If you go into a job interview with any of these weaknesses, you do not deserve to be given the job. Why would an employer want to hire someone who can't do a necessary part of the job? You need to convince the interviewer that you can do the job.

- Poor communication skills
- Poor understanding of the job
- Inability to show initiative
- Inability to manage your time effectively

- Poor ICT skills
- Lack of knowledge of local standards

You need to be prepared to discuss what the employer might perceive as a weakness. So, what is your weakness in their eyes? Make a list of the perceived weaknesses and prepare responses. Some examples of how you might tackle this question...

### So, what is your weakness?

*Well, as far as my job is concerned, I don't think I really have a <u>major</u> weakness. I'm lucky in that I love my job and I think I'm good at it because it allows me to employ my strengths. I enjoy solving problems and working with people from a range of professions – contractors, managers, office staff. I thrive on responsibility and the challenge of doing things I've never done before– learning is a great motivator. But, if you have any concerns with any part of my resume or experience, I'm more than happy to discuss them. Was there something in particular that concerned you?*

### Well, I see you don't have any experience in Australia.

*That's right. But I don't really see that as a weakness. My international experience has been in a company very similar to yours. The road construction projects I've worked on have employed professionals from all over the world. I've worked with a range of standards and I have a good understanding of Australian standards. For example... [demonstrate the similarities and differences between the Australian standards and those you've used internationally]*

**Well, you haven't used the software application we use.**

*That's right. But I don't really see that as a weakness. When I began my last job I hadn't used their package either, but my exposure to a wide range of applications means that my intuition is strong and I can pick up what's required pretty quickly. I believe the program you use is... which, from my understanding, is similar in some respects to ... For example ... [elaborate on a specific similarity]*

The key to the above response is not to sound arrogant, but confident in your ability. You achieve this by talking in specifics (detail) and opening yourself up to questioning. Without substance to back up your claims, you will sound foolish; you can only attempt this if you have done your research. If a true weakness is revealed, it will need to be discussed, and the employer (and you) will need to decide whether it is something that can be overcome, or whether it is a barrier to employment. Either way, you should not be afraid to talk about it. If for example, the role requires you to present publicly to important stakeholders and you have a mortal fear of public speaking causing you to freeze with stage fright, even after months of Toastmaster attempts, I would suggest that you have more work to do before you could be expecting an offer.

Alternatively, you can regurgitate the tried (trite) and true responses to this question suggested on copious websites and forums. Most of these responses will safely move you on to the next question without damage, but you may have just lost an opportunity to win the interview.

**Tell me about yourself.**

This is a great question because the employer has not given you any boundaries. They want to see how you will use the next couple of minutes. So much can be gleaned by simply listening to someone speak. You need to give a summary of your experience that is relevant to the role and reveal a little about yourself. That's right, some personal information about what you like doing in your spare time. Some of the interview panel members could be spending the entire working day with you; they need to warm to you. Nobody is 100% engineer.

To avoid rambling, pepper your speech with questions. After explaining an aspect of your experience, you could say, '*Would you like me to talk more about … or would you like to hear about…?* Again, you are creating a conversation and ending the examination.

'On a personal note, I like to ...

Talk specifics. Instead of just saying, 'I like photography'.

Say, '...*especially beach scenes. I've just returned from the Great Ocean Road where I got some great shots*'.

The aim here is to get someone to bite, to make a connection – that says, we are not different, we are the same.

*Really? What sort of camera have you got?*

Bang! You've made the connection.

## Technical Questions

Know your stuff. Use examples to illustrate and speak as if you are speaking to another expert – don't 'dumb it down', even for HR. You need to sound like the expert they require. All experienced professionals have the knowledge to answer the technical questions, but it is a completely separate skill to articulate that in an interview. Follow the Write-Check-Rehearse steps to ensure your responses are clear and succinct.

## Behavioural Questions

Either presented as a hypothetical scenario or a request for you to tell a story, behavioural questions are designed to reveal your thought process and see how you would respond in each situation, ideally one with which you are likely to confronted while doing the job in question. The key here is to be structured with your response and not to ramble (go off topic).

There are several ways to structure your response to stay on track, one being the **STAR approach**.

*Situation – set the scene: Where? Who? Your role?*

*Task – What was required to solve the problem?*

*Action – What action did you take?*

*Response – What was the result of the action taken?*

Don't spend too long setting the scene, which is where most people get bogged down. The purpose of adhering to a structure is to keep it succinct. If you feel like you are talking too much, think about which letter (STAR) you are up to and maybe it's time to move on. Have a bank of short stories you can use to demonstrate the following:

- How you have handled conflict/a difficult customer
- A disagreement with your manager/colleague
- A difficult decision you have had to make
- How you have dealt with an under-performing team member
- A team you have led, etc.

Google 'Behavioural questions', and you'll find plenty of common ones for which you can prepare responses. The best behavioural questions are ones that reflect scenarios likely to occur in the job. If you're asked, *'What would you do if...?'* , generally, there is insufficient information supplied to give a comprehensive response. A good way to start is by saying, *'Well, that depends...'* This allows you to present several options depending on specific circumstance, or ask more questions about the situation. Remember, the interviewer may not be looking for the 'golden answer', but could be more interested in analysing your thought process. An employer wants someone who is smart, not someone who is going to jump at the first simplistic solution after being given limited information. Sometimes, an intelligent question is more impressive than an answer.

MIGRANT NINJA TIP:

- **Remember to follow up every job application with a phone call to the person in charge to confirm receipt of your resume and to ask for any clarifications about the application process. This highlights your interest in the job as well as helps build a rapport with the employer.**

- **Similarly, after the selection process is complete, if you were unsuccessful in getting the position, call up and ask for feedback about your performance. This will help identify your weaknesses and will make you better prepared for the next opportunities.**

## 6.4 Do's and Don'ts during the Interview Process

**Do**:

- Dress appropriately
- Ask questions
- Smile – culturally, it suggests you are confident, and therefore perceived as being good at your job
- Make good eye contact
- Offer a firm handshake
- Address people by their first name only (We don't use 'Mr' 'Ms' 'Sir' or 'Madam' in Australia)
- Make it a conversation, not an examination
- Know your salary range just in case you are asked. There are plenty of salary guides on the web – SEEK, Hays, Glassdoor, etc.

**Don't**:

- Ask about the salary at the first interview. Job fit comes first, then salary is discussed once you are considered potentially suitable
- Don't be late – punctuality in Australia is paramount

MIGRANT NINJA TIP:

**Remember that the company already has an interest in you. Employers don't interview everyone. They only interview those people who they think have the right skills and experience to succeed in the position. It is vital that you remember this during the course of the interview and you build on the positive image that you have already created.**

**The other important point to remember is that selection is a two-way process. They select you, but you also select them. So don't be afraid to ask questions and maintain a positive body language.**

**Further to Terry's tips, here are some additional Do's and Don'ts:**

**Do:**

- **maintain a positive and confident attitude.**
- **show passion and enthusiasm for the position.**
- **Make sure you fully understand the question and query any point about which you may be doubtful.**
- **Make eye-contact.**
- **Have a list of prepared questions to ask about the company and your particular position.**
- **promote your strengths and sell yourself.**
- **Have a good understanding of the job, the company and the industry. Do your homework before the interview.**

- let the employer know you have a clear career plan.
- highlight how you can benefit the company.
- If you are being interviewed by a panel, ensure that you direct your reply to the person who raised the question, while still including the other interviewers by making brief eye contact.

**Don't:**

- go into the interview without doing your homework.
- arrive late, sweaty and flustered – this will end the interview before it begins.
- leave your mobile phone on. Most basic protocol but one that is often forgotten.
- interrupt the interviewer before they have finished asking you a question
- Never finish the interviewer's sentences for them.
- fidget too much. Display a confident personality even when you are waiting in the reception area.
- Conversely, don't sit rigidly during the entire interview If you feel more comfortable talking with the aid of your hands for emphasis, then use them, but do not overdo the gestures.
- answer questions with a simple "yes" or "no". Elaborate on your viewpoint and give examples whenever you can.
- make negative remarks about past or present employers.
- talk about salary, holidays or bonuses unless the interviewer brings it up.

## 6.5 Challenges Faced by Migrants When Competing in Australian Job Market

Over the past decade, I have heard the same **feedback from employers** regarding interviewee shortcomings. The following is a list of 'Areas Needing Improvement in Interview Performance' (as noted by interviewers):

- Not speaking in the specific "deep" technical terms of your profession – to convince the panel that your CV Profile is an accurate description of your skill level (e.g. no use of technical jargon, acronyms, formulae, "insider" terms for the tools and processes of engineering, science, accounting or IT, etc.; only superficial reference to specific work examples, without any actual descriptions of tasks performed)

- Not speaking to the point / vague generalisations / "motherhood statements"

- lists of either, the attitudes/behaviours, or the specific processes/stages necessary for effective teamwork in the workplace

- Inability to verbalise succinctly regarding effective Quality Assurance / Project Management when required

- Not enough effective research or consideration of what the job in the PD might entail

- No effective knowledge of the employer or their position in the industry. Long preambles and introductions before even beginning to answer a question (sometimes no answer was given at all, just a rephrasing of the question as a statement or "claim"). No understanding of verbal "demonstration" of knowledge or skill, as distinct from "claim".

- Little evidence of the logical thinking and problem-solving that should come with higher education or technical experience – despite CLEAR provision of opportunities to do just that.
- No evidence of recent reading: technical, professional or news and current affairs to do with your profession.
- Poor covering emails (unprofessional, too informal, bad spelling and grammar) and poor application letters (not directed at the actual job in question).
- Overseas born professionals present as overly formal – use of 'Sir', 'Mr',

## 6.6 Questions for the Interviewer

Usually, at the end of the interview, you are asked if you have any further questions or anything else to add. At this point, it is good to have something to say. Some appropriate questions at this point could be...

- How would you evaluate the performance of the person in this role?
- What do you see as the biggest challenge for the successful candidate?
- When do you expect to make a decision?

It is a good idea to take in your notebook with a few 'must say' points jotted down, just in case you haven't had a chance to mention a critical aspect of your skills or experience. You don't want to leave the interview thinking, *'I forgot to tell them...'*

## 6.7 Last Words by Terry O'Reilly

Attending an interview can be a daunting prospect, but with the right preparation and support, it can be an opportunity to relish – a chance to demonstrate the relevance of your skills and experience. Try to stay focused on what the job requires and give examples of having done that, as opposed to waxing lyrical about your glorious career.

Facing an interview presents different challenges for different people. It is worth engaging the services of professional who can diagnose problems, guide you and structure practice exercises to address your specific issues. Video recording mock interviews and evaluating your performance is the quickest way to make a dramatic improvement. You'll be surprised by your progress once you have had a chance to see and hear yourself.

Above all, **listen**. A danger in preparing set responses is that you will go into the interview hell-bent on telling your 'stories', regardless of what you have been asked. At the end of the interview, both you and the interviewer should feel like you've had a good chat; your suitability (or lack of) should be evident to both of you.

Contact Details:
Terry O'Reilly
Website: OBP Australia
Address: 829A High Street Thornbury VIC Australia
Phone: +61 409 330 727 / Skype: OBP Australia

## 6.8 Negotiating Salary

Salary negotiation is a challenging task in any situation, but it is even more daunting when you're negotiating for your first job in Australia. Firstly research average entry-level salaries in your industry. HAYS Salary Guide is a great place to get this information.

Talking about salary up front is not a good thing at best of times. As a new migrant with no local experience, it makes it that much harder. Demonstrate your soft skills like leadership and problem solving along with your core competence and experience to impress the selection panel. So, how can you make a strong case for yourself? Your first action should be to negotiate in a friendly and professional manner when you receive your offer.

- Don't lose your enthusiasm even when the offer is lower than expected.
- Ask to review the offer and weigh all your options before you negotiate – jumping into a negotiation or accepting an offer immediately is a sign of impulsiveness, which you will want to avoid.
- Use the offer to ask about the benefits you may be entitled to above your salary.
- Be prompt and polite with your negotiation for a better salary or more incentives.
- Be thoughtful of what you ask for and make sure it is within reason.

**Negotiate only if you know there is an opportunity to get something more in your favour. Don't over-negotiate or you might end up losing the job. Remember it is not just the salary but also the opportunity to grow in the organisation and within the industry.**

## 6.9 Discussing Relocation Packages

When it comes to relocation packages, negotiating and discussing them with prospective employers involves understanding your own needs before incorporating them into binding agreements. Some of the things to consider when negotiating a relocation package are:

### Cost Of Living

If you are moving interstate or from a new country, you must be aware that Australia has a high cost of living, especially if you're moving to an urban city. You must take into account the cost of living of the place you are moving to so that you can negotiate for a well-planned relocation package. Cost of living involves rent, groceries, entertainment, transport and much more.

### Employment Status

You should know how long your contract is valid for when negotiating the terms of your relocation package. If your contract includes an option for the company to reassign you to a new location once the contract ends, ensure that they offer you an equivalent standard of living in any new location.

**Accommodation Allowance**

If your relocation package involves accommodation allowance, you should do enough research to ensure it meets your needs in the new city. Rents in Sydney and Melbourne tend to be much higher than in regional towns. Don't assume that the accommodation allowance is enough to meet your needs. Be sure to check thoroughly to help you when negotiating for a higher allowance.

**Additional Perks**

If your job requires a lot of travelling within small areas, you may want to negotiate for the use of a car for better productivity. You may also be in a position to negotiate for flight tickets to the new destination. Some companies also offer annual flights as part of their relocation packages.

The most effective technique when negotiating for relocation packages is to choose your battles. Consider the perks that may be available to you and prioritise them based on what you want. You may have to concede some benefits, but this is worthwhile when you consider the ones that are more important for you.

## 6.10 Not Getting Employed? Here are Some Reasons Why!

If you've been trying for quite a while and you still can't find a job, it's likely there are certainly other issues that could probably be the underlying cause of the failures:

## 1. You are only relying on advertised jobs but not tapping the hidden market.

According to one estimate, that's only about 15% of the job market. This is highly disadvantageous and the quicker you start networking the earlier \you may get a job placement.

## 2. You've been applying for the wrong roles or not meeting the selection criteria.

Most of the advertised jobs have a list of mandatory 'must-have' skills and requirements and if you do not satisfy them then you will not be considered for the role. Sometimes these requirements are not clearly laid out and hidden somewhere in the elaborate description.

## 3. The number of applicants for the role is simply too high.

This might be the case if you are applying for an entry or mid-level job, or there is a high unemployment rate in the industry.

## 4. Your skill set is not current.

Your skills are either not current or in demand. You haven't kept up to date with the latest technology.

## 5. Your soft skills need to be addressed.

Maybe your English needs to be improved upon. Maybe you lack basic teamwork skills that an employer seeks in the Australian workspace.

Always take feedback from the recruiter or the interview panel and strive to address your weakness.

## 6. You have pre-conceived notions or fears that prohibit you from performing well during the interview.

You don't get job offers and you question what went wrong - Was it my ethnicity, my name, my age? Although some form of discrimination may exist with certain employers, Australians cannot have such biases by law. Besides, in a country with so many immigrants, they can't afford to have such an attitude. If you have the required qualifications and you are the right fit, you are going to get employed.

# 7. Australian Job Market – An Introduction

Do you fancy the idea of living in a country far away from the rest of the world? Do you enjoy blue skies, pristine seas, outdoor living, sports and a balanced lifestyle? Welcome to Australia – the country that offers you all of this and so much more.

Although spectacular natural beauty, high standards of living and a comfortable lifestyle make this country an attractive proposition, migration is a big decision and there are some hard hitting facts you need to be aware of before deciding to move here, especially when it comes to the local job market.

## 7.1 Major Cities and Regional Towns – A Comparison

Deciding where to live in Australia isn't as straightforward as you assume. The country which is the smallest continent also happens to be the world's largest island.

Whilst job opportunities exist in all states, you should know that the job market is Australia is not evenly distributed across geographic locations. This may influence your decision about where you will eventually settle.

According to the Australian Bureau of Statistics (ABS), nearly 85 percent of migrants live in major urban areas to secure jobs. Based on your skill, visa conditions and family situation, you must assess the feasibility of which area you want to live in.

Living in the big four cities (Melbourne, Sydney, Perth and Brisbane) is usually the top choice for all migrants but you should not rule out moving to other cities or regional towns as they offer certain benefits and lifestyle choices that big city living cannot provide.

In 2009, over two-thirds (69%) of Australians lived in major cities, one in five (20%) lived in inner regional areas, one in 10 (9%) in outer regional areas and around one in 40 (2.3%) lived in remote or very remote areas (1.5% remote and 0.8% very remote). (An Australian Institute of Family Studies (AIFS) Report)

Eventually, the industry you are in and the market conditions at the time will decide where you will eventually move.

### *DID YOU KNOW:*

- *Australia is one of the world's most urbanised countries, with about 70 percent of the population living in the 10 largest cities. Most of the population is concentrated along the eastern seaboard and the south-eastern corner of the continent.*
- *Australia is comparable in size to the continental United States.*
- *It is the world's sixth-largest country by total area.*
- *It takes three days to cross Australia by train and five hours by plane, the country measures approximately 4,000 km from east to west and 3,200 km from north to south.*

## Big City Living versus Small City Living

To put things in perspective, here are a few comparisons of Big City living versus life in regional towns. Although, definition of big and small city is very subjective based on the type of comparison (economic growth, population density, infrastructure to name a few), let's segregate the big cities in terms of urbanization and potential for employment: Sydney, Melbourne, Brisbane, Perth, Adelaide, Gold Coast, Sunshine Coast, Canberra, Hobart and Darwin. These 'Capital' cities offer a different set of opportunities and pose certain challenges which differ from the 'regional' towns across the country.

## Travel Time

Although, public transport is quite good in big cities, the time spent travelling, whether via public transport or by car, usually takes an hour or two depending on the location of suburb and distance from the place of work. Smaller cities provide the luxury of less travel time, but you are better off with your own car as public transport is not comparable to the big cities.

## Home Ownership

Smaller cities and regional areas have a higher level of home ownership compared to urban towns because of the lower cost of real estate, but the return on investment is equally lower.

## Job Opportunities

There's no doubt that bigger cities have access to more jobs than small cities, but the fact remains that competition is also higher. Migrants with specific skills relevant to smaller towns may find them more appealing because of the lower costs and more relaxed lifestyle.

## Education & Social amenities

Bigger cities offer access to some of Australia's top ranking schools and universities. Additionally, healthcare facilities and general infrastructure are much better in the big cities. Even for entertainment, the bigger cities have far more to offer than the small towns. One of the major deciding factors when it comes to migrants with children is the education facilities and future planning in terms of access to universities.

MIGRANT NINJA TIP:

**According to the Australian Bureau of Statistics (ABS), nearly 85 percent of migrants live in major urban areas to secure jobs. Based on your skill, visa conditions and family situation, you must assess the feasibility of which area you want to live in.**

_DID YOU KNOW:_

_FLYING DOCTORS - Australia is a vast land, and for many Australians living in the rural outposts, the nearest doctor can be thousands of miles away. The mission of the Royal Flying Doctor Service (RFDS) is to provide primary health care across the vast continent. It is the largest and most comprehensive aeromedical organisations in the world. They have a national fleet has 66 aircraft, 23 aero-bases, 48 road patient vehicles, and a waiting room spanning 71.6 million square kilometres. The organisation had over 290,000 patient contacts in 2015 alone._

## 7.2 Job Market Demographics across Australia – A Synopsis

### New South Wales

New South Wales has 40% of Australia's ICT employment. Specialist ICT businesses employ almost 100,000 people. This state is also home to 80% of the multinational pharmaceutical companies in the country. The NSW State economy is the largest and most diverse in Australia with the total value of goods and services produced in NSW being greater than many national economies in the Asia Pacific.

Food retailing is the biggest driver of growth in NSW's retail industry.

Mining, resources and energy is a booming part of the New South Wales economy, driven by large and diverse mineral and gas deposits, exploration projects and a burgeoning renewable energy sector. New South Wales is the crown jewel in one of the world's premier tourist destinations and jobs in this industry abound.

Sydney is the third largest financial centre in the region, offering great career opportunities in a range of fields. It is Australia's main industrial city, with manufacturing contributing $31 billion, or 7%, to the NSW economy and employing around 250,000 people.

Regional NSW is also a hub for manufacturing activity, with the state home to more than 60% of Australia's regional manufacturing headquarters. Newcastle in NSW is a smaller regional city in the state offering green spaces, tree-lined streets and good educational facilities, along with job opportunities in healthcare, finance, manufacturing and heavy industries.

## Victoria

Victoria is the hub of Australia's automotive industry - it is responsible for around 60 percent of the country's automotive turnover, and a significant proportion of exports.

Victoria is home to about 150 biotechnology companies, as well as 13 major medical research institutes, 10 teaching hospitals conducting significant research, and 9 universities, together employing about 22,000 people in the life sciences sector.

Victoria has the largest manufacturing industry in Australia, with approximately 30 percent of the country's manufacturing workers employed in Victoria.

According to the '2010-2011 Teacher Supply and Demand Report' released by the Department of Education and Early Childhood Development,  there are over 72,500 teachers employed in schools across Victoria and the demand for teachers is predicted to increase, especially in secondary schools.

Around one-third of all financial and insurance activity in Australia takes place in Victoria. Two of Australia's four biggest banks and hundreds of fund and investment managers are based in Melbourne.

Victoria's hospitality industry is the second largest in Australia.

Approximately one-third of Australia's information and communications technology (ICT) professionals are employed in Victoria

Victoria's manufacturing sector encompasses a broad range of industries, including automotive, advanced electronics and machinery, aerospace and aviation, defence, chemicals and plastics, pharmaceuticals, fabricated metals, textiles, clothing and footwear (TCF) and food processing.

Victoria accounts for around 45 per cent of Australia's communications industry production. Major telecommunications equipment manufacturers and computer companies are also located in the state

Melbourne is one of the largest cities in Australia, and in terms of job opportunities, you are likely to find jobs related to media, finance, technology, real estate, technical services, communications, marketing, sales and much more. Average income tends to be higher in these cities, but so does the cost of living. Most of Australia's large mining and minerals processing companies are headquartered in Melbourne.

Ballarat in regional Victoria offers tourism, retail, hospitality, education, professional services and manufacturing opportunities to people look for jobs.

Agribusiness and high-tech manufacturing, Wheat production, Wineries, Forestry and horticulture, Automotive, Aluminium smelting and Tourism are some of the industries in the regional cities.

## Australian Capital Territory

Canberra has a unique employment market – here, you'll find the best-educated workforce and the highest per capita income in Australia. Their economy is sophisticated and knowledge based, orientated towards service delivery and public administration. The Commonwealth Government is the largest employer and also the biggest customer.

Like any growing city, they have ongoing needs in other key sectors including health and building and construction.

The thriving private sector comprises large multinational companies dealing with government down to small businesses servicing the needs of locals.

Tourism is the largest private sector segment of the ACT economy and offers great employment opportunities on the casual, part-time and full-time basis.

As Australia's capital, Canberra is home to the Australian Public Service – the administrative arm of the Australian Government. The Australian Public Service, or APS, is renowned as one of the most innovative government administrations in the world and is Canberra's biggest employer.

Defence and security are among Canberra's largest industry sectors and over 13,000 military and defence-civilian personnel are located in the capital region. The Department of Defence is based here, along with the Royal Military College and Australian Defence Force Academy.

Around 50 per cent of employment in the ACT is within the public service (federal and territory) and defence sectors.

MIGRANT NINJA TIP:

**It's important to note that employment with the APS will usually require Australian citizenship, however, exceptions are sometimes made.**

## Western Australia

The Western Australian economy is largely dominated by the mining and resources sector. Western Australia's land is rich with resources (iron ore, gold, natural gas and diamonds) that are mined, processed and exported all over the world.

The State produces several Agricultural products for Australia and the international export market: wheat, barley and other grains; wool, lamb and beef; seafood (western rock lobsters, prawns, crabs, shark and tuna); and wine.

The manufacturing of mined resources (engineering metals, shipbuilding, petrol and diesel) form a large proportion of this industry.

Food manufacturing and processing from the agricultural industry contribute strongly to the economy.

Tourism and education industries have grown significantly during the past few years with more international tourists visiting Western Australia and students choosing to study here.

Kalgoorlie in WA thrives on gold mining with active mines acting as major suppliers of gold jewellery to different countries around the world.

## Northern Territory

The Northern Territory's economy is largely driven by mining, which is concentrated on energy producing minerals and petroleum. Tourism also contributes significantly to the economy, especially Kakadu National Park in the Top End and the Uluru-Kata Tjuta National Park (Ayers Rock) in central Australia.

The economy is further supported by agriculture, fishing, tourism, and public administration. This dynamic city is strategically placed as Australia's closest capital to Asia. Darwin is developing this strategic position for shipping, regional freight and as a distribution gateway. Darwin is a fast growing city and this is expected to continue, with population growth driven by economic expansion from new oil and gas projects, mining exports, airport and rail upgrades to cope with increased passenger loads, and defence and port development.

Darwin is a city built on the mining boom, so most of the jobs related to mining, geology and construction are available.

## Queensland

In Queensland, the industries expected to record employment growth to 2016–2017 include health care and social assistance, professional, scientific and technical services, construction and mining. These industries are forecast to provide more than 60% of employment growth in the next 5 years.

Queensland is Australia's second largest tourism market after New South Wales.

Agriculture provides the original base for the development of the Queensland economy. The resources sector has been a key driver of growth in Queensland. The state's coal and bauxite reserves are among the largest in the world. Queensland is the world's largest seaborne exporter of metallurgical coal, with total coal exports exceeding 220 million tonnes in 2014-15. Construction is another key driver of the Queensland economy.

## South Australia

South Australia offers skilled employment opportunities in many industry sectors, including resources, health services, engineering, management and trades

South Australia produces more than half of all Australian wine exports and is the world's sixth largest wine producer. The state continues to be a global exporter of minerals and ores, wine, meat and seafood.

Adelaide is Australia's defence capital, with a strong cluster of defence R&D centres and associated companies and a strong interrelationship with a fast-growing, niche-driven electronics industry. It is also the Asia Pacific base for a growing number of back office, shared service, contact centre, data centre, help desk and administration and processing operations of major global companies.

Bioscience is a rapidly developing new industry, with 50 new companies expected to set up in the state in the next decade. South Australia's information and communications technologies (ICT) industries base are one of the fastest growing in Australia.

Adelaide is well known for its manufacturing sectors, so people engaged in engineering and manufacturing will find this city attractive for settling down.

Mount Gambier in SA offers opportunities related to tourism, hospitality, government administration, agriculture, forestry and transportation.

### DID YOU KNOW:

*If Australia were a city, at 23.5 million, it would still only be the world's seventh largest (after Tokyo, Guangzhou, Shanghai, Jakarta, Seoul and Delhi).*

## Tasmania

Tasmania has a diverse economy with hundreds of significant exporters. The exports go mainly to Asia, and Japan is Tasmania's largest single customer.

The greatest demand is generated by the public sector. There are probably more government jobs per head of population in Tasmania than anywhere else in Australia.

The major industries here are - Metal production, tourism, manufacturing (textiles, machinery, including marine, automotive components, heavy engineering and mining equipment)

About half of all Australian exports of woodchips, newsprint and writing paper come from Tasmania

The City of Hobart operates as a regional service centre with a high proportion of employment in the following industry sectors:

Public Administration & Safety, Health Care and Social Assistance, Education & Training, Retail Trade, Professional, Scientific & Technical Services

***DID YOU KNOW:***

***In the last 100 years, Australia has only created two new cities: places that had no population base and are now stand-alone cities: Canberra (our 8th largest currently) and the Gold Coast (6th largest)!***

## 7.3 Types of Employment

Employees are entitled to different benefits based on their types of employment. Some employment types are:

- Permanent or full time
- Permanent part time
- Part time
- Casual
- Temporary

Read more about types of employees here for more insights.

***DID YOU KNOW:***

***From January 1, 2010, Australia enacted a 38-hour workweek in accordance with the Fair Work Act 2009, with an allowance for additional hours as overtime.***

## 7.3.1 Permanent Jobs

A permanent full-time employee – on an average – works for around 38 hours every week and has ongoing employment with a particular company. A permanent part-time employee enjoys many benefits that full-time employees do, but typically works for less than 38 hours a week. As a permanent part-time employee, you are an employee of an organisation, so you can only leave when your employment contract ends, if you decide to resign or if you are let go. The number of hours and working days are usually set and agreed upon in advance. Some employees may also be hired for fixed terms. While permanent employees are ongoing until one party ends the relationship, fixed-term employment means that the worker is employed for a designated task or time frame. Fixed term employees typically enjoy the same benefits and wages as permanent employees during the period of their employment. The actual number of hours differs in every industry and is subject to an agreement between the employee and employer through a registered agreement. Through the agreement, the employee is paid a salary for the services rendered to the organisation. The frequency of payment will also be determined between the employee and employer, but it is typically subject to the policies and practices of the employer.

If you are in a permanent job, you must keep in mind that your employer cannot change or terminate your employment agreement on the following grounds:

- Discrimination.
- Exercising of working rights.
- Any other reason protected under the law.

MIGRANT NINJA TIP:

**Before signing any registered agreement for permanent or fixed term contracts, make sure you know your employment status, pay rate, hours of work and classification level.**

## 7.3.2 Part Time Jobs

Part-time jobs mean that employees undertake work for a certain number of hours every week, where the hours and days are not set. If you are a part-time worker, then you probably have to complete a certain number of hours every week for a specified rate. In many instances, you may have the opportunity to work more than your set number of hours, which allows you to claim overtime rates for every additional hour. Keep in mind that overtime payments are no longer compulsory or guaranteed under the IR legislation of the government.

If your employment contract doesn't mention permanency, then it's possible that you're on a part-time contract. As a part-time employee, you are entitled to the same benefits as full-time employees on a pro rata basis. Part-time employees are entitled to benefits like holiday leave and sick leave, based on the number of hours they work every week. Read more about part-time jobs here.

MIGRANT NINJA TIP:

**Many enterprise agreements, registered agreements and awards keep records for part-time employees regarding a number of hours of work, so, you should keep track of them as well to ensure that your payment is as agreed.**

## 7.3.3 Casual Jobs

Casual jobs are different from part-time jobs because employees are randomly called in to cover shifts of sick staff or during seasonal periods where more staff is needed. For example, stores need more customer service agents on weekends, so casual workers are usually called in to fill these additional requirements only when necessary. During regular workdays, there may be no need for casual workers. The period of work may range from a few hours to a few months based on the type of work.

Casual workers typically work for irregular hours, but don't get paid for annual or sick leaves.

Many Australian companies employ casual or temporary workers at some point to fill a void in employment – particularly in the front office or clerical positions when staff members are on leave. The casual job industry in Australia has grown significantly in the last few years in the hospitality, food, retail and manufacturing sectors. Downsizing and the need for reducing costs have led many companies to employ casual workers, which is often cheaper and more positively impactful on the bottom line.

### 7.3.4 Temporary Jobs

Temporary jobs are related to filling specific positions for a temporary period, which could be for days, weeks or even months. You could list your details with a temp agency, which is often the best way to help you find temporary work.

When you decide to work with a temp agency, make sure you have a copy of your resume, references, qualifications, licenses and certificates. If you are prepared to work immediately, make sure you have your bank account and tax file number (TFN) details handy. You must also have working rights in Australia, either as a permanent resident or with a work visa.

Department and retail stores are well known for employing casual and temporary workers. Other temporary jobs may be related to hospitality, fast food and corporate sectors.

**MIGRANT NINJA TIP:**

• **Avoid jobs that offer unpaid trials because you will end up working for nothing, which is illegal unless you're a volunteer.**

• **During university holidays, temporary workers face stiff competition from students, so try to get placed before students break for the holidays.**

## 7.4 Voluntary Jobs

Voluntary jobs are typically when a person attempts to get unpaid work experience through volunteering opportunities in a new industry or job. This is a good way for migrants to get the necessary 'local' experience that many employers look for when hiring candidates. It also is the most effective way of networking and building a list of local referees.

If you are looking for new industries that you may be interested in, check out the resources for young job seekers page to help you with ideas.

Through voluntary jobs, you will benefit from:

- Improved understanding of local workplace environments.
- Ability to explore new industries that interest you.
- Developed employability skills.

- References for future jobs.
- An enhanced network of contacts for future opportunities.

Here are some of the Volunteering organisations:

Go Volunteer

Volunteering Australia - Also links to state-based volunteer organisations

Good Company

Pro Bono Volunteer Match

Every state and territory in Australia offer a volunteering centre, which provides information and lists available volunteer positions. It also lists down information of your rights as a volunteer. If you're looking to volunteer in your local state, refer to these local volunteering centres for more information.

- Volunteering WA

- Volunteering ACT

- Volunteering SA & NT

- Volunteering Tasmania

- Volunteering Victoria

- Volunteering Queensland

- The Centre for Volunteering (Volunteering NSW)

Besides state-sponsored websites, most of the job portals have a dedicated section for advertising volunteer jobs. Here are two - SEEK, CAREERONE

**Take adequate steps to protect yourself to ensure that employers don't take advantage of your situation. Refer to information provided in the** Unpaid Work Experience and Volunteer Work **web page to ensure that your volunteering job complies with Fair Work rules and guidelines.**

## 7.5 Trades

Who says hard work doesn't pay? If you are a craftsman and love to work outdoors, then Australia is the right place indeed. According to one 2016 survey, engineers and skilled trades, along with doctors and non-nursing health roles, are among the most difficult to fill in Australia.

Skilled tradespeople include plumbers, electricians, metal fitters, mechanics, chefs, hairdressers and carpenters, to name just a few. These careers generally require manual dexterity and practical training and often require you to complete an apprenticeship where you can begin earning and learning on the job.

According to a research submitted to the Services Seeking website, the average hourly rate for all trades is $60.88 per hour with some construction workers in NSW getting around $78 an hour. As a skilled tradesperson, you can also have the security of working for big or small organisations or even have the freedom of running your own business.

Trades Recognition Australia (TRA) is a provider offering skills assessment services for people with trade skills gained in or out of Australia. The skills assessment service is offered for

191

both skills recognition and migration. The occupations assessed by the TRA can be found on the website of the Department of Immigration and Border Protection. To find out about more programs of the TRA, visit the Programs page of the TRA to choose what you are interested in. TRA offers a number of different programs:

- Job Ready Program
- 457 Skills Assessment Program
- Offshore Skills Assessment Program
- Migration Skills Assessment
- Migration Points Advice
- Optional Skills Assessment Service
- Trades Recognition Service

Check your relevant program for more information.

## 7.6 Working Illegally – A Word of Caution

It is crucial that you have the right visas and permission to work in the country or you may end up breaching the terms of your stay. This is a serious offence in Australia and you will be fined up to $10,000. You will also likely be deported from the country.

Make sure you have proper advice regarding the rules of working in Australia because many visas restrict the number of hours you are entitled to work or the time you can work for. For instance, students on study visas are only allowed to work for a maximum of 20 hours per week while studying.

Employers usually do comprehensive checks of your background and visa details because they could be charged with criminal offences for hiring you. The Department of Immigration, Multicultural and Indigenous Affairs introduced several initiatives to find illegal workers, which include information packs, advertising and information phone lines. Community members and employers are often encouraged to report illegal workers. There is also a free online service to check the working credentials of a non-Australian resident they wish to employ.

Keep in mind that several visas allow you to work, but some like tourist visas don't permit you to work at all. If you're on a working holiday visa, you cannot work with one employer for more than 3 months.

Since every visa has certain conditions, be sure to get proper advice about your own circumstances. According to a particular research, over 51,000 people work illegally in the country.

If you have been working in Australia illegally, it's important that you seek professional advice immediately. Even if you haven't been caught, there's always a chance that you will eventually be found out. Apart from the fine and the threat of deportation, you may be placed in a detention centre until your deportation. Once this happens, it will be extremely difficult for you to come back to the country.

You can apply for legal work in Australia through plenty of ways, so don't risk these opportunities by working illegally in the country.

# 8. Getting Ready for the Workplace

## 8.1 English Speaking Skills

While most of the migrants coming on a Permanent Resident Visa or Temporary Work Visa will have good English speaking skills, there are few migrants for whom English may not be the first language or may need some additional language training. The government of Australia has a programme in place for helping such people.

**Adult Migrant English Program (AMEP)** The Adult Migrant English Program (AMEP) is an Australian government-funded program that provides 510 hours of free English classes to new migrants and refugees. It delivers tuition in the English Language to help eligible adult migrants and refugees settle successfully in Australia.

**Who is eligible for the AMEP?**

You may be able to learn English with the AMEP if you hold a permanent visa, have little or no English, and:

are an adult (18 years or older)

are under 18 years of age and are not attending school. (You may be eligible within the first 12 months of your arrival to Australia)

**Note** - Access to the AMEP is extended to some temporary visa holders.

**Other information about the AMEP**

You are entitled to 510 hours of English tuition. At your first interview with an AMEP Counsellor, he will discuss the best way for you to learn English

You will need to register for the AMEP within six months (or 12 months if you are under 18 years of age at the time of registration).

You must commence your tuition within 12 months.

You will be required to complete the AMEP within five (5) years (this can be changed in special circumstances).

You will also need to complete an AMEP Settlement Course which provides information about Australian society, culture, laws, services and practices.

**Other AMEP services you may need**

**Childcare Services**

When you are attending daytime classes at the AMEP, you can access free childcare for pre-school aged children for the time you are in class. The AMEP will provide childcare if you have children under school age and need childcare to attend AMEP classes. AMEP childcare is only provided during the time you attend AMEP classes. It does not cover time for you to do other activities. Childcare is provided at no cost to you

Where possible, the childcare will be located within 30 minutes of your home or within 30 minutes of your AMEP class. AMEP staff will work with you to provide quality care that also supports your cultural needs Childcare services may not be available immediately as places are limited and in high demand.

MIGRANT NINJA TIP:

**You will need to register for the AMEP within six months of your arrival in Australia (or 12 months if you are under 18 years of age at the time of registration).**

**You must commence your tuition within 12 months.**

The program is available to eligible migrants, from the humanitarian, family and skilled visa groups. The number of hours of free English courses offered depends on individual circumstances.

AMEP teaches more than just English, clients also learn about Australian society, culture and customs. They meet other new migrants, who may have similar experiences and goals, and they make many new friends. Clients will learn about:

Australian culture, Health: doctor, dentist and hospital visits, Water safety, Money and finance, Government services, Rights and responsibilities, The justice and legal system and Current affairs.

**Where can I find out more about the AMEP?**

Call 13 AMES (2637) to find out whether you are eligible to learn English for free. Even if you are not eligible for free AMEP classes, you can still attend the classes for a small fee.

To view further information, go to the Department of Education and Training AMEP webpage. The government assigns the contract to certain institutes and providers in all the states. For example, in Queensland, the AMEP programme is conducted by TAFE

Find your nearest State Run Adult Migrant English Program service provider here

## Skills for Education and Employment

Additionally, if you are without a job and have enrolled at the local jobactive centre, you may also be eligible for the **Skills for Education and Employment (SEE) programme**.

The programme provides language, literacy and numeracy training to eligible job seekers, to help them to participate more effectively in training or in the labour force. The programme is delivered across Australia, from metropolitan and regional areas, right through to remote communities.

The programme caters for job seeker groups with literacy and/or numeracy training needs including Aboriginal and Torres Strait Islanders, youth, people with disabilities, mature aged people, and job seekers from culturally and linguistically diverse backgrounds.

## How does the programme work?

Job seekers are referred to the programme by the Department of Human Services (DHS) and Employment Service Providers, including:

jobactive

Disability Employment Services

Community Development Programme

Eligible job seekers are entitled to up to 800 hours of free accredited Language, literacy and/or numeracy training delivered under the programme. Training is delivered flexibly through full-time or part-time hours, via face-to-face or distance training and may be vocationally contextualised within each stream of training.

Small Group Training allows those participants who are uncomfortable or struggling in a larger class to build their confidence in a class of no more than five individuals, before returning to larger classes.

**SEE** (Skills for Education and Employment) providers around Australia include community organisations, public training providers, such as technical colleges, private providers, and universities.

To see a list of all SEE programme providers, follow the link – SEE Providers page

**Eligibility**

You are eligible for the SEE programme if you:

are 15 to 64 years old

are registered as a job seeker with DHS

are not a full-time student

meet the rules on visa status and benefits.

**How do I find out more?**

Call DHS on 132 850 from anywhere in Australia for the cost of a local call or visit your local DHS office. More Information

Call the Skilling Australia information line on 13 38 73 from anywhere in Australia for the cost of a local call.

Contact your local jobactive provider.

If you live in a remote community, contact the Remote Jobs and Communities Programme.

## 8.2 Etiquettes

Etiquette is the customary code of polite behaviour in society or among members of a particular profession or group. Generally, this is quite standard around the world and common sense and courtesy dictate most of the daily Interactions with society at large. However, every country has some subtle differences which have evolved based on the local traditions, historical background and common observances.

If there are three main traits that make the Australians unique as a nation, then it is the concept of Egalitarianism, Modesty and Mateship.

**Egalitarianism**

This basically means treating everyone equal and a refusal to accept being inferior.

Australia became an egalitarian society because people who were treated as second-class citizens refused to accept that they were in any way inferior. This refusal to accept inferiority greatly differentiates Australia from its eastern hemisphere neighbours, where hierarchical thinking prevails.

Australians prefer people who are modest, humble, self-deprecating and with a sense of humour. When in the company of friends, it's not uncommon for Australians to 'take the mick' out of each other – usually a jovial exchange of mocking and putting down. Modesty is considered a virtue in Australia and this sort of exchange is only meant in jest with no real weight behind any accusations. The subtext of this sort of humour is usually the complete opposite of the jibes – it actually means that the person being mocked is regarded as decent! Remember - Never joke about someone if they're not around, as it will probably be considered as a conniving behaviour.

**Australian Modesty**

Australians are very down to earth and always mindful of not giving the impression that they think they are better than anyone else. They value authenticity, sincerity, and loathe pretentiousness. They do not draw attention to their academic or other achievements.

They often downplay their own success, which may make them appear not to be achievement-oriented.

*"We don't boo Yanks because we think they are better than us. We boo yanks because they think they are better than us."* - Nicole Beatty, Dailey Telegraph Friday, September 29, 2000

**Mateship**

Mateship is a famed Australian character trait. Arguably, no other country celebrates friendships in their national identities as does Australia. In that regard, the celebration of mateship as part of a national identity is a uniquely Australian trait. The concept of mateship was strengthened in World War 1. Australian soldiers found themselves in Europe fighting a war that didn't really seem to have much purpose and certainly had little to do with Australia. They were hence committed to looking after each other and this developed a bond of camaraderie that has shaped itself into the fabric of the society as mateship. Australians place a high value on relationships.

## General etiquette

- The rounds at the pub - The social rules of the round or 'shout' are perhaps the most important of all social rules that need to be mastered. A 'round' is where one individual will pay for the drinks of the other members of the drinking party. Once the drinks have been drunk, another member of the drinking party will get the next round. Every member of the drinking party must buy the same number of rounds.

- Splitting the bill at a restaurant - In most Asian countries, if a group of friends go out for dinner, usually only one person will pay for the bill. Furthermore, if a man and woman go to dinner, irrespective of the level of relationship, the man will usually pay. This is not the case in Australia. If a group of friends go to a restaurant, the bill will be split amongst all the diners. This is mainly because of Australia's core value of Egalitarianism

- If invited to someone's home for a barbeque, etiquette stipulates that you make a contribution to the alcohol that will be drunk. If bringing beer, a six-pack is ok, but a case is more ideal. At the end of the night, it should be left as a gift for the host/s. You could also bring a box of chocolates or flowers for the host, depending on the occasion.

- Contact the hostess ahead of time to see if she would like you to bring a dish.
- Offer to help the hostess with the preparation or clearing up after a meal is served.
- If you are teased, you are expected to reply in kind, with good humour. Such self-confidence will increase an Australian's respect for you. They do not admire a subservient attitude

### DID YOU KNOW:

*Bringing booze to a barbeque - There is an Australian adage that when hosting a barbeque, a knock on the door should never be answered as it means the guest isn't carrying the required case of beer. (One should only answer a kick on the door.)*

## Work Place Etiquette

Work etiquette is an office code that controls the concept of acceptable social behaviour in a working environment. Workplaces can be stressful, so the need to discuss work etiquette is vitally important in an increasingly complex work framework.

Settling into any new workplace can be overwhelming, but it can be especially hard as a migrant dealing with a new job in a new country because you're not familiar with local workplace cultures.

Australia is a multicultural country, so most people have had experience working with migrants at some point or other. The main thing is to not be afraid to ask for clarifications and to learn for fellow co-workers.

**MIGRANT NINJA TIP:**

**The foremost advice to start off on the right note at work is:**

- **Try to connect with at least one person who can be your mentor.**
- **If you do not understand why some did or said something – just ask!**

Although they appear relaxed and casual, most Australians value hard work and talent above everything else, so follow these workplace etiquette tips at all times:

- Always be on time because lateness is not acceptable in Australian workplaces.
- Always shake hands with colleagues when you first meet them – female or male.
- Hierarchy in Australia is not strictly defined like it is in other countries, so show respect for your bosses, but relate to them as your equals. Similarly, speak to your juniors as equals too, not like you are above them.
- You always have to make an appointment with someone before you see them for work-related purposes.
- Stick to meeting time schedules and don't go over time because others may need to use the meeting room after you.

- Always address someone by his or her first name. For example, if you meet John Smith, you would call him John rather than Mr Smith.
- Remember to always make eye contact when conversing, even with your boss.
- Avoid multi-tasking in the middle of a meeting and pay attention.
- Don't take anything from your co-workers without asking.
- Don't judge people based on sexuality, religion and gender. Australia is a multi-cultural country, so even a little discrimination will get you into big trouble.
- Never make jokes about gender, race, sexual orientation and religion at the workplace.
- Respect your work and your work timings —Avoid gossiping about fellow colleagues as this is considered unprofessional and could earn you a bad reputation
- Keep your interruptions of others to a minimum. Always apologise if your intrusion is an interruption of a discussion or other activity
- It's best not to gossip about your fellow workmates. This is considered unprofessional and could get you a reputation as someone who can't be trusted.
- Don't hover around while waiting for a co-worker to get off the phone. Leave a note for them to call you or return later
- Show respect for others workspace. Knock before entering

- Always show appreciation for the slightest courtesies extended to you
- As obvious as it sounds, remember to say, "Please; Thank you; You're welcome", as part of your everyday courtesy
- Keep private phone calls to a minimum.
- If you are teased, you are expected to reply in kind, with good humour. Such self-confidence will increase an Australian's respect for you. They do not admire a subservient attitude.

MIGRANT NINJA TIP:

**Australia puts a lot of emphasis on a good work-life balance. Although this doesn't mean you should leave on time if you still have pending work, it also implies that you should not sit hours beyond regular working schedules to show you're a hard worker.**

## 8.3 Australian Slang

Even people from English-speaking countries sometimes say they find it hard to understand what Australians are talking about.

It is not the Australian accent that is causing the problem; it's more than likely the unique 'Aussie slang'. In time, you will slowly come to understand the accent, the humour and the slang.  In the meantime, this guide will help you understand some of the more common slang words you may hear in Australia. Australian English has many words and idioms which are unique to the dialect and have been written on extensively, with the Macquarie Dictionary, widely regarded as the national standard, incorporating numerous Australian terms.

Internationally well-known examples of Australian terminology include outback, meaning a remote, sparsely populated area, the bush, meaning either a native forest or a country area in general, and g'day, a greeting.

Dinkum or fair dinkum means "true" or "is that true?" among other things, depending on context and inflexion. The derivative dinky-di means "true" or devoted: a "dinky-di Aussie" is a "true Australian".

In informal speech, incomplete comparisons are sometimes used, such as "sweet as" (as in "That car is sweet as."). "Full", "fully" or "heaps" may precede a word to act as an intensifier (as in "The waves at the beach were heaps good.").

Where British and American vocabulary differs, Australians sometimes favour a usage different from either varieties, as with footpath (for US sidewalk, UK pavement) or capsicum (for US bell pepper, UK green/red pepper). In other instances, it either shares a term with American English, as with truck (UK: lorry) or eggplant (UK: aubergine) or with British English, as with mobile phone (US: cell phone) or bonnet (US: hood).

### DID YOU KNOW:

*The most widely said Australianisms are "no worries" (74 per cent of Australians have used this phrase), "arvo" (73 percent), and "G'day" (71 percent).*

Non-exhaustive selections of common British English terms not commonly used in Australian English include (Australian usage in brackets):

artic/articulated lorry (semi-trailer); aubergine (eggplant); bank holiday (public holiday); bedsit (one-bedroom apartment); bespoke (custom); bin lorry (garbage truck); black pudding (blood sausage); cagoule (raincoat); candy floss (fairy floss); cash machine (automatic teller machine/ATM); child-minder (babysitter); clingfilm (glad wrap/cling-wrap); courgette (zucchini); crisps (chips/potato chips); doddle (bludge); dungarees (overalls); dustbin (garbage/rubbish bin); dustcart (garbage/rubbish truck); duvet (doona); elastoplast/plaster (band-aid); estate car (station wagon); fairy cake (cupcake/patty cake); flannel ((face) washer/wash cloth); free phone (toll-free); football (soccer); high street (main street); hoover (vacuum cleaner); ice lolly (ice block/icy pole); kitchen roll (paper towel); lavatory (toilet); lorry (truck); off-licence (bottle shop); pavement (footpath); red/green pepper (capsicum); pillar box (mail box); plimsoll (sandshoe); pushchair (pram/stroller); saloon (sedan); sweets (lollies); utility room (laundry); Wellington boots (gumboots).

Australian English is particularly divergent from other varieties with respect to geographical terminology, due to the country's unique geography. This is particularly true when comparing with British English, due to that country's dramatically different geography. British geographical terms not in common use in Australia include: coppice (cleared bushland); dell (valley); fen (swamp); heath (shrubland); meadow (grassy plain); moor (swampland); spinney (shrubland); stream (creek); woods (bush) and village (even the smallest settlements in Australia are called towns or stations).

Diminutive forms of words are commonly used in everyday Australian English.

In Australian English, diminutives are usually formed by taking the first part of a word and adding an a, o, ie, or y. Alternatively, in some cases, no ending may be used. As with all languages and cultures, the easiest and most effective way to pick it up is to interact with locals and practice as much as you can. Books and language guide can only provide you with a good start. Whilst it is definitely not necessary that you imitate the Australian way of speaking (Australians look down upon false pretences), it is much appreciated if you take the effort to understand and absorb the local culture. If you take a conscious effort then it won't be long before you master the "dinky-di Aussie" vocabulary.

***DID YOU KNOW:***

***Swimming costumes in Queensland are known as togs, in NSW cossies, but in Victoria, bathers. And while Victorians use the word cantaloupe, in the rest of the country the fruit is known as rockmelon.***

## 8.4 Trade Unions

A trade union is a worker organisation with a number of different employees who have come together to achieve a common goal related to the workplace. These goals can be anything from better working hours and better working conditions to higher salaries and job security related to a particular organisation or industry. A trade union seeks to achieve collaborative agreement between the representatives of the union and the employer. This is used to set certain terms and conditions related to the workplace, which is expected to be included in the employment contracts of workers.

In Australia, the Australian Council of Trade Unions (ACTU) is the main body representing different Australian unions and has been around since 1927. The ACTU deals with issues like:

- Workplace violence.
- Minimum wages.
- Superannuation.
- Work and family.
- Health and safety.
- Modern awards.
- Temporary overseas workers.
- Indigenous workers.
- Fair trade.
- Asbestos presence at work.

The ACTU has played a huge role in giving workers rights and has contributed to many fairness policies at workplaces.

## Affiliates and Trade and Labour Councils (TLCs) Of The ACTU

The ACTU has different affiliates and trade and labour councils (TLCs). Here are some TLCs in Australia:

- Queensland Council of Unions

- Victorian Trades Hall Council

- Unions NT

- Unions ACT

- Newcastle Trades Hall Council

- Unions WA

- SA Unions

- Unions New South Wales

- Unions Tasmania

For more information on trade unions related to specific industries, you can visit this website. The ACTU is a body with nearly 46 affiliated unions. Some other important related links:

- -Australian Unions – Offers information about unions and campaigns. This is the go-to website for all information related to unions in Australia.
- -ACTU Worksite – Offers information about rights of people just starting work for the first time.

**MIGRANT NINJA TIP:**

**The ACTU Member Connect team helps unions in their goals by providing added resources when necessary. Get information about the benefits and special offers available if you're a union member on the Australian Unions website.**

## 8.5 Workplace Health and Safety (WHS)

Formerly called the Occupational Health and Safety (OH&S), the Workplace Health and Safety (WHS) Code, lays out guidelines for business owners for maintaining healthy and safe conditions at the workplace. Establishing safety at the workplace is critical to business success to prevent lawsuits and other liabilities. Business owners must ensure that their businesses don't create problems for employees and the public.

As an employee, you must have enough knowledge of WHS laws to know your rights if you face an injury or illness at the workplace. Employers must find ways to reduce safety hazards in the workplace in every way possible by following WHS/OH&S guidelines specific to their industries. Here are some employer WHS obligations that all employees must be aware of:

- Provision of safe premises.
- Ensuring safe materials and machinery at all times.
- Certifying safe work systems.
- Providing instruction, supervision and training for safety.
- Providing a proper working environment.
- Offering workers compensation and insurance for employees.

Complying with these duties helps employers remain within the realm of the law. WHS authorities in every state must enforce WHS legislation. These authorities provide training and education with respect to safety and health at work. You can access information about WHS/OH&S resources from websites in your state.

## 8.6 Rights as an Employee

Employees have a number of different rights in Australia, but they are also expected to follow certain obligations. Some rights of employees are:

## Right to Protection against Discrimination

Discrimination occurs in the workplace when an employer takes adverse action against an employee or prospective employee because of a protected attribute.

Protected attributes include: race, colour, sex, sexual orientation, age, physical or mental disability marital status, family or carer's responsibilities, pregnancy, religion, political opinion, national extraction and social origin.

If you've lost your job, contact the Fair Work Commission (the Commission) first if you think you were sacked because of: discrimination, a reason that is harsh, unjust or unreasonable and another protected right.

MIGRANT NINJA TIP:

**You have 21 days from the day you were sacked to lodge an application with the Commission. For more information, visit – Fariwork.gov.au**

## Right to Privacy

An employee's right to privacy is covered under the Privacy Act 1988. Similar legislations have also been set up in some individual states and territories in Australia. For instance, if you let your employer know about a certain health issue, they cannot disclose these details to anyone else without your permission. They must only use the information for a specific purpose, like adjusting certain situations to your role at the workplace.

## Right to a Safe and Healthy Workplace

Australian legislation gives employees the right to a safe and healthy workplace, which means that certain steps must be undertaken to ensure that the workplace doesn't harm employees' physical and mental wellbeing. Employers are compelled to take action and reduce potential risks to employees. If you are looking for more information, check about WH&S laws on the SafeWork Australia website. The obligation of employers when it comes to safety at the workplace is known as 'duty of care' and this applies to all employees.

## Right to Minimum Wages

Under workplace laws, no worker over 21 can be paid below the minimum set wage. This is created as a safety net to prevent workers from being exploited. An award or agreement for the employee will confirm the minimum wage and any additional rates for overtime. For more information about employee agreements, you can go to the Fair Work website. If you are paid less than the minimum rate, you can lodge a complaint with the Fair Work Ombudsman.

## 457 Visa Holders Rights

If you are in Australia on a 457 visa, you have certain rights under the Migration Act 1958 and the Fair Work Act 2009. The Fair Work Ombudsman and the DIBP work in collaboration to help you know your legal rights as an employee working in Australia. If you think that your employer is not giving you correct entitlements, you can complain to the Fair Work Ombudsman. Get more information about your working rights as a 457 visa holder here.

**The Fair Work Act 2009 also governs all visa and migrant worker rights. You can get more information about your rights on this** webpage **to ensure that you protect your interests in the event of difficulties in the workplace.**

## 8.7 Obligations as an Employee

Apart from rights, employees in Australia have certain responsibilities and obligations that they are compelled to follow. Here are some employee obligations:

- If your mental health issue doesn't affect your job, then you have no legal obligation to inform your employer about it. But if it does, then you must inform your employer.
- You must take adequate steps to protect yourself at the workplace and must cooperate with employer guidelines when it comes to health and safety.
- If your disability can put others at risk, then you are compelled to inform your employer or you could be breaching your obligations declared under the WH&S legislation.
- You must comply with any instructions and policies laid out by your employer.
- Wear protective clothing if your job calls for it without cutting corners.
- Report hazards and ill health to employers.

**As an employee, your 'duty of care' obligation applies to apprentices, contractors and labour-hire workers.**

## 8.8 Work Cards

A work card is another form of an identity card related to your workplace. It verifies that you are employed and are eligible to perform work in your profession. Keep in mind that this work card is not a visa that enables you to work. It is used together with your work visa or permanent residency when you seek local employment in Australia.

Work cards are typically used in industries where specialised training skills or background credit checks are necessary to reduce crime rates. For instance, workers need to have training certificates to work in the construction industry. They will be issued with work cards as part of their employment in a particular building site. Similarly, employees engaged as teachers in schools or as dealers in casinos will have extensive background checks undertaken to prevent any crimes from taking place in the work premises.

### White Cards In Construction

The construction industry typically uses work cards more than any other workplace and use the terms 'white card' or 'white card training' to describe the nature of employment. White card training is a course providing basic information about construction work. It covers applicable Work Health and Safety (WHS) laws, along with common dangers associated with construction work.

A white card is a type of plastic card issued to a worker by a Registered Training Organisation (RTO). This card indicates that the worker has gone through construction training and is ready to undertake work on behalf of the employer. The WHS legislation in Australia rules that construction site workers must have this training and must have sufficient evidence of their course before they can work on construction sites. Any worker that doesn't have this general induction training will not be allowed employment on any construction site.

The website of the National Register for the Vocational Education and Training offers information about various Registered Training Organisations that are able to administer 'White Card' training through a course –– 'CPCCOHS1001A - Work safely in the construction industry.'

Workers who have gone through the training in one state may be accepted for employment in construction sites in other states. These white cards typically don't have expiry dates, but certain sites may require workers to take refresher courses when necessary.

## Blue Cards (For Working with Children in Queensland)

Under the Working with Children (Risk Management and Screening) Act 2000 in Queensland, blue cards are issued by the Queensland Government. People who work with children (teachers, caregivers, tradesmen and cleaners) mist have blue cards in the state.

If you are a volunteer or education provider and hire people as paid employees or trainee students in schools or around young children, you must ensure that they have blue cards. You cannot force all employees to have blue cards unless they provide specific child-related services or are around children under the Act.

Some states do not recognise checks done in other states, so workers will have to apply for a local blue card to seek work in the region. Currently, all states have their own laws about working with children checks. Refer to the information below if you are based in another state in Australia:

- Victoria Working with Children Check website.

- Western Australia Working with Children Check website.

- New South Wales Working with Children Check website.

- ACT Working with Vulnerable People website.

- South Australia Screening and Background Checks website.

- Northern Territory Working with Children website.

- Tasmania Working with Children Check website.

## Other Occupations Requiring Work / Accreditation Cards

Some other occupations and trades also have similar work card requirements.

*Example:* Taxi Drivers in Queensland require a 'Driver Authorisation Card'

This is a qualification required when providing particular public passenger service. This helps to maximise confidence in the driver's skill and to ensure that the driver is safe to be around – particularly when it comes to vulnerable community members like elders and children. Application forms for driver authorization in Queensland can be found here.

Information for drivers licensing and accreditation in New South Wales can be found here. Driver accreditation for Victoria is available here. Driver accreditation for South Australia is available here.

MIGRANT NINJA TIP:

**Work cards are popular in industries where specialised training skills are necessary, like construction, teaching, plumbing, driving and other trade skills.**

## 8.9 Certificates & Clearances

Certificates and clearances are typically issued to determine whether an employee is able to take on a specific type of work based on their employment type. Certificates and clearances may be needed for the following situations:

- If a new worker has been employed in a sector.
- If a worker has been injured temporarily and is unable to perform regular work for a specified period of time.
- If a worker is moving from one industry to another.

**What is Certificate Of Capacity?**

If an employee has been off work because of an injury, medical clearance is necessary to return to work. WorkSafe Agents and employers typically use Certificates of Capacity to determine whether an employee is able to work after an injury. Medical professionals like doctors, physiotherapists, chiropractors and osteopaths issue these certificates.

Injured workers must have a Certificate of Capacity if they are to receive compensation for loss of income. An appropriate Certificate of Capacity helps an injured worker get back to work eventually, but takes care of him/her in the meanwhile.

Certificates of capacity are important when it comes to lodging compensation claims and for returning to work eventually. If the employee fails to fill out the form correctly, he/she will not receive benefits or they may be delayed.

## 8.10 Employee Entitlements

Australia is governed by several rules regarding what employees are entitled to at work, which covers everything from the number of working hours to break times. These can be set out as awards, employment contracts or registered agreements.

Every employee is entitled to minimum benefits, which are detailed in the National Employment Standards (NES). An employment contract or registered agreement can provide for additional entitlements, such as bonus leaves and benefits, but they cannot be less than what exists in the NES or the applicable award.

MIGRANT NINJA TIP:

**Rules are clearly set out regarding employee entitlements, so make sure that your employer isn't giving you less than what you deserve. Refer to the employee entitlements page for more information.**

## 8.11 Work Flexibility

Australia is one of the most progressive countries when it comes to workplace flexibility. Workplace flexibility enables employees and employers to arrive at certain working conditions that best suit them. For instance, a single working mother can arrange to work on certain days of the week to ensure that she can be available for her kids. An employee with elderly dependents can arrange to work for a certain number of hours in a day to relieve the caretaker's duties. This enables employees to maintain a healthy work/life balance while allowing employers to maintain efficiency and productivity of their business.

While employees are still eligible for their entitlements, they can negotiate conditions with their employers to make the workplace more flexible. Employees and employers can introduce more workplace flexibility through:

- **Flexible Working Arrangements:** Some employees can ask for flexible working conditions based on their personal situations.
- **Individual Flexibility Agreements:** Employees and employers can agree to alter certain terms in awards, registered agreements and employment contracts when applicable.

MIGRANT NINJA TIP:

**Employers may not always accept or reject a flexible working schedule in full. Often, employers and employees negotiate an arrangement that works for both parties. More information can be found on the Flexible Working Arrangements page.**

## 8.12 Protection from Adverse Action

Adverse action refers to unlawful action undertaken for specific reasons. Adverse actions can include any of the following:

- Firing employees without a legitimate reason.
- Hurting an employee at the workplace by not giving proper pay or leave.
- Modifying jobs to the disadvantage of employees.
- Not hiring a prospect on the basis of religion, caste or gender.
- Discriminating between employees.
- Offering unfair terms to employees for jobs.
- Ending contracts without legitimate reasons with independent contractors.
- Altering contracts without notifying employees that go against their best interests.

Employers cannot take adverse action against employees if:

- They use their workplace rights.
- They choose to belong or not belong to a union.
- They choose not to participate in a voluntary workplace activity.

If an employee feels that he/she isn't getting the correct pay and reports this to the Fair Work Ombudsman, the employer cannot demote or change the duties of the employee suddenly. This could be termed as adverse action and is considered illegal as per Australian law.

## 8.13 Protection from Coercion

Coercion effectively means compelling a person to do something that is against their will through intimidation, threats and fear. A person cannot be forced to not use or use a workplace right. For instance, if an employee votes against a certain management decision, the employer cannot:

- Threaten to fire or demote employees.
- Change their role without proper consent.
- Make life more difficult at the workplace.
- change their roster.

This type of coercive behaviour is considered illegal, even if the person chose not to do something against his/her will. Employees can get protection and help from the Fair Work Ombudsman to ensure that they don't feel coerced into doing their jobs. Find out more about how the ombudsman can help <u>here</u>.

## 8.14 Resolving Disputes at the Workplace

If you and your employer have a dispute at the workplace, then you will need to find a way to resolve it amongst yourselves by holding meetings and internal intervention. If you are unable to resolve this dispute, you or your employer can approach the Fair Work Commission for assistance.

The Fair Work Commission provides effective and accessible ways to resolve disputes and grievances. In some instances, this is done directly with employees and employers. In other instances, it is undertaken through unions, employer organisations and other representatives. The Commission can help in different ways:

- Conciliation: This is a semi-formal process where both parties are involved in discussions before arriving at an agreement.
- Mediation: This is a more informal process where all parties come together with the Commission to arrive at a viable solution for everyone.
- Arbitration: This is a more formal process where the Commission will need to decide the ideal solution. This decision is made once all parties present their arguments.

# 9. Your First Job

## 9.1 Employment Contract

An employment contract states the conditions of employment between you and your employer, which should ideally be in writing to ensure no discrepancies in the future. Your employment contract must contain at least the legal minimum entitlements as stated in the National Employment Standards (NES). Keep in mind that you are covered under the NES, irrespective of your employment contract.

The NES covers all Australian employees, irrespective of an employment contract. The contract cannot make an employee worse than the minimum legal rights. Learn more about employment contracts here.

**What Should Go Into Your Employment Contract?**

The terms of employment in Australia are either defined as contracts, agreements or awards and are usually written from the NES with applicable federal or state laws. Information that should ideally be included in an employment contract includes:

- Basic pay
- Job title
- Employment type (full-time, part-time, casual)
- Overtime pay rates
- Working hours
- Annual salary
- Leaves and allowances
- Settlement of disputes escalation matrix

- Redundancy
- Flexible terms to match individual needs

If applicable, other information like allowances, job duties, bonuses and performance standards should also be clearly listed.

Apart from clearly describing what you will do for the company, your employment contract should ideally address these details:

- Duration of employment
- Information of all your responsibilities
- Your benefits like leave, health insurance and workplace rights
- Grounds for termination
- Your ability to join a competitor once you leave
- Confidentiality
- Ownership of work
- Dispute resolution matrix

Employment contracts can be extremely valuable in the event of any disagreement between you and your employer. For instance, if there is a sudden change in hourly rates paid to you, you may want a written contract, so that your employer cannot change your pay. The contract can also protect you from being indiscriminately fired from your job without a suitable reason.

An employment contract is also valuable when you or your employer wants to ensure confidentiality. If your employer treats you poorly, then you can hold them responsible for breaching the terms of the contract based on the agreement drawn up.

## 9.2 Wages

In Australia, wages can be paid weekly, fortnightly or monthly, depending on the type of industry you are employed in. An employee contract or award will stipulate how you get paid. Wages can either be paid by cash, cheque, money order or electronic funds transfer based on the policies of the company. Employees must at least be paid monthly, if not more frequently.

Your employer typically has to pay superannuation and tax for you (if you earn above a certain threshold) and you can claim a tax refund from the government every financial year. If you decide to leave Australia permanently, you may also be eligible to get your superannuation. However, if you continue to live in the country, you cannot access your super, even if your switch between employers.

### National Minimum Wage in Australia

Australian law details information about minimum wage rates. This amount must be legally paid to people as a minimum for different types of jobs. It is okay to receive more money than the minimum wage rate, but it is illegal for your employer to pay you less.

The national minimum wage in Australia is currently $17.70 per hour. This translates to approximately $672.70 for a 38-hour working week before paying tax. Casual employees who are also covered by the national minimum wage get a 25 per cent casual loading.

The Fair Work Commission's Minimum Wage Panel usually determines the minimum wage rate for employees in national workplaces.

## What Influences Wages in Australia?

The average wage in the country can vary because of several different factors:

- The place where a person applies for a job (big cities and urban centres offer higher wages)
- The period when a person applies for the job (holiday seasons pay more)
- A person's experience, education and skill

If you're on an hourly wage, then weekends and holiday wages are typically higher than otherwise. The average calculation is 1.5 times your regular wage, but this is not the general rule for all employers.

Migrants on independent or sponsored permanent residency visas will be able to work provided they remain within the stipulations of their visa conditions.

## Wages on Pay Slips

You should ideally get a pay slip every time you are paid your wages so that all payments are put on record. The pay slip can either be electronic or it can be given to you as a printed sheet. Pay slips typically include the following details:

- Payment period and date

- Number of days/hours worked during the payment review period
- Gross pay before tax and net pay after tax
- Tax deductions made from gross pay
- Superannuation payments made for you

For more information, contact the Fair Work Ombudsman.

MIGRANT NINJA TIP:

**If you get paid your wages in cash, make sure you and your employer sign a record for the amount of money paid during the payment review period to avoid future conflicts.**

## 9.3 Superannuation

Superannuation, or 'Super', refers to the arrangements which people make in Australia to have funds available for them in retirement. Superannuation in Australia is government-supported and encouraged, and minimum provisions are compulsory for employees. Super plays huge roles in ensuring Australians are able to enjoy their retirement without relying on social welfare. It is also taxed at a lower rate than other investments or salary, so the system is designed to encourage you to save for your own retirement since you'll get a better after-tax return. Most super funds offer additional benefits, such as life insurance cover, and total and permanent disability insurance. In this case, it is "super" because it comes to your rescue in your later years.

**How do I pay my Super? Money can find its way into your fund in four ways:**

From your employer, from you, by government co-contribution, and Rollover from other super funds.

Generally, if you are aged 18 or older and earn AUD$ 450 or more in a month, your employer must pay superannuation into a superannuation account for you. However, if you earn less than the AUD$ 450 a month, or if you work for less than 30 hours a week, and your work is of a domestic or private nature, your employer is not required to pay superannuation for you.

The Australian government guarantees a minimum of 9.5% of your salary as super contributions from your employer (it was 9.25% until July 1, 2014, and 9% up to a year before that). This requirement is set out in the superannuation legislation that employers must adhere to and is known as the superannuation guarantee and covers full-time, part-time, and casual employees. This money comes from your employer directly, and not from your pay packet (although total remuneration can be quoted inclusive of the superannuation amounts, so you should check).

However, you are able to put extra money into your superannuation yourself (by way of salary sacrificing and co-contributions described later in this chapter), although there are contribution caps regulating the maximum amount you can put in without being hit with a penalty tax. Your money then gets invested by the fund on your behalf and is yours to use when you retire (or meet another condition that allows you to access your money).

**Your salary may contain other additions but the fundamentals are a base amount plus the statutory superannuation payment. Salaries can be advertised excluding or including the statutory superannuation, so, always make sure you know which way round it is as it makes a big difference to your take home pay. These are the basics anyone from overseas should understand.**

## When can I get my superannuation?

As your superannuation is meant to be for your retirement, you generally cannot get access to your fund until you reach preservation age and retire, or reach age 65. There are some exceptions regarding personal circumstances – if you have a terminal illness or injury, you may be entitled to access your super as a tax-free lump sum payment. However, this will need to be organised through your super fund as it is their decision, and has to meet the conditions in the superannuation law as well.

## What about temporary residents – do they pay super, and can they take it with them when they leave?

Yes, they do have super contributions paid on their behalf, and yes, they can take it with them. If you are a temporary resident and would like to find out more about claiming your super back, visit DASP (Departing Australia Superannuation Payment)

## What is Low-income boost?

A super tax "refund", called the Low Income Super Contribution (LISC), is a government superannuation payment of up to

AUD$ 500 each financial year to help low-income earners save for their retirement. If you earn AUD$ 37,000 or less per year, you may be eligible to receive an LISC payment directly into your super fund account. Visit LISC for more information.

## What are the benefits of saving through super?

Certain advantages make saving through superannuation more tax-effective than other investments, which means your savings could grow faster. For example, any contributions your employer makes, as well as any returns you earn on your super, are taxed at a maximum of 15%, rather than at your marginal tax rate. If you make super contributions on your own, you could also be eligible for special tax concessions. Having your super locked away until you reach retirement ensures your savings will be used for one purpose only – to help you achieve your financial goals and secure the retirement you're looking forward to.

## What is Salary Sacrifice for Superannuation?

Salary sacrifice can be a great way to get a part of your remuneration in a form other than cash – and not personally pay tax on it. This is where you agree to take part of your wage as a benefit of some kind, equal in value to the salary it is exchanged for. The upside in you doing this is that your income tax is then based only on the reduced amount of salary that results. If your employer agrees to go into a salary sacrificing arrangement with you, the benefit you get should, of course, be equal in value to the portion of salary that you give up. Options include a car, shares or payments for your expenses, such as school fees, child care or home phone costs for example. On top of these, one of the most popular ones is superannuation. Your employer already has to pay 9.5% of your salary into your super fund, but many people choose to top it up with salary sacrificed amounts to further prepare for their retirement.

## Other Things you should know about Super

Most people are entitled to compulsory super contributions from their employer. These Superannuation Guarantee Contributions must be at least 9.25% of your ordinary earnings, up to the 'maximum contribution base'. You are entitled to choose the fund your super is paid into. If you leave Australia because your visa requires you to leave, then you may apply to reclaim some of the super contributions made on your behalf. You can do this online within a certain period of leaving. This is known as DASP – Departing Australia Superannuation Payment. Check the ATO site for details.

The performance of your super really depends on the types of things (asset classes) you are invested in. Growth assets like shares and property are more likely to produce shorter-term fluctuations in their price. History has shown that shares have performed in this group over the past 100 years, but to get these returns, you must invest for at least 10 years to weather the volatility they can create. This requires discipline, calmness, and the ability to stay focused on the long-term result above the noise of today.

At the other end of the spectrum, putting your money in cash is more stable, but when interest rates are low – as they are now – you risk losing your earnings to inflation. Generally, you need to aim to produce an overall return from your super after tax and fees that are 2-4 % better than inflation to enjoy a decent retirement. Adding in more than the regulated 9.5 % of wages is also required.

*This information has been reproduced with permission of ASIC. Source: ASIC's MoneySmart ,08.10.2015*

## 9.4 Taxation

It is prudent to familiarise yourself with the Australian taxation system before you arrive so that you are aware of the regulations. Visit this link for more information

**Tax Returns**

Australian tax returns for the tax year, beginning from 1 July and ending 30 June of the following year are generally due on 31 October after the end of the tax year. The main tax that Australians will know about first-hand is income tax, such as that levied on salary and wages, investment income, and business income. Generally, taxpayers pay income tax during the year as it is earned – for example, employees will see a portion of their wages held out by their employer for income tax. The amount of income tax you pay is linked to how much you earn and whether you're an Australian resident. The more you earn, the higher your rate of tax.

At the end of the income year (June 30), most people need to lodge an annual income tax return to notify the government (through the Tax Office) how much income they received, the tax they paid, and to list any deductions or offsets. Employees will get most of this information on a payment summary their employer prepares. The annual tax return is a person's declaration of income received and if there is anything that may reduce tax, such as tax already paid during the year, deductions, and tax offsets.

Apart from declaring your income, the tax return also allows you to tell the government if you have any deductions to claim, are entitled to any offsets or if there are any special circumstances which will affect the amount of tax you paid – such as your age or other situations. The Tax Office examines the information you provide on the form and calculates if you have paid the correct amount of tax (for example, through PAYG withholding throughout the year), if you are entitled to a refund, or if you owe the Tax Office money.

MIGRANT NINJA TIP:

**Before you begin working in Australia, you might consider applying for your Tax File Number, which is issued by the ATO. It's not essential to get one, but you'll pay more income tax if you don't.**

There are several ways to fill in a tax return. The cheapest and easiest option would be the new myTax online tax return.

There are also individual tax return instructions. You can also approach a professional tax agent to calculate your tax for you – they will submit your return on your behalf. The tax year ends on June 30. You have from July 1 to October 31 to lodge your tax return unless it is prepared by a registered tax agent (in which case, you are likely to qualify for an extension). If you do not lodge your return in time, you may be penalised.

The Tax Office contact number is 13 28 61.

If you need to lodge your return early, find out how by reading early lodgment.

The tax you pay depends on how much you earn and the tax brackets often change as they are set by the Government of the day, according to the nation's budgetary requirements. Income tax will normally be deducted from your pay directly by your employer. The ATO website also has a calculator to help you work out your tax rate. Part of the amount deducted from your income is for something called the Medicare Levy. This pays for the free (or heavily discounted) public health system in Australia.

Australians who pay income tax must fill in a tax return at the end of the tax year. This means filling in a form with all your earning details – and information about any work-related expenses on which you can claim your tax back – to the ATO. This can result in a refund if you have paid too much tax. Most people who are only earning wages and therefore have a simple tax return prefer to do it themselves using the ATO's online e-Tax.

**Tax File Number (TFN)**

In the United States, it is called a Social Security Number, in Britain, a National Insurance Number, and in Australia, we call it a Tax File Number (TFN). Everyone who pays tax gets a TFN. Tax file numbers are obtained from the Tax Office when individuals commence their working life and are used to help identify your tax records. Your TFN is identifiably yours and yours alone, and you shouldn't share it with friends, or online. Sharing the details of your tax file number could result in identity theft.

**What do I do with my TFN? When do I use it?**

You will be asked to provide or declare your tax file number in certain situations, such as starting work for the first time, or changing jobs, or applying for allowances and benefits from Centrelink. Of course, you'll also have to provide it to lodge a tax return or deal with the Tax Office. The people or organisations most likely to ask for your details are your Employers, the Tax Office, your bank or other financial institution, Centrelink, your university, and your superannuation fund.

When you start a new job, you provide your TFN by filling in a form from your employer. You have 28 days to give them your tax file number before tax begins to be deducted at the highest rate. Once you've filled out the form, your employer will use the information you have provided (regarding any dependents or higher education loan schemes) to determine how much tax is taken out of your salary or wage payments. To ensure your TFN is used appropriately, you have the right to: ask what legal basis the organization has in asking for the tax file number, be told that if you don't provide it, you're not doing anything wrong, and be told what the consequences of not providing the tax file number will be.

**Do I have to have a tax file number?**

No, it is not compulsory to have a TFN, but life is difficult without one. An employer that does not have your tax file number is legally required to hold back tax from your pay at the top marginal rate; even if you are earning so little that you'd almost be paying no tax at all otherwise. And any interest from bank accounts, unfranked dividends from companies or dividends (franked or unfranked) passed to you through unit trust distributions, will have the highest possible level of tax taken out if a TFN isn't provided.

You also need a TFN to be able to access government benefits or support, such as unemployment benefits, that you are entitled to. Tertiary students will need one to access the government's higher education loans. Only one TFN will ever be issued to you. Once you have a TFN, you don't need to re-apply for one if your circumstances change, for example, if you change your name, have investments or claim government benefits.

**Who can apply for a tax file number online?**

Foreign passport holders, permanent migrants and temporary visitors

You can apply for a tax file number online if you meet these three conditions:

You are a foreign passport holder, permanent migrant or temporary visitor.

You are already in Australia.

Your visa is one of the following: a permanent migrant visa, a visa with work rights, an overseas student visa, or a valid visa allowing you to stay in Australia indefinitely.

**NOTE** - During this application process, checks will be made with DIBP to verify that you have the relevant visa

To apply online, you must have a valid passport or relevant travel documents. You don't have to provide proof of identity documents – The Tax Office will compare your personal and travel document details with Department of Immigration and Border Protection (DIBP) records. Visitors and permanent migrants need authorization from the Department of Immigration and Border Protection (DIBP) to work in Australia.

**NOTE** – You must be in Australia to use this online application process. Again, this information will be verified with DIBP.

Within 28 days, the ATO will send your TFN to the Australian address you had provided in your application.

MIGRANT NINJA TIP:

**Solely receiving a TFN is not an authorization for you to work in Australia.**

**Applying for a TFN should take about 20 minutes. You will be asked to enter details including your passport or travel document number, a postal address in Australia where you're TFN can be sent, your legal name and other names you use or have used and contact details for yourself or your preferred contact person.**

## Deductions you can claim

When completing your tax return, you're entitled to claim deductions for some expenses, most of which are directly related to earning your income. To claim a work-related deduction: you must have spent the money yourself and weren't reimbursed, it must be related to your job, and you must have a record to prove it (there are some limited exceptions). If the expense was for both work and private purposes, you can only claim a deduction for the work-related portion.

Further reading – Deductions you can claim.

The Australian taxation system is based on a tiered structure; the more you earn, the more you will be taxed. There is a tax-free threshold of AUD$ 18,200, which you can earn under and effectively not pay any tax at all. The highest rate of tax is 45% if your taxable income is over AUD$180,000 in the year.

**The following rates for 2016–17 apply from 1 July 2016.**

**Taxable income - Tax on this income**

0 – $18,200 - Nil

$18,201 – $37,000 - 19c for each $1 over $18,200

$37,001 – $87,000 - $3,572 plus 32.5c for each $1 over $37,000

$87,001 – $180,000 - $19,822 plus 37c for each $1 over $87,000

$180,001 and over - $54,232 plus 45c for each $1 over $180,000

The above rates do not include the:

Medicare levy of 2%

Temporary Budget Repair Levy; this levy is payable at a rate of 2% for taxable incomes over $180,000.

For the latest ATO tax brackets visit:  <u>Individual Income Tax Rates</u>

## 9.5 Salary Packaging

Salary packaging is a clever way to optimise your income because it enables you to pay for certain expenses with your before tax salary, which is permitted under the law by the Australian Taxation Office (ATO). This amount is usually removed from salaries before you spend it and you end up paying for all your expenses with your net pay. This option is generally available for permanent employees only.

With salary packaging, you get paid the same salary by your employer. But in this case, instead of paying for any expenses you incur after-tax, you will pay for some expenses before you are taxed. You will naturally pay for these expenses anyway. Salary packaging could be used for the following expenses:

- Car repayments
- Tablet computers
- Mortgages
- Rent payments
- Work-related laptops

The expenses that you can salary package will depend entirely on your employer and the type of industry you work in. Before finalising, make sure you are aware of all your options in terms of salary packaging to help you optimise your income as best as possible.

## 9.6 Leave Entitlements

The National Employment Standards (NES) has declared the minimum leave entitlements for every employee based on occupation. Some types of leaves employees may take are given below:

**Annual Leave**

Annual leave enables an employee to be paid while taking time off work to go on a vacation or to spend some time with family. Employee contracts and agreements typically detail the number of annual leaves an employee is entitled to take. Full-time and part-time employees usually get four weeks annual leave based on ordinary working hours. All employees within a company are entitled to annual leave. Shift workers may be able to get up to five weeks of annual leave every year.

Annual leave typically starts from the time the employee starts working, even if he/she is on probation. The leaves gradually collect over the year and any unused leave will move on to the next year. Annual leave will continue to accumulate even when an employee of the company is on:

- Paid leave or carer's leave
- Community service leave
- Long-service leave

But it doesn't accumulate when the employee of the company is on unpaid carer's leave, unpaid parental leave or unpaid annual leave. The Paid Parental Leave Scheme of the Australian government is not paid leave, so the employee will not accumulate annual leave under this scheme.

## Parental and Maternity Leave

You may be able to get parental or maternity leaves when your child is born or adopted. Based on the specifics, you may be entitled to maternity leave, paternity leave, partner leave, special maternity leave and adoption leave. After this leave, you have a right to return to your old job. This type of leave can be taken when:

- The employee or employee's partner gives birth
- The employee adopts a child below the age of 16

Employees are typically entitled to 12 months worth of unpaid parental leave and can even request for another 12 months of leave. Employees who are on leave to care for adopted children are entitled to unpaid pre-adoption leave for 2 days, which is used for attending examinations and interviews.

Every employee in Australia is entitled to parental leave, regardless of his/her occupation. The employee should have worked in the company for at least 12 months before the expected date of birth or adoption.

Casual employees are also entitled to unpaid parental leave if they have been working for the employer on a regular basis for at least 12 months. Even if you have taken parental leave, you don't have to work for another 12 months before you can take more parental leave when you work with the same employer. If you start to work with a new employer, then you will need to work for at least 12 months before you are entitled to parental leave.

## Long Service Leave

You may be entitled to long service leave if you have worked for a specified period of time with the same employer. Long service leave will depend on how long you have been working in the company. In some territories and states, casual workers may also be eligible for long-service leave. Check your specific state or territory for information about long-service leave entitlements.

- WorkSafe ACT
- Commerce WA
- NT Government
- SafeWork SA
- Business Victoria
- NSW Industrial Relations
- Queensland Industrial Relations
- WorkSafe Tasmania

Australian states and territories can provide employees in coal mining, building and construction industries with portable long-service leave. This effectively means that employees can keep their long-service leave even when they work on different projects. You can get some more information on long-service leave with this fact sheet.

## Sick and Carer's Leave

You can apply for sick and carer's leave if you need to take time off to deal with your own illness or to care for someone with an illness. This leave is also known as personal leave and can be taken when an employee is injured or ill.

Employees may need to take some time off to care for household members who are sick and injured. This is known as carer's leave and is taken out of the same sick/personal leave balance. This kind of leave may be both paid and unpaid. You can get more information about paid sick and carer's leave here and unpaid carer's leave here. This type of leave can be taken to care for immediate family members like:

- A de facto partner
- A spouse
- A parent
- A child
- A grandparent
- A grandchild
- A sibling

A household member may also be defined as any person who lives in the same accommodation as the employee.

You may also be entitled to other leaves like public holidays, compassionate and bereavement leave, community service leave and worker's compensation leave. If you want more information about the kind of leave, you are entitled to in your industry and company, visit this help web page for more information.

## 9.7 Salary Slip and PAYG Summary

Small and large businesses alike find it invaluable to keep records, not only for their own accounting purposes, but also from a taxation and legislation point of view. Giving every employee a pay or salary slip is a good way to ensure that correct entitlements and wages are given at all times.

Salary slips are given to employees on the first working day after getting paid, even when the employee is away on leave. They are either given as hard copies or in an electronic form and should have the exact same information. Salary slips should include the following:

- Employee and employer name
- Employer ABN
- Date of payment
- Pay period
- Net and gross pay
- Hourly rate
- Number of hours worked at the rate
- Bonus
- Tax cut
- Penalties
- Expenses incurred for the employee
- Paid entitlements
- Superannuation contributions made during the period of pay

Employees can easily find out their leave balance by checking directly with their employers. If you don't receive a salary slip, you must talk to your employer.

The PAYG summary is a document that you will receive from your employer for the salary that you have received during a financial year. This summary shows the total amount of payments you received, including the money that was withheld in the year. Payments will include income accrued as a part-time or casual employee. Payments include wages, commissions, salaries and bonuses. The PAYG summary will include:

- Gross income from the employer
- Tax withheld
- Employer ABN or withholding payer number (WPN)

If your PAYG summary is missing or lost, you can obtain it by asking your employer for another copy. You may also request for an employer letter declaring income and tax details. You can get information about lost or misplaced PAYG summaries here.

For a standard Salary Template sample see here - **_Pay-Slip_**.

# 10. Job Seeker Support

## 10.1 Career Advice and Counselling

The Australian government provides support to people looking for jobs through counselling centres. Work counsellors are professionals who help you identify occupations that you may be able to undertake after you move to Australia.

The government helps you with career advice through several channels, while also providing you with enough support to help you find a job.

When you are eligible to work, the Australian Job Search website offers free tools for migrants and other workers to help you with job vacancies throughout the country. This helps job seekers identify employment opportunities and to make contact with service providers who may be able to help them in various aspects of their search for work.

If you have been terminated or made redundant from an employer, the Australian Government provides you with the necessary support as you search for a new job through local employment services available to provide you with the needed support to find a job. These services include help with preparing your resume, providing access to computers and telephones and similar assistance in finding a job.

MIGRANT NINJA TIP:

**The Australian Government offers several free tools to help migrants look for work in the country. The government also**

**organises Community Development Programmes for those who live in remote parts of the country.**

## 10.2 Support for Job Seekers / Unemployed

The Australian Government supports job seekers in their search for a new job. While you look for jobs, you may be eligible for certain payments under different government programs.

Centrelink is an Australian Government program managed under the Department of Human Services, which offers a range of services and payments for people. Centrelink is the entry point to a range of services available to people who may be in need of government support.

### Government Support While You Look for Work

Support while you look for work includes income support like Newstart Allowance, Sickness Allowance, Youth Allowance, Widow Allowance and Disability Support Pension. Each of these support systems has their own requirements.

### New Start Allowance

This allowance is given to individuals above 22 years of age, but below pensionable age. The individual should be looking for paid work and should meet the mutual obligation requirements. A prerequisite for this allowance is completing the income and assets test. The payment rates for new-start allowance are given on the website. There is normally a waiting period before you receive your first payment. The minimum waiting period is one week and can extend up to 104 weeks, depending on circumstances.

## Sickness Allowance

This payment is given to individuals above 22 years of age who cannot work due to injury or sickness. There are also residential and other requirements to avail this payment. To see that you are given the right amount of payment, officials undertake a periodic review. Read more about sickness allowance here.

## Youth Allowance

This allowance is provided to youth between the age group of 16 to 21, who are searching for a job. The payment amount is calculated using an income and assets test. This test will depend on your personal situation. To avail this allowance, you need to be an Australian citizen and reside in the country during your claim.  You also need to be studying at an approved institution and undertaking an approved course. Get more information about youth allowance here.

## Payments to help you Study

The Australian Government also gives a payment to full-time students and Australian Apprentices to help them study or train.  For more information, visit -  Austudy

## 10.3 State Government Support

Migration is a crucial part of the Australian economy. Most migrants who enter the country want to work and make a valuable contribution to the nation. Finding the right support can be challenging for migrants, so the government has set up online and offline resources to help support you find a new job in your new country.

Local workforce centres help you make career choices and are located across different parts of Australia. Most of them are designed to provide free or highly subsidised advice to residents. They offer:

- Career guidance and training course information.
- Training providers and access to career development tools.
- Skill improvement workshops.

These centres may offer in-person, online or phone advice and can make a big difference to you when you first enter Australia and are trying to get a grasp of the local culture. Some workforce centres across different states include:

- Western Australia
- Victoria
- Queensland
- Tasmania
- Northern Territory
- South Australia

These workforce centres can help you at any point in your life to make informed choices about your career and training options. The government has also started an initiative where Welfare Support workers offer information and support to people on issues related to finance, health, housing and social welfare. The scope of work for these social welfare workers includes:

- Assessing needs and offering educational and training support programs.
- Interviewing and understanding the extent of client difficulties.
- Referring people to specific agencies that can provide added help for work, training and employment.
- Working with government bodies, private businesses and welfare agencies to promote community awareness.

**Job Services Australia (JSA)**

Job Services Australia (JSA) is a free service provided by the government to help you identify possible jobs. JSA also helps employers get access to employees based on screening and skill training. For more information, refer to **Australian Job Search** website. You can also get more details about job services Australia providers **here**.

MIGRANT NINJA TIP:

**Most of the Australian capital cities have JSA providers, so should be able to get access to them. You can also confirm about a JSA specialist in your area.**

## 10.4 Local Council Support

Each local council is an independent group that works together in the best interests of the local community. Services provided by local councils range from providing building permits and planning events to creating local rules and maintaining public parks.

Get in touch with them to find out whether they provide any free training or employment opportunities. Often, local businesses get in touch with local councils seeking workers, so if you are a good fit, they may connect you to prospective employers through their platform.

- If you are based in Queensland, you can find information about local QLD councils here.
- If you are based in NSW, you can find information about all local NSW councils here.
- If you are based in WA, you can find information about all local WA councils here.
- If you are based in SA, you can find information about all local SA councils here.
- If you are based in NT, you can find information about all local NT councils here.
- If you are based in Tasmania, you can find information about all local TAS councils here.
- If you are based in ACT, you can find information about all local ACT councils here.
- If you are based in Victoria, you can find information about all local VIC councils here.

**MIGRANT NINJA TIP:**

**Many local councils in Australia have started some specific initiatives to help people find work in the region. Many also offer educational and training programs to help workers find their footing in a competitive Australian job market. Contact your local council to see what free advice and employment support you can get.**

## 10.5 Support for Families

This chapter covers payments for parents who are either employed or unemployed and looking for work. The actual circumstances, income threshold, family structure and various other factors will determine the payment one can actually expect.

MIGRANT NINJA TIP:

**For being eligible for most of these payments, you need to fulfil the residency requirements, amongst many other conditions. For most new migrants, the general wait period before access to these payments is 104 weeks.**

## 10.5.1 Family Tax Benefit

Family Tax Benefit is a two-part payment to help families raise children without feeling pressure. To be eligible, you must:

- Have a dependent child not receiving a pension or any other payments like youth allowance.
- Provide care for your children at least for 35 percent of your time.
- Meet the criteria in the income test.

The Family Tax Benefit (FTB) Part A is a payment made for every child, which is a certain amount you receive based on your situation. You are eligible for this payment if you have a dependent child up to 19 years. Other requirements mean that your child should be undertaking some training or education in approved courses. Your child should also have an acceptable study load or should be granted exemption from training or education. If you homeschool kids, you will not satisfy the study requirements to be eligible for FTB. If you are a single parent, you can also obtain child support. Else, you may only be eligible for the FTB Part A base rate.

If you are eligible for FTB Part A payments for a newborn or recently adopted a child, you can also claim for Newborn Upfront Payment and Newborn Supplement. This is a component paid over a period of 3 months as part of the FTB payment. To be eligible for this supplement, your kids should be updated with immunisations based on the early childhood vaccination schedule for your kid's age. Learn more about immunising your children.

The Family Tax Benefit (FTB) Part B is a payment for giving added assistance to single parents, non-parent carers like grandparents and great grandparents, and couple with only one income. A one-income household usually occurs when one parent stays home full time to care for your child or manages some paid work while taking care of the kids. This payment is generally income tested.

You are eligible for this payment if you take care of a child less than 12 years, at least for 35 percent of your time. If you are a single parent or a non-parent carer, you may be eligible for this payment if the child is younger than 16 and is a full-time student. You must take care of the kids at least for 35 percent of your time. Once again, home schooled children will not meet the study requirements. You cannot receive this payment if you are on paid parental leave, but you can claim it when that ends.

Income tests for FTB Part A and B are subject to income tests. Get more information about the income test for FTB Part A and the income test for FTB Part B. For FTB part B payments, the primary earner should have a regulated taxable income of less than or equal to $100,000 per year. Learn more about taxable income because this is used to calculate your payments and benefits.

You must satisfy residency criteria for Australia to be eligible for Part A and B payments. You should be living in Australia as a citizen or a permanent resident. You can also have a special category or temporary visa like a Temporary Protection visa or Partner Provisional visa. If you are a grandparent carer, refer to more information presented here.

## 10.5.2 Child Care

Childcare payments have been set up to help you with the costs involved for registered or approved care like outside-school day care, vacation care, kindergarten and pre-school. To be eligible for these payments, you may use only registered centres and should be responsible for paying the fees. You should have also immunised your child.

Any childcare service must be approved by the government to be eligible for childcare benefits. Childcare doesn't include schooling from primary level. Find out from the childcare service whether they have been approved for childcare benefits. You can also get this information on the mychild website. If you get access to approved childcare, your benefits will be:

- All eligible families get up to 24 hours per week per child.
- Up to 50 hours per week per child if you are a grandparent, working parents, looking for work, studying or any other exemptions.
- Over 50 hours may be available to some families based on specific circumstances.

Childcare rebates may be available for guardians and parents who meet the requirements of the Work, Training, Study test with out-of-pocket expenses. You will be automatically assessed for any rebates if you submit claims for child care benefits. If you want more information, check out this website for a Child Care Rebate. You can also get more information about childcare benefits here.

### 10.5.3 Parental Payments

Parental Payments is income support provided to parents or guardians to enable them to take care of children more appropriately. To be eligible for parental payments, you should be:

- A single parent caring for a child below 8 years.
- A co-parent caring for a child younger than 6 years.
- Meet the eligibility criteria of an income and assets test.

The parental payment amount you are eligible for depends on your personal family situation. These rates are updated on 20 September and 20 March every year. This table will help you understand how much you may receive if you are eligible for the parental payments scheme.

## Family Circumstance - Maximum Payment Per Fortnight

Single - $737.10 (with Pension Supplement)

Couple - $476.40

Couple, respite care, prison, separation-causing illness - $570.80

The parental payments you are eligible for depends on income and assets for you and your partner. Read more about income and assets here. For eligibility, you must be an Australian resident and must satisfy these requirements:

- You should have been a resident for at least 104 weeks.
- Be exempt from this need if you are a refugee or become a single parent.
- Be physically present in the country when you lodge your claim.
- Meet all residential requirements when you receive this parent.

If you live or have worked in a country where Australia has a social security agreement, you may meet these residency requirements more easily. Depending on your own individual circumstance, you may need to wait for some time before waiting for your income support payment. You can get more information about waiting periods here.

MIGRANT NINJA TIP:

**If you are looking for child support or other types of income support, you may still need to lodge a tax return to be eligible. Seek advice from the Australian Taxation Office for this.**

## 10.5.4 Single Income Family Supplement

To be eligible for a single income family supplement payment:

- You must have one eligible child.
- You must have one main earner with an income between $68,000 and $150,000.
- If the second person earns an income below $18,000, you will still be eligible for this supplement.

You must satisfy residency requirements where you are a citizen, a permanent resident, a special category visa holder or a provisional protection visa holder. This annual payment is made to you of up to $300. The payment rate is usually determined based on your household income and the number of days an eligible child is in your care. Find out how much you can get using this rate estimator.

## 10.5.5 Energy Supplement

If you receive income support payments of FTB, an energy supplement is usually paid automatically with regular payments. The amount of energy supplement payments you are eligible for will depend on your personal circumstances. You can read more about it here. The Essential Medical Equipment Payment is a yearly payment of $147 made to people who experience increased home energy costs because of using essential medical equipment to manage medical conditions or disabilities. Read more about it here.

## 10.5.6 Low Income Supplement

The Low Income Supplement is a payment of $300 that you can claim every year. You may be eligible for this supplement if you received any benefits or pension from the Australian government for over 39 weeks. Find out more information about Low Income Supplement. The Low Income Family Supplement is a payment of $300 that low-income families can claim every year. You may be eligible for this supplement if you or your partner received any family tax benefits from the Australian government for over 39 weeks. Find out more information about Low Income Family Supplement.

## 10.5.7 Family Assistance Payments

All family assistance payments are managed after every financial year ends by comparing the income estimate to actual income of the family. This ensures that families are paid correct amounts. This balancing payments process has been simplified, so you don't need to call your local authorities. Get more information when it comes to balancing your family assistance payments.

MIGRANT NINJA TIP: **If you need information about other organisations providing support services use the Service Finder for finding assistance in your area. Use the payment finder tool to help you establish what payments you may be eligible for based on your personal situation. Find this tool here.**

# 11. Website Links and Resources

## 11.1 Job Portals

NOTE- This is not an exhaustive list of job websites and job seekers are encouraged to do further research online as there are numerous websites that list job vacancies in Australia.

Most employers will advertise on job seeker websites. New job advertisements are published daily. You can set up a personal account on the job portals (which is generally free) so that suitable job advertisements can be emailed to you.

Most of these job websites also have a blog which provides useful information to help you in your job search and hand tips on an array of topics such as resume writing and presentation and preparing for interviews.

There are numerous internet-based job seeker websites in Australia. Here is a compilation of some of the leading websites.

Seek - SEEK is Australia's premier jobs site with the most visible presence across all industries, regions and locations. You can Search or browse for jobs right across Australia. Their motto and call line is "SEEK and you shall find".

Career One - This website launched in 1999 is a part of the Fairfax family group. It delivers a national base of jobs and job seekers. Careerone also provides support in writing and building resumes provides career advice and online courses. Their job board offer a collection of career advice, job hunting tips, company profiles and job listings.

Indeed - Indeed is rated as one of the top job sites worldwide, with over 200 million unique visitors per month. Indeed is available in more than 60 countries and 28 languages, covering 94% of global GDP.

Apart from these leading job sites below are a list of some of the other prominent job portals.

Jobjobsjobs

Adzuna

LinkMe

LiveHire

Jora

Glassdoor

Apply Direct

Mitula

Careerjet

Aussie Employment

Australia.recruit.net

Simplyhired

Oneshift

Working in Australia

Jobserve

Casual Staffing

Neuvoo

Anywork Anywhere

SpotJobs

## 11.2 Recruitment Agencies

For the average person looking for jobs in Australia in the current economic situation, it can take weeks, even months to find work. You can imagine how much longer it would take newly arrived migrants with no local experience. With the slowing economic climate, partnering with a specialist recruitment agency within your chosen industry can be the best course of action in securing a job.

Recruitment specialists are in constant contact with employers within your industry, which means they'll be the first ones to know if your dream job has just opened up. They know your industry like the back of their hand and they will be able to give an accurate evaluation of where your experience and skills would be best utilised, and also provide you with advice on how to remedy any gaps in your knowledge.

Here is a list of Australia's top recruitment agencies.

RCSA- Recruitment and Consulting Services (Australia and New Zealand) – With a comprehensive list of recruitment firms segregated over 78 industries and locations, this website provides a one-stop shop for access to a range of recruitment firms across Australia and New Zealand

Australian Recruiting

Ignite

Rpb Consulting

Chandler Macleod

Greythorn (IT Recruitment)

Clicks (IT Recruitment)

Michael Page

Morgan Consulting

Hays

Hudson

Randstad

Nspire Recruitment

Six Degrees Executive

SHK (For Senior Management Roles)

Carmichael Fisher (For Senior Management Roles)

Devlin Alliance

Charterhouse

Robert Half

Xpand (Digital, Technology, Media, Sales and Marketing)

Command Recruitment

## 11.3 Industry Specific Job sites

Jobs in Mining: Mining related jobs.

Environmental Jobs: Environmentally related jobs.

Salon Staff: Jobs in the hairdressing industry.

Bluecollar - BlueCollar.com.au is a leading Trades & Technical job board matching skilled blue collar workers to Australian manufacturing, construction, mining and agricultural businesses.

Health Job Search - Jobs in healthcare.

Health Care, Nursing – Nursing Sector

Care Careers - Jobs, Careers Advice & Courses for The Care Sector.

Jobnet – This Company was established in 1995 and has quickly become one of the leading sites for IT and technical jobs in Australia.

Webjobz - is a group of International, and domestic Generalist and Niche Job Boards

Jobswiregurus.com.au - JobsWireGurus.com.au was founded by Australian IT professionals for Australian IT professionals and is committed to growing the most relevant and effective IT employment destination in Australia.

Mining Australia - is not a mining company nor is it a recruitment agency. What they do is provide recommendations on the best way to get work in the industry, and provide an in-depth assessment on such issues as the types of roles which may be best suited to you, trainings you may need to undertake to improve your employment prospects, as well as providing assistance with improving resumes.

## 11.4 Career Guidance, Psychometric Testing & Career Expos

### Career Guidance and Coaching

There is a difference between coaching and guidance. Career guidance is necessary when the individual (adolescent or adult) has little or no idea where to head in a career. They lack a career goal. It is generally applicable to young people fresh out of university or looking for their first job.

Career Coaching, on the other hand, is undertaken when individuals know their career goal or have a career pathway in mind, but want help on HOW to get there. For migrants who have just arrived in the country, career coaching acts as a compass that provides a direction one must take to achieve the objective of gainful employment.

You may think you don't need any professional help for getting your first job. But no matter what anyone says, as a migrant, it is never going to be a level playing field and the only way to compete with local talent when applying for jobs is to outshine other candidates at the very onset. This means having a winning Resume and cover letter, great communication skills and the confidence to ace the job interview. Most of the career guidance and coaching institutes charge a premium, but in the long run, the cost is justified as your chances to land the dream job shoot up exponentially with the right guidance and their professional support. The way forward is to think of these costs as a part of the migration expenses where you most certainly have spent thousands of dollars to get your visas.

Most of the professional companies offer a variety of services, which could include career advice, career counselling, executive career coaching, resume writing, selection criteria, LinkedIn Profiles, interview coaching, outplacement services, psychometric testing and career development. You should decide which services you require based on your industry, your current skill set and the type of job you are looking for.

Paid professional help is not the only way you can get career coaching. You can seek advice from your friends and family who have already established themselves in Australia. They most probably will have a solid network of friends who are in a position to help. The main thing to remember is to ask for help.

NOTE – As I have mentioned in the Foreword, please note that I am not affiliated to any of the businesses and I do not get any commission for recommending their services. The information provided is based on my own research as well as on reviews by candidates who have utilised the services.

The Career Development Association of Australia (CDAA) is your first stop when seeking expert help. This particular website has a searchable list of private career counsellors. Note that these counsellors will charge a fee for their services.

Apart from the paid services, each state government also offers free or subsidised training for job seekers that also cover most of the above topics. See Chapter 10.3 for more details.

**What you should ask a Career Practitioner?**

Their experience, training and qualifications

Their specialised skills and knowledge

What types of services they can offer you and how they work

Can you meet them first to discuss your issues?

Do they belong to a professional association and if so which one?

Cost and length of sessions?

What tools do they use?

You may also want to ask for a written quote and their terms of business.

## Psychometric, Personality and Aptitude Tests

### Psychometric Tests

Psychometric testing is commonly used to assist employers when deciding whether candidates are suitable for specific roles. Psychometric testing is designed to find job-relevant information about you which an interview wouldn't be able to do. Psychometric testing typically includes a combination of aptitude and personality tests online which measure your job-relevant cognitive abilities and personality. Psychometric testing has become a powerful tool and a proven method of delivering significant business value. Psychometric assessment ensures hiring managers select candidates based not only on their skills and experience but also on their cultural fit and potential for growth.

## Personality Tests

Personality tests are used by employers to assist them in gauging your personality and behavioural style as they relate to the job you have applied for.

## Aptitude Tests

An aptitude test is one of the most popular methods employers use to measure your work-related cognitive ability. Aptitude tests are always timed, as the key to these tests is how quickly you can finish answering the test. Aptitude test questions only have one correct answer and the test is designed so that only 5% of the population can answer all the questions in the given time frame. The aptitude test helps employers measure your intelligence; your ability to effectively solve problems; and your ability to think strategically and quickly draw accurate conclusions. Employers will look at your aptitude test results to determine your ability to handle work-related challenges

Psychometric Institute - Offers free tests

Practice Psychometric Tests Online

Hudson - Psychometric Testing Examples

JobTestPrep - provides you with a unique opportunity to learn how you are perceived through personality testing and to increase your employability skills. Receive a detailed analysis of your personality profile, customised to your job level, delivered through a smart online test preparation system.

## Job expos

At job expos, industries and employers promote themselves and provide detailed information about themselves, including their current and future job vacancies.

Whether you're a job seeker, or thinking about changing careers, job expos are a great way to connect with career advisers, employers, education and training providers, and job opportunities.

Job expos are also known as:

- Employment expos
- Skills expos
- Career fairs, markets or expos.
- Careers and Employment Expo

The Careers and Employment Expo series make up Australia's largest free careers, employment, education and training events. The annual events are a showcase of employment, skills, and education and training opportunities across many industries.

These expos are conducted regularly and in various locations. To find out the nearest one to you just search the web for 'Skill Expo or Career and Employment Expo" for your city. Official State Websites and local council websites also advertise any upcoming events.

## 11.5 Government Support and Job Websites

My Skills  -  My Skills website is the national directory of vocational education and training (VET) organisations and courses. It is a federal government initiative to enable consumers to search for, and compare, VET courses and training providers.

Job Outlook - is a career and labour market research information site to help individuals decide on their future career. For new migrants, it provides an overview of your specific industry, job or trade qualification. It provides statistics, job listings state wise), training required, outlook and prospects covering around 350 individual occupations.

Australian Job Search - Australia's largest free online jobs website.

Job Search - This is a government initiative that helps the unemployed find Jobs, employment & browse career opportunities

Myfuture.edu.au – is Australia's national online career information and exploration service. It is aimed at all Australians wishing to explore their career options, especially students. It is an interactive, user-driven website, which contains a personal career exploration and decision-making tool, comprehensive career-related information and help for those assisting others making career decisions.

National Centre for Vocational Education Research - The National Centre for Vocational Education Research (NCVER) aims to be Australia's leading provider of quality, independent information about vocational education and training (VET). The NCVER is responsible for collecting and managing national VET and Australian Apprenticeship statistics and managing national surveys of TAFE graduates and students, and employers' views of training.

Jobactive - jobactive is the Australian Government's way to get more Australian's into work. It connects job seekers with employers and is delivered by a network of jobactive providers in over 1700 locations across Australia.

More information about jobactive is available at Jobactive –Help for Job Seekers

Labour Market Information Portal - The Department of Employment publishes a range of products that can help you explore industries, occupations and skill shortages. They tell you about which industries and occupations have the largest number of jobs, where the new jobs will be over the next five years and where the skill shortages are.

Training.gov.au - Training.gov.au is the National Register for Vocational Education and Training. It is the authoritative source of information on Training Packages, Qualifications, Courses, Units of Competency and Registered Training Organisations (RTOs) and has been developed for experienced training sector users.

Jobs and Workplace – States and Territories - Information provided on state and territory employment and workplace pages can include career development and training, jobs, conditions and entitlements and occupational health and safety. New South Wales links to their main government entry point where you can search for specific employment information.

Each **state government** also provides advice and information to help local job seekers consider their vocational education and training options:

In the Australian Capital Territory – the Skilled Capital website

In New South Wales - the Smart and Skilled website

In Victoria - the Victorian Skills Gateway website

In Queensland – the Queensland Skills Gateway website

In South Australia – the Work Ready website

In Tasmania – the Skills Tasmania website

In Western Australia – the Future Skills WA website

In the Northern Territory – the VET NT website

Australian Jobs  - The Australian Jobs publication presents an overview of the current labour market and highlights the major changes which have occurred, including for industries and occupations. It is designed to meet the needs of a range of users, such as people exploring careers, those supporting people into employment and students who want a better understanding of the labour market.

Australian Public Service (APS) Jobs – APS jobs will help you discover Jobs and diverse career paths the public service has to offer and link you to vacancies in the APS, the Australian Parliamentary Service and many other Australian Government agencies. Note – Most gazette and federal jobs are offered only to Australian citizens so check Selection Criteria.

For State and Territory Links visit - State and Territory APS government jobs

LG Assist - is Australia's largest local government employment network serving Councils throughout Australia.

National, State and Territory Governments Job Websites – Are you interested in a career in state or territory government? Find out about the public service in Australian states and territories. This portal provides access to state-wide links with listings for job opportunities, graduate programs, cadetships, etc. and application information.

**Something different**

*Harvest Trail **links job seekers with** harvest jobs **Australia wide. It offers a great way for people to travel around Australia at their own pace while working and earning money.***

# 11.6 State and Territory Links

**Australian Capital Territory**

**Job Sites**

Careers with ACT Government

ACT –Looking for Jobs: Government Website

**Information**

ACT- Looking for Jobs

Moving to ACT: Government Information Portal

ACT - Government Information Portal for Employment  -

## New South Wales

## Job Sites

Careers with NSW Government

## Information

Living and Working in NSW

Moving to NSW: Government Information Portal

Multicultural NSW – Information for New Arrivals

## Northern Territory

## Job Sites

Careers with NT Government

NT – Looking for Jobs: Government Website

## Information

NT – Looking for Jobs

Living and working in NT

Moving to NT: Government Information Portal

## Queensland

## Job Sites

Careers with Queensland Government

Queensland- Looking for Jobs: Government Website

## Information

Queensland – Looking for Jobs

Moving to Queensland: Government Information Portal

## South Australia

### Job Sites

Careers with South Australian Government

South Australia – Choosing Your Career – Search Careers & Industries

### Information

South Australia – Support for Migrant Job Seekers

Moving to South Australia: Government Information Portal

## Tasmania

### Job Sites

Careers with Tasmanian Government

Tasmania – Looking for Jobs: Government Website

### Information

Tasmania – Resources for Job Seekers

Moving to Tasmania: Government Information Portal

## Victoria

### Job Sites

Careers with the Victorian Government

Victoria – Looking for Jobs: Government Website

### Information

Victoria and Melbourne – Looking for Jobs

Moving to Victoria - Government Information Portal

**Western Australia**

**Job Sites**

Careers with WA Government

Western Australia – Looking for Jobs

**Information**

WA – Looking for Jobs

Moving To Western Australia

Office of Multicultural Interests

# 11.7 General Research and Handy Information Websites

Payscale – Find out how much your skills are worth. Do career research and find in-depth salary data for specific jobs, employers, and more.

Department of Social Services – Settling in Australia Guide – This area provides information to all new arrivals, including skilled migrants, family migrants, refugees and humanitarian entrants.

Centrelink  - Delivering a range of payments and services for people at times of major change.

Australian Tax Office

Border.gov.au - Immigration into Australia information

Australian Government Website – Career Information and Services – Find information on a range of jobs, get advice on what might suit you, and pathways to get you there.

Employment Research and Statistics – The Australian Government undertakes research and analysis of employment trends across Australia to support government policy development. Employment related research in the areas of skill shortages, recruitment experiences, labour and skills needs and industry and employment trends is available.

Fairwork Ombudsman - Provides information and advice about your workplace rights and obligations.

Best Practice Guide - These best practice guides by fairwork.gov.au aim to help small businesses and employees with a range of workplace issues. By adopting best practice initiatives, employers and employees can achieve happier, fairer and more productive workplaces.

Employment.gov.au - The Australian Government Department of Employment is responsible for national policies and programmes that help Australians find and keep employment and work in safe, fair and productive workplaces.

Australia.gov.au Helping you find government information and services

Jobs and Workplace – State and Territories - Information provided on state and territory employment and workplace pages can include career development and training, jobs, conditions and entitlements and occupational health and safety. New South Wales links to their main government entry point where you can search for specific employment information.

Finder.com.au – One of Australia's leading and fastest growing comparison websites. This website provides abundant information about various aspects of Australian life; from banking and personal loans to the best phone deals and money transfer companies. It also has a great blog with handy tips and information

SBS settlement guide – for resources and information in more than 30 languages to help you settle in Australia

Australian Demographics

Carsales - Useful pricing and availability information on new/used cars

Choice - Australian Consumer Association

Dial an Angel - Australia's Leading Agency in Home and Family Care

My School - *My School* is a resource for parents, educators and the community to give readily accessible information about each of Australia's just over 10,000 schools and campuses.

Realestate - Useful real estate resource

**Resumes & Interviews**

How to Write a Resume

Tribuslingua/Skilled-migrants that need Australian CV Resume

Expat Arrivals

40 Interview questions you should be prepared to ask answer

Resumes and Cover Letters – UTAS Fact Sheets

Interview Question Tips –Hays

## Local Newspapers

The majority of vacancies advertised in the major regional newspapers are usually advertised in most major Job Portals as well, however, there are some Small Business Enterprises, local businesses as well as council jobs that are only advertised in the Classifieds Sections of local Newspapers. The Job Listings are usually in the weekend editions, however, the weekday papers also have daily listings.

Online Newspapers

The most exhaustive list of online Newspapers all in one convenient location. The Australian Section has over 400 listed newspapers, from the national papers to the local dailies.

The website also has a listing of newspapers created by and specific to ethnic communities (For example – there are newspapers in Hindi, Nepali, Greek, Farsi and Arabic to name a few)

The Australian - This is Australia's national newspaper. It carries job advertisements through the week, with the largest job section in the Saturday edition. Certain daily editions will also focus on specific industries, for example 'Epicure' on Tuesdays focuses on the food and hospitality industry.

## Australian Capital Territory

Australian Capital Territory Newspapers – A Comprehensive List

Canberra Times - Wednesday and Saturday editions

The Advocate

The Examiner

**New South Wales**

New South Wales Newspapers – A Comprehensive List

Daily Telegraph

Herald (New Castle)

**Northern Territory**

Northern Territory Newspapers – A Comprehensive List

NT News

Katherine Times

**Queensland**

Queensland Newspapers – A Comprehensive List

Brisbane Times

**South Australia**

South Australia Newspapers – A Comprehensive List

The Advertiser

**Tasmania**

Tasmania Newspapers - A Comprehensive List

The Mercury (Southern Tasmania)

The Examiner (Northern Tasmania)

**Victoria**

Victoria Newspapers – A Comprehensive List

Herald Sun

The Age

The Weekly Times Regional Jobs in Victoria

**Western Australia**
Western Australia Newspapers – A Comprehensive List

The West Classifieds

The Courier

# 12. Additional Training

## 12.1 Upgrading Skills

If you are looking to become employable in Australia, you can seek opportunities to upgrade your skills through TAFE (Technical and Further Education) and VET (Vocational Education and Training) courses. TAFE campuses are available throughout the country and can help you find diplomas or courses that help you get straight into the local Australian workforce.

TAFE courses are relatively cheaper and can help you gain relevant qualifications and skills. Check out information about some TAFE courses here.

TAFE offers you the opportunity to benefit from vocational training courses from top education providers in the country. Many courses can be completed online, so you don't have to worry about being physically present somewhere.

Offering courses like certificates, diplomas and short courses, TAFE points you to the right training skills that you need. Courses are available in a myriad of occupations – creative fields, financial services, healthcare, tourism, hospitality, building & construction, IT and much more.

The online resources allow you to find what you're looking for with your final job outcome in mind. Finding relevant skills at TAFE can put your local Australian career on the fast track and can make a real difference when you start going for interviews to employers.

# TAFE Institutes in Australia

Most states have a TAFE Institute. Get more information about them here. TAFE is the largest education sector in Australia with over 59 institutes spread across several hundreds of campuses across the country. These government-funded training institutes are also known as Registered Training Organisations (RTOs).

These training centres offer practical Vocational Education and Training (VET) courses designed to equip you with training and skills needed for the workforce. Relevant state and territory governments regulate these TAFE institutes, so fees and policies will vary across different parts of the country. Visit the different TAFE institutes for more information:

- NSW: TAFE NSW

- ACT: CIT

- TAS: TAFE Tasmania and Tasmanian Academy

- QLD: TAFE Queensland

- VIC: Victorian Skills Gateway

- NT: CDU VET

- WA: Training WA

- SA: TAFE SA

**MIGRANT NINJA TIP:**

- **TafeCourses.com.au isn't part of TAFE institutes. It belongs to Training.com.au and provides information on a multitude of vocational training courses provided by** educational institutions in Australia. You can get more information about TAFE institutes in Australia here.

• My Skills offers a directory of VET courses to help you find what you are looking for.

• National Centre for Vocational Education Research (NCVER) offers statistics and research on VET courses.

## 12.2 Additional Courses for Developing Soft Skills

If you want to become more employable in Australia and feel you need help with certain soft skills, then you may consider undergoing some training in that regard. You can find a range of training organisations and short courses that they offer when you search for the relevant skills training online.

One of the best ways of mastering these skills on your own is by attempting to self-learn by joining the local library and investing your time in learning about the soft skills, watching YouTube Videos and researching online.

Listed below are some of the soft skills which are just as important as your skills and experience when looking for suitable employment. I have refrained from recommending any training institutes which offer courses in these subjects because, firstly, I do not have any personal experience with regards to the quality of courses, and secondly, there are so many establishments out there that you can pick and choose from a multitude of training providers who offer the relevant course.

**Technical skills may get you the interview, but soft skills will help you shine above other candidates in your desired field. As a migrant, you will need all the help you can get to succeed in the Australian workplace, so building these soft skills will boost your employability.**

## Personality Development

In today's highly competitive business environment, confidence, attitude and determination are what makes you stand apart from the competition and will help you succeed. Concentrated courses on personality development will enable you to master your skill so that you can excel in your desired occupation.

## English Language Development

English is a global language and is the official language in Australia. It is necessary for working and even your daily living in Australia. Studying English will help you be more successful during interviews with potential employers and will help you interact with your colleagues more easily. See earlier chapters for training provided in this regard.

## Public Speaking

Applying for a job where you need to make a presentation or speak up in team meetings? Speaking at events, conferences and networking activities is a vital part of ongoing professional development. Through preparation and practice, you can overcome your nervousness and perform exceptionally well.

## Confidence Building Classes

Not everyone finds confidence naturally. It can be hard to develop confidence if you suffer from low self-esteem. Healthy self-esteem is essential for growth and achieving success. Single-day workshops are available to help you learn practices to intensely change your feelings towards yourself. You will also learn how to enhance your communication skills and relationships, which is important when you want to succeed in your new Australian work environment.

## Leadership Training

Investing in a leadership training program is a good way to build your workplace fundamentals if you are looking to acquire a management role. Leadership skills will help you build your professional intellect and will advance your employability.

## Critical Thinking Skills

Critical thinking is designed to teach you the art of reasoning through problems. You will also learn to present your arguments in a compelling and logical manner. The best part is that critical thinking can be imparted so that you are equipped to think more critically in a workplace environment.

## Negotiation Skills Training

Negotiating successfully requires you to explore opposing views with the ultimate aim of achieving an outcome in your favour. Learning how to successfully negotiate can make a big difference to your employability because organisations are always looking for smart people who can resolve conflicts in a calm and collected manner.

**Mastering Interviews Training**

An interview is your stepping stone to a job, so you should ideally learn to develop your skills before you head into the job market. The Australian marketplace pays tremendous heed to impressions, so you'll obviously want to ensure you succeed through proper preparation. Single-day workshops will help you with the interview preparation process.

MIGRANT NINJA TIP:

**Toastmasters International is a not for profit training organisation that focuses on communication and leadership development. There are over 800 clubs with over 17,000 members throughout Australia, New Zealand and Papua New Guinea. If you want to address all the above mentioned soft skills free of cost (a small fee is charged to cover running costs) and experience overall personal growth, then, I would highly recommend joining this organisation.**

## 12.3 Apprenticeship

Planning of changing jobs? If the industry you are currently working for is not able to provide you with suitable employment or if you are in between jobs and would like to change your profession, then, this option may open new avenues for employment. Australian apprenticeships are great for gaining on-the-job training and expertise in specific industries. Australian Apprenticeships are available in different certificate levels for over 500 Australian occupations – whether traditional or emerging trades. Some occupations are listed below, while the full list can be found on this web page.

- Agriculture

- Building and construction
- Financial services
- Food
- IT
- Government
- Printing
- Process Manufacturing
- Retail
- Sport
- Telecom
- Tourism

  If you are looking for apprenticeships and industry-specific training, check Internet job sites and local newspapers daily to see whether anything is available in your interest areas. Here is a list of some websites that can help you find apprenticeship training programs:

- AMA Apprenticeship & Traineeship Services WA: For apprenticeship vacancies in WA.
- Year 13: For apprenticeship jobs throughout Australia.
- Group Training Australia (GTO): GTO employs apprentices for different industries and is present in every State and Territory. Some hire apprentices for all industries, while others are hired for specific industries only.
- MAS Jobs National: For apprenticeship vacancies throughout Australia.
- ApprenticeshipCentral: Job site for apprenticeship vacancies throughout Australia.

- MRAEL QLD: For apprenticeship vacancies throughout Queensland.
- Skillsroad jobs board: For apprenticeship jobs throughout Australia.
- MEGT Apprenticeship jobs: For apprenticeship vacancies throughout Australia.
- Skill 360 Far North QLD: For apprenticeship vacancies throughout Far North Queensland.
- Trade apprentices QLD: A government website for apprentices in Queensland.
- Apprenticeships in minerals and energy sectors: For apprenticeship jobs in minerals and energy sectors.
- Apprentice Match : For apprenticeship vacancies in Australia.
- Need an Apprentice (NSW & VIC): For apprenticeship jobs in NSW and VIC.

Apprentices looking for jobs can also visit general job portals by using apprenticeship and training in keywords.

MIGRANT NINJA TIP:

**The Australian Government has made it easier for people with financial difficulties to undertake Australian Apprenticeship programs. Get more information about it here. Follow these key steps in your goal to become an Australian apprentice.**

## 12.4 Additional Australian Government Initiatives

The Australian Department of Education has started a website as the National Register for VET programs in Australia. This nationally recognised training offers information related to:

- Qualifications
- Training packages
- Competency units
- Accredited courses
- Skill sets

Approved RTO's will deliver this Nationally Recognised Training under the purview of legal obligations in Australia. The website is managed by the Education Department for state and territory governments.

The Australian Skills Quality Authority was also started by the government to promote quality training to help students and employers have confidence in the sector. The ASQA regulates training and education providers to ensure that quality is maintained at all times.

The Australian Qualifications Framework determines the quality of local qualifications. It is the national policy to regulate qualifications in the training and education system of the country. The AQF provides regulations and standards that education departments and training courses must adhere to for students.

MIGRANT NINJA TIP:

**The Australian Government offers various initiatives to help people looking for jobs or wanting to up skill. Knowing the initiatives available will help you develop your skills in accordance with regulations and guidelines prescribed by the government.**

# 13. Alternate Professions

Although, finding an alternate profession when you first arrive in Australia and when you are seeking employment may not be something you would initially consider, however, it is worthwhile to be aware that Australia offers a range of labour intensive jobs that are always in demand. They also work as a great secondary income, especially if you are employed as a temporary or part-time employee in your current job and may help you sustain when you look for your 'Big Break'.

MIGRANT NINJA TIP.

**If it is mentioned in your present contract, always check with your current employers if it is legally allowed to work in the desired occupation and if there could be a potential conflict of interest.**

**Taxi Driver**

Becoming a taxi driver is quite straightforward, but you do have to satisfy certain state regulations and be suitably licensed. The area where the taxi driver provides the service sets this fare. This is a good alternative profession and you can set your own work hours and schedule. An average salary for a taxi driver in a full-time position is around $45,000.

For licensing in your specific state, visit:

- Western Australia
- New South Wales
- South Australia
- Queensland

- Victoria
- Tasmania
- Northern Territory
- Australian Capital Territory

When looking for job opportunities, just search for 'becoming a taxi driver' in your relevant state. Most of the private companies provide in-house training, but the cost of licensing and training is borne by the candidate.

**Photographer**

If you have a flair for photography and possess the drive for changing your passion into a profession, then, this is a great option. Photographers use lights and surrounding environments to produce images on a variety of subjects. Photographers can either be employed full-time, part-time or work on a freelance basis for newspapers, online websites and magazines. Salary and fees vary based on your experience and employer. There is an ever-growing need for professional photographers to cover local events, family ceremonies and special moments. One great way to begin is to start offering your services in your local community and then build your network from there. Get more information about photographers in Australia here. The average salary of a photographer is around $58,000

**Farming**

The agricultural industry in Australia is ever growing and supports the Australian economy in a very big way. Although farming in rural areas is generally considered a backpacker's short-term option, it does offer a range of jobs from beginner level to advanced positions such as farm managers or supply chain managers. It is a hard life in remote locations, with early hours and long days. However, many migrants have made a fortune from farming and have turned it into a family owned business spanning generations.

From shearing sheep to picking bananas, from working in sugar cane farms to rounding cattle, the job profiles are as abundant as the variety of produce in the industry.

Learn more about how to get farm jobs in Australia here.

The average pay for a Farmer is AU$59,664 per year

For Jobs, visit:

Ruralenterprise

Queensland Farmers Enterprise

Seek – Farm Jobs

Jobsearch - Harvest

### *DID YOU KNOW:*

*There are approximately 134,000 farm businesses in Australia, 99 percent of which are family-owned and operated. Each Australian farmer produces enough food to feed 600 people, 150 at home and 450 overseas. Australian farmers produce almost 93 percent of Australia's daily domestic food supply.*

*As of 2010-11, there are 307,000 people employed in Australian agriculture. The complete agricultural supply chain, including the affiliated food and fibre industries, provide over 1.6 million jobs to the Australian economy.*

## Private Tutor

Private tutors have extremely adaptable jobs since they are able to set their own salaries and working hours. Some private tutors may work with individuals, while others may set classes based on the needs of students. Find out how to become a tutor here. You can also join the Australian Tutoring Association for more information on your chosen field.

## Landscape Gardener

Landscape gardeners help to maintain and develop parks, landscapes and gardens. Salaries will differ based on your skill level and employer. Gardening professions have risen in demand in the last few years because homeowners have less time to manage their yards. More information about how to become a landscape gardener is available. In its simplest form, you can join a local lawnmower company and make a part-time job out of it.

## Retail Jobs

Retail jobs are something you can consider as soon as you arrive. You don't always need qualifications to get a foot in the door and there can be great opportunities for training and development.

Besides, as a migrant, it will enhance your communication skills, help you network and provide an insight into the local work culture. There are lots of different jobs that you can do in retail, from junior customer service roles, right up to area manager, responsible for several key stores. Customer service assistant, Sales assistant, Merchandiser and retail manager roles are some other positions. The top categories in Australia for these industries are chefs and cooks, management and waiting staff, and retail assistants, management store and department management. During the holiday season, the need for temporary workers jumps and so does the average hourly rates.

For Jobs visit:

Seek – Jobs in Retail Industry

Spotjobs

## Franchising

Franchising is a way to distribute goods and services of the franchisor, who is the original owner of the business. The franchisor assigns his business to be run independently (franchisee) with certain rules and regulations stipulated for a specified period. If you are planning to get into your own business when you migrate, this is an excellent opportunity contributing over $131 billion annually to the Australian economy (based on data from the Franchise Council of Australia). Some reports have also revealed that franchise businesses are growing at a better rate than other small businesses. Over 400,000 people are employed in nearly 73,000 franchise businesses in the country, which makes this a lucrative proposition if you want to start something on your own, but don't have much knowledge about local market conditions in Australia. Get more details about franchising in Australia here for more knowledge of the industry as a viable alternative career choice for you.

## Online Business/Jobs

## Uber Driver

Uber has transformed the taxi industry in Australia by allowing regular people to make some extra money. There is a massive opportunity to make some good money by signing up to become an Uber driver in Australia. You will need to meet basic state-regulated requirements, which includes owning a car less than 9 years old and gaining a driver authorization from your local transport department. Once you complete your induction with Uber, you'll have the freedom to pick up as many customers as you want. Learn more about how to become an Uber driver in Australia here. Average earning for an Uber driver is around $ 35 to $ 40 per hour before Uber takes its 20% cut.

MIGRANT NINJA TIP:

**Australia is still in the process of legalising Uber in most states and territories, so, whilst you may be on the right side of the law in once city, you could possibly be in breach of regulations when you enter a different town or state.**

### Airtasker

Airtasker is an online community where people can outsource certain tasks to trusted professionals and tradesmen online or through mobile. If you want to offer a service, simply sign up to Airtasker and let people contact you when the need for your type of job arises.

These alternate professions offer the opportunity to earn reasonably good salaries for a decent standard of living or even as a temporary recourse until you get your first break in the preferred field. Remember that in Australia, there is a dignity of labour in every trade and profession. So while you may not have considered doing some of these jobs in your home country, rest assured, they are equally respected professions in Australia.

# 14. Q&A with Judith Leeson AM, Director – Vector Consultants

*This chapter is provided by Judith Leeson who, with her husband, Brian, are the founding Directors of Vector Consultants and have been providing career development and transition services to a diverse range of job seekers since 1991. They have a clear understanding of the challenges faced by people seeking employment or looking to change the direction of their career. Both have made significant career transitions themselves – Brian as a skilled migrant to Australia from England, and Judith as an Australian moving to England to live and work. Both have enjoyed significant careers in other industries (science, early childhood and disability), and then periods of transition and development through learning and mastering new areas of work, They have considerable interest and experience in working with skilled migrants, and have provided some answers to some frequently asked questions observations which may be helpful.*

## a) What are challenges faced by new migrants when they enter the job market in Australia?

The biggest challenge is responding to the inevitable gap between expectations and the reality of the labour market. While there are many wonderful opportunities here in Australia, there are also many challenges faced by migrants as they adapt to a completely different culture of employment, including differing workplace conditions, a demand for workers who are both qualified and experienced locally, legislation that is demanding, and the lack of an established professional network and often family support. Many migrants are disappointed if they are not immediately able to transition to a job of similar status to the one they previously enjoyed in their country of origin and may struggle to manage their resources when these opportunities do not emerge quickly. Some may need to undertake training to add value to their qualifications and meet local Australian requirements. Others may need to gain local experience before they obtain employment, and should anticipate and prepare for this delay and financial cost.

English language skills that are highly regarded in their home country may be not reaching the professional levels expected in Australia, and some may need to upgrade their English language skills, both spoken and written. Fluency of expression, clear articulation, the ability to interpret nuanced communication, and to write fluently and succinctly, are highly desirable professional qualities. A sense of humour and the ability to laugh at oneself are also considered part of engaging communication, as are honesty, openness and warmth.

Skilled migrants come to Australia with a clear understanding of the culture of the labour market in general and their industry or profession in particular in their former country of employment, but may need some time to adapt to the workplace culture of Australians. In the early days of settlement here, it is important to take some time to explore Australian culture, and it is helpful to start with the community in which you take up residence. Exploring the unknown will gradually result in more confidence, and involvement as a volunteer, a participant in an English language group, member of a playgroup or school volunteer, sporting, religious, or other community activities will hone your appreciation of the nuances of Australian expressions and values, and the ongoing development of your English language skills if needed.

Early contact with a group of your own heritage and culture will provide you with time to relax and share your early experiences, and may also provide some you with the nucleus of your network in Australia, and an enjoyable meeting place where you are able to connect with migrants who have been here for a few years and clearly understand some of the issues you will face.

Early support from a career development practitioner will ensure that time is not spent unproductively. It may take up to six months to secure a positon, and for some, it may take longer, depending on the perceived match between desirable and actual skills, fluctuations in the economy and influences of the global labour market. Skilled migrants usually have clear career goals in the days following their arrival in Australia, but will often benefit from an analysis of their existing résumé and some coaching in interview skills to enable them to maximise the initial effectiveness of their job search. An investment in working with a career coach will also benefit them in looking more laterally for work, and developing strategies for employment other than merely applying for advertised vacancies. In some cases a change of career direction may provide a faster pathway to financial independence and participation in the local workforce.

For some skilled migrants, the early time spent in the job search may precipitate a questioning of their career goals, and a desire to explore alternative options. A professional career practitioner will be able to facilitate effective exploration of other viable options and a training pathway to achieve these aspirations. It is increasingly the norm in Australia for people to move between industries up to five or more times in their career and they may undertake up to ten or more different occupations in their life time. A realistic strategy, to ensure that skilled migrants are able to access professional career management support and further education and training, is to sequester some funds specifically for that purpose.

There are a number of generic, free government services designed to help people find employment, but there are limitations on eligibility, and the type and length of support available. Professionally qualified and experienced career development practitioners who can target career coaching, career management and mentoring services to meet the individual needs of skilled migrants are able to offer longer, more in-depth support usually on a fee-for-service basis. A list of professional career practitioners can be obtained from Find a Practitioner on the website of the Career Development Association of Australia, www.cdaa.org.au where you can identify people with appropriate skills, qualifications, experience and professional standing.

**b) What advice can you provide new entrants when looking for a job?**

New job applicants will need to undertake considerable research when looking for paid employment, not only about the national and local labour markets, but also about the transferability of qualifications and experience from their home country.

Although qualifications may be officially verified as having an Australian equivalent, there is no guarantee that industry bodies, unions or employers will accept these equivalents. Before embarking on your journey of migration you actually need to contact professional associations, industry bodies and even employers to enquire if you have the pre-requisites for applying for work in an occupation where you may consider that your experience and qualifications should be more than adequate. You may need to consider enrolling early in appropriate courses to provide some Australian context to your knowledge and experience. For example, an overseas qualified accountant will need to demonstrate knowledge of Australian Tax Laws; an HR professional will need to have knowledge of industrial relations and Occupational Health and Safety legislation. Often, this additional knowledge can be gained through a Vocational Education Certificate III or IV qualification which would take only a few months to complete part-time.

While some overseas Diplomas are verified as being of Diploma level in Australia (comparable content and degree of difficulty), there may be no real equivalent to the qualifications that are expected by the industry bodies. New arrivals may need to gain Recognition of Current Competencies from a Registered Training Organisation or from an employer as an Adult

Apprentice. This process is expensive and an Adult Apprenticeship is difficult to obtain in the skilled trades area.

The list of skilled vacancies is helpful, but there needs to be much more research on the part of the job seeker to see if there are actually advertised vacancies in the local press or through recruitment companies on the internet. Understanding what is required for an application to be considered by an employer is critical to the whole process, including format, content, examples, and style.

Transport is another significant consideration, and although, larger Capital Cities are well served by public transport, smaller cities and towns may not be so well served by cross-regional transport. In many areas you will need a car to travel to employment that is not located in the Central Business District.

In South Australia, we are seeing a trend for employers to advertise only on their own website, using their own internal recruitment processes. Once you have identified potential employers, you will need to check these websites regularly, as well as the more popular Recruitment Agencies and Job Boards like Career One and Seek. A career practitioner can assist you with this process, and also with on-line applications if necessary.

The Yellow Pages Business Directories are an excellent source of information regarding industries, businesses, community organisations, education and training providers and other essential products and services, their locations and contact details.

## c) What advice can you provide for writing a résumé?

Research the industry, the employer and the occupation thoroughly. Look for the key attributes required in the advertised vacancy and make sure that you address them thoroughly. Provide a one-paragraph Summary of your relevant experience, qualifications and values, focussing on the relationship between the advertised vacancy and what you can contribute. Avoid extravagant and unsupported claims. Concentrate on how you can add value to an employer rather than providing an old-fashioned Curriculum Vitae, which is essentially a history of everything you have done.

Many employers now use an initial computer scan of résumés to deal with the sometimes overwhelming numbers of applications for advertised vacancies. The computer searches for key words, and the context in which you use them, before they are passed on to a human being. It is very important that you analyse all advertised vacancies and job descriptions for the key skills, qualities and experience, to include a targeted response in your applications. As some of the key-word software has limitations in reading some formatting, it is best to avoid the use of tables, cells, text boxes, headers and footers.

Look at using a STAR (Situation, Task, Action and Results) formula for providing evidence of previous achievements that are relevant to the position for which you are applying. Include details of your employment history over the past ten years or so, as well as relevant accredited education and training. Identify referees who can comment on your workplace performance with current contact details. Invest in advice from an experienced and qualified career coach and résumé consultant.

Don't clutter your work history with too many details of the tasks you have performed. It is better to provide a brief summary of your principal responsibilities. Present the list of your applied skills as a summary in the early part of your résumé, but only include those which are relevant to the positon for which you are applying.

Overseas companies and universities may not necessarily be familiar to an Australian employer so it is often a good idea to add a brief description of the company you have worked for (e.g. the largest paper manufacturer in China), or an indication of the status of your university (e.g. respected provincial university in the north of India) if you feel that will add to the level of understanding.

## d) How much income is enough to have a decent living In Australia?

People survive on government assistance if they are eligible, but a reasonable annual wage would be from $55,000 - $65,000 depending on the needs of each family. Professional salaries are higher, and there is a good guide in this e-book to shape your expectations.

## e) What government assistance is provided for people looking for jobs?

A wide range of financial support is provided to people who are eligible, depending on the status of their Citizenship or Visa category. The Commonwealth Department of Social Services administers this through a central agency – Centrelink. State Governments may also offer free or subsidised support programs of various types, including assistance with job search. The emphasis is on helping people identify the skills they need for job search, rather than trying to place anyone in employment. People who find their own jobs are seen as empowered and accountable individuals who have initiative and not dependent on welfare agencies.

**f) What are some of the specific challenges for skilled migrants who do not find work immediately?**

My knowledge and advice is strongly influenced by the cohort of the people with whom Brian and I work. They are either unemployed, underemployed or in positions that do not match their qualifications, former experience or high level skills, and many are disillusioned and frustrated. We are deeply saddened that many of them have been strongly influenced to come to Australia without the level and depth of research that would enable them to make an effective transition into the Australian workforce. Some have been provided with inadequate and outdated information, but have unlimited enthusiasm and are very resilient. Many have postgraduate qualifications Masters and PhDs, but can't find work immediately that will utilise their obvious skills. They use their savings to supplement their welfare payments (if they are eligible for them), and eventually find that they have to accept unskilled or lower skilled jobs, casual employment, or retrain at their own expense for jobs far below their capacity. Some migrants have anglicised their first and/or family names as they perceive that they may be more likely to get interviews with a name that is easier to pronounce – a sad comment on the risk management strategies of some employers.

Strategic planning, early intervention and professional career support will assist you to maximise your opportunities here, and bring a return on your considerable investment, while you and your family enjoy the benefits of living in Australia and being part of a vibrant, diverse and inclusive community.

If your early applications are not successful, a local career specialist may be able to shed light on the reasons why you are not obtaining interviews or receiving offers of employment. Sometimes, it may simply be that you have not understood what is wanted by way of the required application format – locals also may experience this!

It is important to understand the current state of the local economy and labour market, and its fluctuations. The initiation of the migration process may coincide with a boom in one or more industries, but by the time you arrive in Australia, this boom may have passed. Employment that has been generated in a densely populated overseas country to meet development needs may not be such a priority here, and a shifting political agenda may mean that sometimes essential work is delayed or abandoned until the next political cycle. Ironically, some skilled migrants find that the work in which they are so experienced has been moved off-shore to their country of origin.

I hope that these reflections and observations are somewhat helpful. They are a result of our professional experiences with many skilled migrants, and other job seekers, over twenty five years, but these observations may not be reflected in promotional material or "official" news releases. We believe that early investment in career coaching, mentoring and informed job search support is a wise move that is supported by evidence in the career development literature, and is a way of enjoying the next phase of your career journey as you make a new life here in Australia.

Australians will welcome you, as we appreciate your wonderful skills and professional and personal experiences that will enrich our country and our culture. This is an amazing country and it is true that fortune favours the brave. You are able to construct an amazing life and career here, and enjoy the bounty and the challenges of our wonderful country.

This e-book will give you a head start when you arrive, and provide you with many genuine contacts with people and agencies that can walk with you on the first stage of your great adventure.

My warmest wishes to you all.

Judith Leeson AM, FCDAA (Life)

Inaugural CDAA Lifetime Achievement Award 2014

Master of Career Development (Counselling and Coaching), B. Ed., Dip T.

Director, Vector Consultants Pty Ltd

Adjunct Lecturer, Edith Cowan University

Former National President CDAA

Founding Member & Inaugural President CICA

 PO Box 553 Echunga SA 5153

Phone: (08) 8388 8183

Email: judith@vectorconsultants.com.au

Web: www.vectorconsultants.com.au

**MIGRANT NINJA TIP:**

**It is advisable for all migrants and job seekers to pay attention to what Judith has to say in this chapter. One of the most pertinent points she has made is the fact that we as skilled migrants come to Australia with a clear understanding of the culture of the labour market in our former country of employment but may need some time to adapt to the workplace culture of Australians. The other crucial point she raises is the fact that strategic planning, early intervention and professional career support will assist you to maximise your job opportunities here.**

**It does appear like this constant repetition of the need for professional help is just a way for the Career Guidance Professionals and Resume Writers to get more business. However the fact of the matter, and one that I realised the hard way, is that we need their services more than they need our business.**

**This book is an attempt to empower and provide you, the reader, with self-help tools as well as access to experts and the choice to go one way or the other is entirely up to you.**

# 15. Sample Formats and Checklists

## 15.1 Sample Resume 1 – Successful Resumes

# JOHN SMITH

00 0000 0000    88 Success Street, Sydney    name@email.com

We use this critical real estate to write a compelling summary that articulates what you offer and persuades the reader that you are the strongest candidate

### PROFILE

- We work with you to understand and articulate your key skills and what you offer to potential employers
- We talk about your previous experience and how you add value
- We don't just talk about generic skills that almost everyone has. We delve into your work history to find the moments that you have shined.
- We get to know your personality so we can articulate who you are and how you fit into teams
- We don't just position you for your next role, we prepare you for career leaps!

### WORK EXPERIENCE

| | |
|---|---|
| Position | Company Name | Date - Date |
| Position | Company Name | Date - Date |
| Position | Company Name | Date - Date |
| Position | Company Name | Date – Date |

### KEY EXPERIENCE SUMMARY

**Role | Company**                                                                        **Dates**
*We assist potential employers understand the company's you have worked within the past and highlight the contributions you have made to their operations and success.*

- Our unique and personalised consultation process helps you identify your achievements
- We write these in a persuasive and compelling manner to help potential employers understand what you offer and the contribution you would make to their business
- We don't just state it, we help you demonstrate it. We strengthen your resume by using quantifiable data that provides evidence of your skills and experience

### EDUCATIONAL BACKGROUND

| | |
|---|---|
| Qualification | Provider | Date |
| Qualification | Provider | Date |

### ADDITIONAL INFORMATION

| | |
|---|---|
| Languages: | We include these if you are bilingual or multilingual |
| Community involvement: | Do you volunteer, help coach the local sports team? Telling potential employers how you spend time outside of work can often help build rapport |
| Licenses: | We include these if you have them and/or the job requires them |
| Interests: | We like to include your authentic interests. Things like reviewing movies on a blog, climbing Mount Everest, deep sea fishing or travelling around Australia in a campervan are all more engaging than your typical reading and watching movies. |

## 15.2 Sample Resume 2 with notes - Vector Consultants Pty Ltd

Penny CASHMAN

20 McHenry Road, WEST PERTH WA 6005

Home: (08) 9388 7183, Mobile: 0417 885 000

Email: pencash@vectormail.com

---

### POSITION SOUGHT

*Senior Medical Receptionist*

### CAREER SUMMARY

Diploma in Reception and Office Management with additional training in Medical Reception and Medical Office Management with twenty years' experience in Reception/Administration including 12 years in the medical area. Held the position of Medical Receptionist with Selby Medical Imaging in Perth from 1998 to 2007 leading to my appointment as Senior Medical Receptionist with Peterson & Partners, a well-known Medical Specialists Centre in Perth. Strong customer service and interpersonal skills with experience in all aspects of Medical Reception and Administration support. An earlier career in banking, including responsibility for staff supervision and performance has provided me with a knowledge and confidence base for handling in-house financial matters at the level of a large medical practice. Returning to the workforce after a refreshing break parenting, undertaking rewarding voluntary work with hearing-impaired children, and completing refresher training relevant to the medical area.

## *KEY SKILLS*

- Customer Service • Interpersonal Skills • Team and Independent Work

- Audio-Typing (80 wpm) • Telephone and Email Skills • Administration and Clerical Skills

- Financial Skills • Multi-Tasking • First Aid

## *AREAS OF PROFESSIONALISM*

- Medical reception duties – telephone and front desk enquiries

- Organising doctors' day sheets and theatre/anaesthetist group lists

- Making and managing patient appointments

- Booking patients into hospitals or specialists' rooms

- Emailing results to other practice rooms

- Familiar with current medical terminology

- General administration, mail in/out, filing, photo-copying

- Able to work flexible hours

- Waiting-room house-keeping and hospitality

- Audio-typing of medical reports and letters

- Entering and maintaining computerised database of patient information

- Understanding of client confidentiality and medical protocols

- Familiar with OH&S and first aid procedures

- Computing – MS Windows 10 / MS Office 2010 (word; excel, data base; in-house medical software)

Penny CASHMAN_____

## *RELATED ACHIEVEMENTS*

- Coordinated the Reception and other Front Desk services of a major Specialist Consulting Rooms in Perth from 2007 to 2010 as Senior Medical Receptionist, combining new patient meet and greet procedures with a high standard of waiting room comfort and hospitality, while attending to the full-range of medical reception duties.

- Supervised and supported a team of 5 tellers at the Rural Bank, Mt Wellington, from 1988 to 1991 with responsibilities for staff performance assessments, staff rosters, staff counselling and cash clearances to the Central Bank, while organising and attending weekly management liaison meetings, providing a high standard of personal customer service and monitoring the CCTV surveillance unit and other security systems.

- Worked in a voluntary capacity as a part-time Education Assistant at King's Park Special School, East Perth, from 2012 to 2016 assisting with classroom activities including taking small groups of hearing impaired students for language and other activities, liaising with Medical Specialists, Occupational Therapists, parents and the classroom teachers, to work out best program for the students.

### *EXPERIENCE*

Parenting, study and part-time voluntary work - 2010-current

Senior Medical Receptionist

*Peterson & Partners, Perth, WA* - 2007-2010

Medical Receptionist

*Selby Medical Imaging, Perth, WA* - 1998-2007

Receptionist (part-time)

*Mt Wellington Clinic, Mt Wellington, WA* - 1991–1998

Supervisor

*Rural Bank, Mt Wellington, WA* - 1988–1991

## *RECENT TRAINING*

Certificate in Medical Office Management, *Brownlow College, Perth*

Medical Terminology; Preparing and Processing Medical Accounts; Medical Computing

Mandated Notification Training, *Denham Training Institute*

AUSLAN 1 Certificate, *Institute for the Hearing Impaired, Perth*

## *REFEREES*

Andrew Peterson

*Practice Manager, Peterson & Partners, Perth*

John Selby

*Selby Medical Imaging, Perth*    (08) 9204 1234

## *RESUME - EXPLANATORY NOTES*

## NOTES ON SECTIONS

### *OBJECTIVE / POSITION SOUGHT*

A one or two-word description of the sort of work or position you are looking or applying for. E.g., **Clerical Officer**. This immediately tells the reader what the document is all about. It also creates the focus for what you put into the résumé and what you leave out.

### *CAREER SUMMARY*

- This is an edited, focused statement of about 6-8 lines summarising what you are offering to support your objective. It will probably present a mixture of experience skills, education and training and career focus. Importantly it says what you can do for the employer

### *KEY SKILLS or COMPETENCIES*

- Up to 10 of your best basic skills/competencies particularly those that the potential employer is looking for: e.g., customer service, communication, problem-solving, team effectiveness, change management, innovation, leadership, coaching, computer literacy. These are often referred to as 'soft skill' and are very highly regarded by employers – but they must be realistic (you must be able to justify them). Importantly, these are often the KEY WORDS which will get you resume past the computer to be read by a human being.

## *AREAS OF PROFESSIONALISM / AREAS OF EFFECTIVENESS*

- How do you apply your key skills/competencies in the workplace? The AREAS OF EFFECTIVENESS are the components of the job which are your best marketing aspects. For example: **Problem Solving** might be expressed as - Resolving accommodation problems for single parents. The Areas of Effectiveness should match as closely as possible what the potential employer is looking for.

## KEEP ALL THE ABOVE ON THE FIRST PAGE – THIS IS YOU MAIN MARKETING PAGE

### *RELATED ACHIEVEMENTS*

- This section provides the opportunity to tell the employer of your success in applying these competencies in terms of the bottom (profit)-line i.e., the outcome. By describing something you have done in the past and stating what the benefit was (to your employer), you are making a promise of a similar level of performance or achievement to the future. Try to expand on some of your Areas of Effectiveness. Use the STAR formula to put these together and quantify as much as you can, e.g., dollars and cents; numbers of people; numbers of processes; length of time, etc.

Develop several of these examples and if you keep them relevant to the sort of work you are applying for.

## *EMPLOYMENT HISTORY / EXPERIENCE*

- Clear statement of your employment history, giving the position, organisation and dates (years to and from

- Because you are from overseas, you may want to add a brief description of the organisation e.g., largest paper manufacturer in India.

- You can, if you wish, include a brief listing of overarching responsibilities, but you should not write more than 3 or 4 lines on these: as a rule of thumb the older the job, the shorter the description. Do not add a long list of your day-to-day duties – IT WON'T BE READ,

- Generally, list your employment from the most recent at the top to the oldest at the bottom.

- You don't have to include your entire work history - you may wish to include only the last 10 years or so, in which case, call it **RECENT EMPLOYMENT.**

- If you have done several types of work, you may wish to highlight that which is most relevant to the job you are going for under **RELEVANT EMPLOYMENT** and the rest under **OTHER EMPLOYMENT.**

- **Voluntary work** should be included if it adds to your marketable skills. It can be listed under a separate heading or you can choose to include it with your paid employment, in which case, you should identify it as voluntary work.

## *EDUCATION AND TRAINING*

- You can combine **EDUCATION AND TRAINING** or separate them into **EDUCATION** (TERTIARY EDUCATION / QUALIFICATIONS) and **ADDITIONAL TRAINING** (OTHER TRAINING / SHORT COURSE TRAINING / OTHER RELEVANT TRAINING) to highlight your major qualifications (e.g., Trade, Tertiary qualifications). Choose whichever you prefer.

- **EDUCATION** - include major qualifications (degrees, certificates, trade qualifications). Where you are coming from overseas; you may need to have the level of your tertiary assessed in terms of Australian equivalent. Australian employers may not know the reputation of your ex University, so you may want to add a brief note expanding on it e.g., Stafford University, Isle of Man – a new University with a current enrollment of 5,000 students and a global reputation for research into the overpopulation of tertiary students.

- Only include school if your leaving level was high, the experience was recent, or you went to a "big-name" school.

- **ADDITIONAL TRAINING.** Omit anything which is not relevant to the position you are going for, or which has been superseded by later courses. Aim for a clear presentation.

## *REFEREES*

People who can verify what you claim in your work history, voluntary activities or education and training

- Include the name, position, organisation (no street address), and contact telephone number. You may need to include an **email address where the referees are from overseas** and there are difficult time differences; or the referees are in Australia but likely to be hard to contact by telephone. They should be <u>mainly work related</u>. If you are a recent arrival and have done some Voluntary work you can use the names of the Supervisors. You can, if necessary, use the name of a Course Presenter if appropriate.

- Make sure that it is obvious how your referee relates to your work or voluntary history (if the person has moved on to another organisation you may need to say *former supervisor, etc.)*

- Make sure that they are willing to be a referee, and provide them with a copy of your Résumé and information about the job you are applying for.

- You should list two or three referees. At least one should be from your current or most recent job.

- Only include referees who will give you a good reference. You may need to side-step an unfavourable referee (possibly a former boss) by nominating someone else from that organisation.

- You could quite reasonably include a referee from outside your organisations e.g. a client with whom you have regular dealings – but again make it clear what the relationship is.

# 15.3 Sample Resume 3 – UTAS Nursing Resume

*Reproduced with permission of University of Tasmania, Student Leadership, Career Development and Employment team*

Susan McKenzie • 7 Howard Street • Launceston  TAS  7250

phone: 03 6343 2323 • mobile: 0418 662 112 • email: s.mckenzie@iinet.com

Career Objective

To consolidate my knowledge and clinical placement experiences to achieve excellent patient care skills with the longer term aim of specialising in cardiac or emergency nursing.

> A *Career Objective* is optional. It needs to be genuine, tailored to the organisation and highlight what makes you right for the position.

Education

| | | |
|---|---|---|
| 2010 – 2013 | **Bachelor of Nursing** | |
| | University of Tasmania | |
| 2008 – 2009 | **Tasmanian Certificate of Education** | |
| | Newstead College, Launceston | |

Academic Achievements & Awards

| | |
|---|---|
| 2012 | Awarded High Distinction grades in Medication Management for Nurses and Bioscience |

Clinical Placements

| | |
|---|---|
| May/June 2013 | **Northside** (312 hours) |
| | CNA319 Community & Mental Health Nursing Practice |
| | Ward 1E |
| Sep 2012 | **Launceston General Hospital** (160 hours) |
| | CNA227 Integrated Nursing Practice |
| | Oncology |
| May 2012 | **Hobart Private Hospital** (160 hours) |
| | CNA227 Integrated Nursing Practice |
| | Maternity |
| April 2012 | **Aldersgate** (160 hours) |
| | CNA226 Contemporary Nursing Practice |
| | Aged Care |
| Aug 2011 | **North West Regional Hospital** (80 hours) |
| | CNA111 Introduction to Nursing Practice |
| | Surgical Ward |

> Guide only.  Your placements are important. Some employers may require details of skills demonstrated/gained, responsibilities and achievements.

1

UTAS    Career Development & Employment – **sample only** resume for nursing

Key Clinical Placement Experiences

- Developed, implemented and evaluated nursing care plans with patients/clients
- Worked collaboratively as part of a health care team which included doctors, physiotherapists, occupational therapists and enrolled nurses
- Documented patient/client care, including admission assessment, care planning, nursing notes and discharge
- Observed established procedures such as angiogram and blood transfusion

Key Skills

> *Key Skills* are optional.
> Please refer to individual
> employer requirements and
> use your judgement.

**Communication**

- Successfully communicated, both verbally and non-verbally, with clients in an easy-to-understand manner, which ensured confidentiality and sensitivity
- Effective teamwork skills demonstrated during placement in Department of Emergency where timing highly important
- High level of empathy when liaising with client's family members

**Next skill**

- Successfully communicated, both verbally and non-verbally, with clients in an easy-to-understand manner, which ensured confidentiality and sensitivity
- Effective teamwork skills demonstrated during placement in Department of Emergency where timing highly important
- High level of empathy when liaising with client's family members

**Next skill**

- Successfully communicated, both verbally and non-verbally, with clients in an easy-to-understand manner, which ensured confidentiality and sensitivity
- Effective teamwork skills demonstrated during placement in Department of Emergency where timing highly important
- High level of empathy when liaising with client's family members

Professional Memberships

2013      **Nursing and Midwifery Board of Australia**
Student Registration Number: 56448955

2

UTAS    Career Development & Employment – **sample only** resume for nursing

## Employment

| | |
|---|---|
| Feb 2013 to current | **Disability Support Worker (casual)**<br>Eskleigh Home, Perth |

Responsibilities
- Assist with daily living activities and collaboratively plan a weekly schedule with clients and their families
- Coordinate transport and logistical arrangements to enable clients to engage in the wider community

## Professional Development

| | |
|---|---|
| March – Nov 2012 | **Mental Health – Carer Information Workshop**<br>Launceston General Hospital |
| Nov 2010 | **Apply First Aid Plus (2 full days)**<br>St John Ambulance Tasmania |

## Volunteer Work

| | |
|---|---|
| 2012 | **Volunteer Counsellor**<br>Lifeline Telephone Counselling, Launceston |

## Referees

**Dr Michael Harvey**
Senior Lecturer, School of Nursing and Midwifery
University of Tasmania
Newnham Drive
NEWNHAM TAS 7249

03 6324 5621
0402 621 552
michael.harvey@utas.edu.au

**Ms Lucy Bowen**
Nurse Unit Manager, Department of Emergency
Launceston General Hospital
274 – 280 Charles Street
LAUNCESTON TAS 7250

03 6344 4652
0411 784 888
lucy.bowen@dhhs.tas.gov.au

> Remember to ask for their permission to list as referees and provide full contact details.

3

UTAS Career Development & Employment – **sample only** resume for nursing

# 15.4 Sample Cover Letter 1 – Successful Resumes

## EXAMPLE COVER LETTER

Name
Address
Telephone
Email

Name
Position
Company
Street Address
Suburb   State   Postcode

Your contact details

Date

Dear Mr / Ms Surname,

Salutation - make it personal. If you don't know a specific name, do some more research

Re: Application for Operations Manager

Thank you for the opportunity to discuss the role of Operations Manager for Centre Stage on the phone. After reviewing the advertisement and our discussion, I believe my strategic and operational experience managing similar venues coupled with my passion to create strong teams, positions me to meet and exceed the expectations of the role.

Open with details of the position you are applying for

I have been following the development of Centre Stage with interest and am aware of the investment all stakeholders have contributed to develop a dynamic and vibrant facility.  I have over ten years experience managing cultural venues for both community and government organisations. My previous roles, as detailed in my resume, have allowed me an opportunity to develop strong skills in programme development, facilities and building management, and capital development projects.

Demonstrate what you know about the role and the company along with how your skills are a good fit

My experience opening new venues includes detailed knowledge on product suppliers, furniture and fit outs and managing launch events for public spaces. I am also experienced at developing and implementing processes and procedures that ensure effective operational management from day one.

I have excellent communication and interpersonal skills and use a respectful and collaborative approach to develop successful and sustainable relationships with stakeholders. I currently manage an annual budget of $1 million and consistently exceed budgetary expectations by increasing revenue and reducing expenditure. In my current role, I have increased revenue by an average of 300% year on year for more than five years.

Emphasise the skills, experiences and qualifications that you would bring to the role or company to make it successful

I am confident that the intent and aspirations of the venue to provide a mix of professional and community events is aligned with both my personal values and skill set. I look forward to discussing my application and what I offer in further detail with you at an interview.

Kind Regards
Winning Candidate

Wrap it up

successful
**resumes**

324

## 15.5 Sample Cover Letter 2 with notes - Vector Consultants Pty Ltd

## APPLICATION (COVER) LETTERS

## GENERAL CONSIDERATIONS

There are three types of 'application' or 'cover' letters:

- Responding to a simple advertisement – usually requiring a letter plus a résumé

- An unsolicited letter following-up a cold canvass telephone call

- A cover letter sent as part of a package together with a separate document giving responses to selection criteria plus a résumé

Here we are dealing with the first type.

Before you start to put your letter together, you must fully understand what sort of application they want. There may be hidden messages in the small print at the end of the advertisement. Or if it is an online advertisement, via a tick-box (opens a new page). You may have to download an application package. Some organisations include a separate document which tells you exactly what they want - follow the instructions carefully; if you don't, your application may not be considered. If you have any doubts ring up and find out.

Be particularly careful about any jobs advertised on the internet. Quite often, jobs are left up long after they have been filled. Again, if you have any doubt, ring up and find out.

So, you have done all that. The next thing to do is to go through the advertisement very carefully to see what they are looking for. Underline all keywords. If you have any doubts – again ring up, and check it out.

Now, you need to be absolutely honest and ask yourself; do you really have what they are looking for – if you don't, it's not worth wasting their time and yours. Also, it is a good idea at this stage to look at the organisation's web-site (if you know the identity of the employing organisation) to get to know a bit more about the organisation before you start your letter.

The following sample letter gives a reasonable idea of a good, effective layout.

20 McHenry Road

WEST PERTH WA 6005

Home:  (08) 9388 7183

Mobile: 0417 885 000


16th April 2016


Dr R. W. Caruthers

1 Smith Road

FREEMANTLE, WA 6160


Dear Dr Caruthers,


I wish to apply for the position of **Senior Medical Receptionist** which you are currently advertising in the Western Courier Mail. I am coming back into the workforce after a refreshing break parenting, undertaking rewarding voluntary work with hearing-impaired children, and completing refresher training relevant to the medical area.


I have a Diploma in Reception and Office Management from Prides Business College and followed this with specialised training in Medical Reception. I recently revisited this training with a refresher course in Medical Office Management.  I also have Mandated Notification training and a Clearance for working with children. I am currently renewing my First Aid Certificate.

I spent nine years from 1998 to 2007 in Medical Reception in a large General Practice Clinic and a Medical Imaging Center, leading to my appointment as Senior Medical Receptionist with Peterson & Partners, a well-known Medical Specialists Centre in Perth. I have strong customer service and interpersonal skills and experience in all aspects of Medical Reception and Administrative support, including taking telephone and Front Desk appointments, organising Doctors' Day Sheets, theatre and anaesthetist bookings, client database maintenance and audio-typing. I have a strong understanding of client confidentiality and medical terminology and protocols. My general and audio-typing speed has been certified at 80 wpm. An earlier career in banking included the supervision of 5 tellers, staff performance assessments, rosters, staff counselling and cash clearances to the Central Bank. From this period, I have brought a knowledge and confidence in handling all in-house financial matters at the level of a large medical practice, which was one of my tasks at Petersons. A confidential reference from this period can be obtained by ringing the Practice Manager, Andrew Peterson, on (08) 9XXX XXXX.

Over the last few years, I have learnt the Australian sign language, AUSLAN, so that I could undertake voluntary work at a nearby Special School for hearing-impaired children. For this reason, I am particularly attracted to your Practice which has helped a number of the hearing-impaired children I have been working with.

My attached resume will give you details of my work history and training and a summary of my skills. I am looking forward discussing my suitability with you and your team. I am able to offer the ability to work very flexible working hours thanks to the support of two very active and devoted grandparents.

Yours sincerely

Your name

## THE STRUCTURE

**Your contact details:** Your address and telephone number(s). It is OK nowadays to add your email address here or after your name at the end of the letter. Please <u>don't set out your details as a letterhead</u>; this is essentially a personal letter, not a business letter.

**Date:** Use the date when you plan to send the letter.

**Their address/addressee:** Please ring up to find out the **name of the recipient (spelling and gender)**; don't be satisfied with writing to the General Manager; you then have the problem of whether to address the letter to Dear Sir or Dear Madam – it's not a bloke's world anymore.

**Salutation:** Refer to the comment above. If the recipient is female, find out how she prefers to be addressed – Ms, Mrs, or Miss (some ladies get upset if you get it wrong). If you are in a technical area, check whether there is a title e.g. Dr. Don't use first names unless you really are on first name terms, otherwise, address it to Dear Mr Smith (NOT Dear Mr Brian Smith), followed by a comma. If you can't find out the personal name, then resort to Dear Sir/Madam or Dear Manager – **NOT** 'to whom it may concern'. That belongs in only one document, and it isn't an application letter.

**First paragraph:** I believe this should tell them why they are getting the letter. State the title of the position you are applying for and any reference number*. *you can also put this as a 'heading' above the Salutation line, e.g.:

**ref: Senior Medical Receptionist, Western Courier Mail**

My preference is that you should be direct and say something like 'I am applying for the position of....' It is often a good idea to mention where you saw the advertisement or use a covering phrase such as 'which you are currently advertising'. Some advisors advocate a strong opening statement to catch the reader's attention – such as your strongest qualification for the position.

**Second paragraph:** A brief statement of your overall fit for the position. You could merge this with the first paragraph to produce the 'strong opening statement'.

**Third paragraph:** (This is the most meaty one.) How you meet the key requirements stated in the advertisement.

**Fourth paragraph:** Your special selling point that makes you stand out from the others.

**Fifth (and last) paragraph:** Refer to your attached résumé in a dynamic way ...'My attached résumé will give you ...' Cover any special conditions such as availability for out-of-hours work, or having a driving licence. Close with a phrase indicating an expectation of an interview, such as 'I look forward to discussing the position with you in person.'

**Closing:** If your salutation is Dear Sir/Madam, end with Yours faithfully. If your salutation is the personal name (e.g. Dr Caruthers) then end with Yours sincerely. Don't be tempted to use 'Regards' unless you are a personal friend of the recipient. Type your full name and sign above it.

## MORE COMPLEX APPLICATIONS

For some jobs, you may be required to submit a more complex application responding to Selection Criteria. Usually, you are required to respond to each item with a paragraph stating how you match the criterion, in which case use each criterion as a heading. Sometimes, you are asked to respond the criteria collectively in a 2-page document. Occasionally you are asked NOT to respond to the criteria, but instead, answer a few competency statements. It can be confusing.

## EXAMPLE FROM A CHILD CARE APPLICATION

*Give an example of how you prepared stimulating and fun environments for play groups.*

Use the **STAR** formula to develop your statement

**S** – SITUATION; **T** – TASK; **A** – ACTION; **R** - RESULT

## APPLY THE STAR FORMULA:

**SITUATION:** As part of my Certificate III training, I spent two weeks on a work experience placement at the Happy Tots Centre, Frewville.

**TASK:** On the first day, I was asked to prepare a simple activity for ten new arrivals.

**ACTION:** I decided to do a simple 'Dragon' game. I made ten simple hats out of coloured paper - one for the head, seven for the body, and two for the tail.

**RESULT:** The children took it in turns to be different parts of the dragon and they went around the Centre holding on to each other's' waists, making appropriate dragon noises. They really enjoyed it and it helped them to overcome their initial shyness.

**RE-WRITE THE RESPONSE:**

As part of my Certificate III training, I spent two weeks on a work experience placement at the Happy Tots Centre, Frewville. On the first day, I was asked to prepare a simple activity for ten new arrivals. I decided to do a simple 'Dragon' game. I made ten simple hats out of coloured paper - one for the head, seven for the body, and two for the tail. The children took it in turns to be different parts of the dragon and they went around the Centre holding on to each other's waists and making appropriate dragon noises. They really enjoyed it and it helped them to overcome their initial shyness.

## 15.6 Checklist – Moving to Australia

**A CONCISE GUIDE TO HELP PLAN YOUR MOVE TO AUSTRALIA FROM THE TIME YOU APPLY TILL THE TIME YOU ARRIVE IN AUSTRALIA**

### Twelve to Eighteen Months to Go

1   Plan a visit to learn more about Australia or else do as much research as possible.

2   Check visa(s) eligibility for you and your family.

3   Assess your finances and resources to cover visa costs and the cost of moving and settling down in Australia.

4   Check your passports to make sure they are valid for at least another two years.

5   Consider hiring a migration agent or applying for the visa online by yourself.

6   Initiate the application process and submit the necessary documents to obtain your requisite Australian visa.

7   Ensure you have provided all the required information. Evidence will need to prove work experience, Overseas qualifications, Police clearances, Medical checks, English proficiency tests. The DIBP website provides precise and up to date information and guidance for applicants.

8   Brainstorm your city and state of choice. Some of the things to consider - Job availability, cost of living, school and university options.

## Three to Six Months Out

1   Research where to live and potential job opportunities in the area.

2   Narrow down your suburb preference based on budget.

3   Prepare an 'Aussie Ready' Resume.

4   Start applying for jobs and contacting potential employers in Australia.

5   Make budgets for your move based on cost of living.

6   Book your flights to Australia.

7   Get quotes from freight companies for moving your belongings.

8   Apply for school admission and plan your arrival to match the beginning of school term of the relevant school.

9   Open an Australian bank account.

10  Look for accommodation rentals and research the facilities in the suburb you have chosen for the initial period.

## Eve of Departure (Two weeks out)

1   Finalise packing. Be aware of baggage allowance & Custom/Quarantine Restrictions.

2   Convert currency to Australian dollars.

3   Book temporary accommodation in Australia.

4   Enrol your children in their new schools.

5   Give a forwarding address to all your contacts.

6    Cancel accounts and direct debits for all utilities (If not already done so).

7    Transfer your funds with a foreign exchange specialist.

8    Confirm bookings with travel agents and freight companies.

9    Make a photocopy set of all documents. Additionally, upload all files on Google Drive Cloud or similar cloud based system for easy access.

10   Say Farewell!

## Upon Arrival

1    Get Connected. Buy a SIM Card.

2    Apply for Medicare Card.

3    Apply for Driving Licence.

4    Obtain a Tax File Number (TFN).

5    Visit your bank and provide identification proof to activate account.

6    Enrol your children in local schools.

7    If you are in temporary accommodation, then start looking for rental property to move into.

8    Establish utilities for your rental or own home in Australia.

9    Connect your new home to the Internet to be able to search for job opportunities.

10   Update your resume with Australian address and contact number.

## 15.7 Checklist - Writing a Resume

*Reproduced with permission of University of Tasmania, Student Leadership, Career Development and Employment team*

**LAYOUT**

• Is resume visually clear with even spacing between words and lines?

• Have you used a clear font throughout (Times New Roman, Arial)?

• Are your name and contact details visible and professional at top of the page?

• Is resume 2-4 pages maximum?

• Are tabs/margins aligned throughout the document?

• Is layout gimmick-free? – no coloured paper, fancy fonts, photos, cover page, borders.

• If using reverse chronological format, are most recent details first throughout the document?

• Appropriate use of BOLD or CAPITALs to highlight section headings?

• Good use of bullet points to keep information concise?

• Have you included page numbers as a footer? (especially important for online applications)

**CONTENT**

• Is content relevant and up to date?

• Does resume clearly highlight your skills, achievements and knowledge?

• Is your resume tailored to the job/audience?

• Have you thought about explaining gaps in your employment?

• Are unpaid work / voluntary experiences listed as well as paid?

• Are referees listed clearly with full contact details, and did you get their permission?

• Is your personal information, e.g. age, gender, marital status, left off the resume?

## LANGUAGE

• Have you used strong, active words to describe your tasks/responsibilities? (i.e. organised, produced, developed)

• Is grammar, spelling and punctuation correct throughout? Proofread!

• Have you avoided long wordy paragraphs?

• Have you used language that reflects the language of the Position Description?

• Is document jargon free? (Except to explain technical terms the employer would understand)

• Have you made positive claims about your skills?

## 15.8 Checklist – Writing a Cover Letter

*Reproduced with permission of University of Tasmania, Student Leadership, Career Development and Employment team*

**COVER LETTER – CHECKLIST LAYOUT**

• Is your letter addressed personally to the appropriate contact?

• Have you set out your letter professionally – employer's details on the top left, your details on the top right?

• Is your letter 1-page maximum?

• Have you included your address, phone numbers and a professional email?

• If applying for an advertised position, did you state the job reference/title at beginning of the letter?

**CONTENT**

• Have you highlighted your enthusiasm and interest in the job and organisation?

• Are your skills, qualifications and attributes described strongly and linked to the requirements of the job?

• Have you included information about your educational qualifications?

• Have you tailored your letter to the job, rather than use a template letter?

• Have you clearly and concisely expressed how your skills and experience will assist the organisation in achieving their goals/aims?

• Have you mentioned what you have attached (resume, selection criteria?)

## LANGUAGE

• Is your letter grammatically correct – with no punctuation or spelling mistakes?

• Have you used positive language to describe your background and key qualities?

• Is the letter written in a professional way – no casual terms/references

• Have you avoided using negative statements about yourself / your qualifications?

## 15.9 Selection Criteria

*Reproduced with permission of Successful Resumes Australia*

**THE WRITING PROCESS**

The following writing process is designed to help:

- Organise your information and flow of ideas to make it easier for you to write
- Make your application stand out from the others
- Make it easy for the selection panel to understand and assess
- Get you to the interview stage

For every Selection Criteria, cover each of these five steps in the order shown:

1. **Underline the key words** in the Selection Criterion and **break them down into meaningful components**
2. Provide **your viewpoint** on why the selection Criteria is important to the job
3. **Give an example** to demonstrate how you have applied (or would apply) the Selection Criteria
4. **Describe the step-by-step** process you used in the example
5. Say how **you were successful.**

When you are describing your examples and the step-by-step processes you have used, it may help to use the **STAR** model:

- Situation – provide a brief outline of the situation/setting/task
- Task – outline what you did, what role you played

- Approach or action – explain how you did it
- Result – describe the outcomes of your involvement and the project, and explain the benefits to the organisation/team/department/target audience

When you write your response, make sure you write in a direct, persuasive manner.

This means:

- Use the first person "I" and active, present tense language (i.e. "I implemented a new system" rather than "A new system was implemented.")
- Include the keywords used in the position description and organisation values statement
- Use short, concise sentences
- Use bullet points where necessary rather than long lists
- Explain each example in a logical, step-by-step manner.

## SAMPLE ANSWERS

Let's have a look at a Selection Criteria common to all Public Sector positions. The wording of this criterion changes depending on the level of the position applied for.

This criterion comes from an AO3 position for a Job Placement Officer advertised by the Queensland Dept. of Employment, Vocational Education & Industrial Relations

Criterion:

"Well-developed interpersonal and communication skills as evidenced by the ability to liaise with employers, community groups and agencies on employment and labour market issues."

Most applicants answer Selection Criteria poorly. They typically answer in a brief paragraph, for example:

*My interpersonal and communication skills have been well developed through my work in the industry and the public sector. As a Secretary, I have worked for senior management and in typing pools. I have been a member of two Schools Councils and travelled to statewide conferences. I had to speak publicly.*

Let's work on improving this answer! Ask yourself:

• Does my answer relate to the Selection Criterion or am I telling them about a different job?

• Can I expand on what I have written without using unnecessary padding?

• Is my language positive?

• Have I supplied evidence to back up my claim?

Using the above writing process let's rewrite the sample answer above using the five steps. Headings are only shown so you can see how they will help to write the answer. You won't need to show them in your written application.

1. Keywords of Criterion: "Well developed interpersonal and communication skills as evidenced by the ability to liaise with employers, community groups and agencies on employment and labour market issues."

interpersonal: relationships, respect, social, personal, interactive communication: sender, receiver, feedback, verbal, non-verbal, level of person, listening, questioning, mediation, negotiation, clarification.

2. Your viewpoint: Well developed interpersonal and communication skills are important so that one can relate to others at all levels, verbally and nonverbally. Interpersonal and communication skills include the use of active listening and questioning. Feedback must be given and mediation used. Being able to negotiate with clients, both inside and outside the organisation is vital. Being able to communicate within a team structure is also important.

3. Example: Think of a challenging situation you have faced and use that as your example. Draw up a table like this to pre-plan the examples to be used in your written answers and at the interview.

Examples

**Selection Criteria Number** - 6.3 Interpersonal & Communication Skills

**Written answer** - example - Head Hunters Personnel agency

**Interview** - example - Office Team

As a Secretary, I have worked for senior management. This put me in contact with many employers and employment agencies. For example, I had to help arrange the employment of new staff for our Front Counter at ABC Pty Ltd. This made me aware of the plight of people looking for work and also the processes to be used to recruit employees.

4. Step-by-step Process: I was asked to contact the Head Hunters Personnel Agency and list the job vacancy with them. I had to have a Job Description so that I could answer any questions asked of me. I used active listening skills as I knew how important it was to get the right person. I gave feedback to clarify the information the personnel agency wanted. When the interviews were held, I was on the Selection Panel. My role in the team was to ask questions applicable to that job and to assess how the applicant might fit into the Front Office team. I looked at the type of body language the interviewee showed so I could put them at ease. When the interviews were over, I composed a letter thanking all the applicants for their interest.

5. Evidence of Success: I knew I was successful because I clarified very carefully the needs of the position. This resulted in several people with the right skills being referred to the Company for an interview. My boss congratulated me on the way I handled the liaison and kept to the deadlines needed. She complimented me on the wording of the final letter to all applicants. Head Hunters Personnel Agency was always able to get the information they needed when necessary. The Front Office team was happy with the choice of their new team member.

The written response would now look like:

*Well-developed interpersonal and communication skills are important so that one can relate to others at all levels, verbally and non-verbally. Interpersonal and communication skills include the use of active listening and questioning. Feedback must be given and mediation used. Being able to negotiate with clients, both inside and outside the organisation is vital. Being able to communicate within a team structure is also important.*

*As a Secretary, I have worked for senior management. This put me in contact with many employers and employment agencies. For example, I had to help arrange the employment of new staff for our Front Counter at ABC Pty Ltd. This made me aware of the plight of people looking for work and also the processes to be used to recruit employees.*

*I was asked to contact the Head Hunters Personnel Agency and list the job vacancy with them. I had to have a job description so that I could answer any questions asked of me. I used active listening skills as I knew how important it was to get the right person. I gave feedback to clarify the information the personnel agency wanted. When the interviews were held I was on the Selection Panel. My role in the team was to ask questions applicable to that job and to assess how the applicant might fit into the Front Office team. I looked at the type of body language the interviewee showed so I could put them at ease. When the interviews were over, I composed a letter thanking applicants for their interest.*

*I knew I was successful because I clarified very carefully the needs of the position. This resulted in several people with the right skills being referred to the Company for an interview. My boss congratulated me on the way I handled the liaison and kept to the deadlines. She complimented me on the wording of the final letter to all applicants. Head Hunters Personnel*

*Agency was always able to get the information they needed when necessary. The Front Office team was happy with the choice of their new team member.*

What a difference between the first version and second! The first version shows that the person is stumped for ideas on what to write. The second is much more interesting to read. It's the way you tell your story that can make a difference in getting to the interview stage.

To improve your chances of getting that job, you need to invest time in writing a good application.

## 15.10 Interview Preparation

**Reproduced with permission of *Successful Resumes***

*One of the key elements to a successful interview is confidence. With confidence on your side, you are more likely to build good rapport, articulate responses well and make a good impression. Preparation is an essential part of building your interview confidence and you can prepare effectively by following these steps.*

### KNOW THE DETAILS

Know exactly where, when and with whom the interview will take place. Ask about parking or the best public transport to use in advance so you are not trying to figure it out on the day. Give yourself extra time and arrive early for the interview.

### RESEARCH THE ORGANISATION

Before you go to any job interview, it's important to find out as much as you can about the organisation. Research is a critical part of interview preparation. It will help prepare you to both answer interview questions and to ask the interviewer questions. Things to consider are: the size of the organisation, the vision or mission statement, current projects or goals that they are working on, the products or services they are selling, competitors, industry issues, and recent changes in the organisation.

### DRESS THE PART

Have an interview outfit ready to wear, so you don't have to think about what you're going to wear while you're focusing on the job interview. It's important to be neat, tidy, and well-groomed, and to present a positive image to the employer so dress in the appropriate attire. Don't forget to pay attention to detail - your hair, nails, shoes, should all look polished and professional.

## PRACTICE MAKES PERFECT

In advance of the interview, prepare answers to possible questions as well as prepare questions to ask at the interview. Taking the time to practice answering mock interview questions will help you develop your responses and calm your nerves on the day because you won't be scrambling for an answer while you're in the interview. Practice interviewing with a friend or family member ahead of time and it will be much easier when you're actually in a job interview.

## KNOW YOUR OWN FACTS

Before the interview, read your résumé and refresh your memory about your past achievements. Remind yourself about every example you've used and the timeframes, budgets, percentages, numbers of staff/customers/suppliers/ agents or whatever is relevant to your background. By taking the time to remember the details and by using specific facts and figures, you will build credibility during the interview. Familiarise yourself with your own salary package so that if discussion about salaries comes up, you'll be prepared.

## HAVE IT ON HAND

It's important to know what to bring to a job interview - a portfolio with extra copies of your resume and cover letter, a list of references, a copy of the position description, and a list of questions you can ask the interviewer.

## IMPRESSIONS COUNT

Proper interview etiquette is important. Greet people you meet politely and with enthusiasm, shaking hands firmly. Relax and lean forward a little towards the interviewer so that you appear interested and engaged. Pay attention, be attentive and look interested. Maintain eye contact with the interviewer as you respond. The more positive an impression you make, the better you'll do during the interview.

## LISTEN UP

During a job interview, listening is just as important as answering questions. If you're not paying attention, you're not able to give a good response. It's important to listen to the interviewer and take the time to compose an appropriate answer. Also, be ready to engage the interviewer. You want to build a relationship with the interviewer rather than just answering questions.

## SELL YOUR PERSONAL ATTRIBUTES

You need to prove that you are the right *cultural fit* for the organisation. *Cultural fit* refers to your likeability, and the potential to fit in with the organisation. Make sure you demonstrate your personal attributes during the interview – your reliability, work ethic, attitude, emotional intelligence, personality, organisational skills and initiative.

If you are confident, pleasant and well-presented, you will make a positive first impression. You know you're nervous –

but take a moment to consider things from the interviewer's perspective, and then make an effort to put them at ease. When you flip the tables and make them the focus of your attention, you'll be surprised at how quickly you can build rapport with your interviewer. Most importantly, try to be *likeable*. Ultimately, you want the interviewer to like you and to see how you can add value to the organisation without threatening the existing culture or hierarchy.

## FOLLOW UP

Follow up a job interview with a thank you note or email reiterating your interest in the job. This thank you letter is also the perfect opportunity to discuss anything of importance that your interviewer didn't ask or that you didn't answer as thoroughly or as well as you would have liked.

## KEEP YOUR REFEREES INFORMED

Have two or three professional/work-related referees and one or two personal/character referees (non-family members) lined up in advance. As soon as you are invited to an interview, contact your referees and send them a copy of your application, job description and résumé. Your resume will be a good reminder of your achievements and strengths. After the interview, tell your referees the names of people who may be contacting them so that they will be mentally prepared when they answer the phone. Treat your referees like gold - they can make or break you.

## INTERVIEW QUESTIONS

The types of questions you will be asked will depend on what kind of organisation is conducting the interview. If a government department is conducting your interview, questions will be based strictly on the relevant selection criteria (you may even be given a list of interview questions before the interview). If a private sector organisation or recruitment agency is conducting your interview, the questions may be more behaviour-based. It is critical to prepare in advance and practice your responses. It is also helpful to prepare a list of questions to ask at the interview.

## BEHAVIOURAL INTERVIEW QUESTIONS

Behavioural interviews are based on the premise that a person's past performance on the job is the best predictor of future performance. The questions require you to give specific "real life" examples of how you behaved in situations relating to the questions. Most companies will include at least a few behavioural questions into each interview.

Employers are looking for evidence that you have the qualities that will lead to success in the job. Because they are asking you to demonstrate how you accomplished results in your answer it can be helpful to follow a formula when responding to behavioural questions.

There are many formulas available but we recommend a simple SAR (Situation, Action, Result) formula.

S: Describe a situation or a problem you were confronted with

A: Discuss the action that you took to improve the situation or solve that problem

R: Describe the results that occurred from your action

For example, if the interviewer asked you for an example of your organisational skills, you might respond with:

[Situation] "When I took on the job as an assistant at Marketing Solutions, I found that there was no easily accessible system for retrieving information on the past campaigns. Each of the five consultants had their own computer file.

[Action] I suggested to the director that we set up a shared online filing system with past campaign materials that would be accessed by all staff, I reviewed each of the staff to get input about how to categorise the files and proposed a system which was implemented.

[Result] My supervisor mentioned this accomplishment as one of the reasons for my raise at my recent performance review."

Below are some examples of behavioural questions that may be asked in an interview. These are great questions to practice with friends and family members.

Give an example of how you set goals and achieve them.

Give an example of a goal you didn't meet and how you handled it.

Describe a stressful situation at work and how you handled it.

Tell me about how you worked effectively under pressure.

Have you been in a situation where you didn't have enough work to do?

Have you ever made a mistake? How did you handle it?

Did you ever make a risky decision? Why? How did you handle it?

Have you ever dealt with company policy you didn't agree with? How?

Have you gone above and beyond the call of duty? If so, how?

When you worked on multiple projects, how did you prioritise?

How did you handle meeting a tight deadline?

What do you do when your schedule is interrupted? Give an example of how you handle it.

Give an example of how you worked with a team.

Have you handled a difficult situation with a co-worker? How?

What do you do if you disagree with a co-worker?

Have you handled a difficult situation with a client? How?

What do you do if you disagree with your boss?

## CHALLENGING INTERVIEW QUESTIONS

### TELL ME A LITTLE ABOUT YOURSELF

This is a well-used opening question in an interview and it's the perfect moment for you sell your strengths and value - not to tell your life history. Your answer should be a quick overview of your qualifications and experience. Talk about your education, work history, recent career experience and future goals.

*"I graduated from University X and since then, I have been working in public relations with an agency where I have generated millions of PR hits for my clients. While I've enjoyed working on the agency side, I'm looking to expand my horizons and start doing PR for corporate companies such as this one."*

## WHY DID YOU LEAVE YOUR LAST JOB?

This is your chance to talk about your experience and your career goals, not to speak badly about a former boss or company. Focus on your desire for career progressions what you learned in your previous position and how you are ready to use those skills in a new position.

*"My previous position was excellent and I really enjoyed my work there, however, I am looking for new challenges and opportunities to support my career progression. When this position became available I felt that this was the perfect opportunity to personally and professionally grow and develop in another fantastic company"*

## WHERE DO YOU SEE YOURSELF IN FIVE YEARS?

This is a good opportunity to let the employer know that you're stable and you want to be with this company for the long haul. This question is really geared towards professional aspirations, rather than personal ones.

*"In five years, I would like to see myself in a middle management position that provides me with the opportunity to create success and drive positive change and growth for a company. I am particularly interested in working for a young company, such as this one, so I can get in on the ground floor*

*and take advantage of all the opportunities a growing firm has to offer."*

## WHAT ARE YOUR WEAKNESSES?

The key to answering this question is not to respond literally. Your future employer won't care if your weak spot is that you can't cook, nor do they want to hear the generic responses like you're *"too detail oriented" or "work too hard."* Respond to this query by identifying areas in your work where you can improve and how they can be assets.

*"In my last position, I wasn't able to develop my public-speaking skills. I'd really like to be able to work in a place that will help me get better at giving presentations and talking in front of others."*

## TELL ME ABOUT THE WORST BOSS YOU HAVE EVER HAD?

Never talk badly about your past bosses. A potential boss will anticipate that you'll talk about him or her in the same manner somewhere down the line.

*"I have been fortunate with some really fantastic managers in the past who have helped me develop my skills; however, there are some who taught me more than others did. So I have learnt what types of management styles I work with the best."*

## HOW WOULD OTHERS DESCRIBE YOU?

It's a good idea to be regularly asking for feedback from your colleagues and manager so you can gauge your performance. With this information, it is easy to provide an honest and accurate response to this question. Doing so will also help you identify strengths and weaknesses.

*"My former colleagues have said that they have enjoyed working with me because I am very solutions based and they have found that encouraging and positive. My previous manager frequently provided me with feedback he had received from our clients who felt I was always very approachable and easy to work with."*

**WHAT DO YOU KNOW ABOUT OUR ORGANISATION?**

Demonstrate your interest in the job and your understanding of the organisation (and industry) by mentioning some of your findings from your research. This might include your knowledge of their products and services, the location of offices, the number of staff, the company's mission statement, their core values, and recent media coverage of the company.

**WHAT IS YOUR CURRENT SALARY / WHAT FIGURE DO HAVE IN MIND FOR THIS POSITION?**

In advance, research similar positions where the salary is stated so that if you are asked this question, you can talk about it with some reference points in mind. Refer to the whole package (benefits, salary packaging, car expenses etc.) but ensure that you show more interest in the job than the money.

**WOULD YOU BE WILLING TO TAKE A SALARY CUT?**

Salary is a delicate topic. In today's tough economy, how much a company can afford to pay might be the deal breaker in whether or not you are offered a position. A potential response could be:

*"I'm making $X now. I understand that the salary range for this position is $XX -$XX. Like most people, I would like to*

*improve on my salary, but I'm more interested in the job itself than the money. I would be open to negotiating a lower starting salary but would hope that we can revisit the subject after I've proved myself to you."*

## DID SOMEONE ELSE WRITE YOUR RÉSUMÉ AND/OR APPLICATION LETTER FOR YOU?

It's unlikely you would be asked this question, but if you have had help with your documents, do not lie or shy away from the fact. It is very appropriate to get help with such important documents and it is important for a prospective employer to see how serious you have been in preparing for the opportunity.

*"I did get professional help and advice with my documents, and I believe it was money well-spent because this is very important to me. I have not had to write a résumé for some time and like most things, it's always helpful to ask the experts if you want to do a great job and learn from the process. The writer who helped me was very collaborative and there's nothing in my documents that isn't completely accurate."*

## QUESTIONS YOU SHOULD ASK AT AN INTERVIEW

Job interviews are not a one-way street. Not only is it an opportunity for an employer to determine if you have the right skills and cultural fit for the job and the organisation, equally, it gives you an opportunity to determine if the role and the company is a good fit for you.

Asking questions at the interview has two key purposes, the first is that it gives you an opportunity to clarify any information that will help you decide if this is the right job for you and second, it demonstrates that you are interested in the role and working for the organisation.

To make your questions valuable, you need to invest some time before the interview to research the company. Research can come from looking at their website, reading the job description carefully, searching for news items about the company and talking to people who have worked at or dealt with the organisation. Ideally, you should have a few questions written before the interview and decide which one or two to ask once the formal part of the interview has finished. That way, you can make sure you are not asking questions that have already been covered.

Below are some generic examples of questions you could ask at an interview, however, the more specific to the role and the organisation the better, so have a think about ones that suit the role you are being interviewed for.

### WHAT WOULD MY AVERAGE DAY IN THIS ROLE LOOK LIKE?

It is essential that you clearly understand your role and the tasks that you would be expected to undertake prior to accepting a job offer if provided. It is easy to make assumptions and get the wrong impression of what the work would be so it is vital for both sides that there is clarity in what is expected of you.

### WHAT ARE SOME OF THE CHALLENGES YOU THINK I WOULD FACE IN THIS ROLE?

This questions couple be interpreted by the employer in two ways, they could respond to the areas of the role that have shown difficulty in the past, such as managing clients high expectations with limited resources or they may respond with feedback on how they think you personally would fit the role.

## WHAT ARE THE OPPORTUNITIES FOR TRAINING AND CAREER ADVANCEMENT?

This question helps you to understand where the job might lead and what skills you might acquire. It also demonstrates that you are ambitious and thinking ahead.

## WHAT IS THE BIGGEST CHALLENGE FACING THE ORGANISATION TODAY?

This sort of question takes the interview away from the detail and towards strategic issues. It allows to you discuss the bigger picture. It proves that you are interested in more than just the 9 to 5 aspects of the job and can lead to interesting discussions that can further demonstrate your fit for the position.

## WHY DO PEOPLE COME TO WORK FOR YOU RATHER THAN A COMPETITOR? AND WHY DO YOU THINK THEY STAY?

This question will help you understand what core values other employee respect.

## WHAT KINDS OF PEOPLE REALLY THRIVE IN YOUR ORGANISATION?

This question will help identify if the company is a good cultural fit for you.

## WHAT ARE THE POTENTIAL GROWTH AREAS THAT PEOPLE ARE MOST EXCITED ABOUT IN THE COMPANY OVER THE NEXT COUPLE OF YEARS?

This type of question gives you an opportunity to understand where the company's focus and attention will be and discuss how you may contribute to that growth.

### WHAT ARE YOU REALLY SAYING?

Non-verbal language accounts for 55-65% of what people see when they interview you, Considering your body language is critical to winning the job. Common body language mistakes often made in job interviews include:

- Weak handshake
- Invading personal space
- Crossing your arms
- Playing with your hair
- Bad posture
- Lack of eye contact
- Looking disinterested
- Not smiling
- Fidgeting
- Hiding your hands

It is also essential to be mindful of your other actions and to avoid the following pitfalls:

- Don't arrive late — if it is unavoidable, apologise sincerely
- Don't wear jeans, other unsuitable clothing or inappropriate jewellery

- Don't have your mobile phone turned on
- Don't chew gum
- Don't mention other job applications during the interview.

# 16. Final Word

We have come a long way together, you and I, through the pages of this book and we now stand at the launch pad ready for lift-off. What you do from here on and how you utilise the information provided in this book to your advantage is entirely up to you.

As I keep repeating occasionally in my books and my blog, it is not my intention to paint a rosy picture of a great life in Australia. Nor am I beating the doomsday drum and issuing dire warnings of a life of hardships and constant struggle. I aim to provide an unbiased view and factual information to empower you as you commence your new life in Australia. Eventually, it is you who decides what to do with the opportunity that was given to you by the Australian government the day you were issued your visa in good faith.

Remember, it is about the journey and not just the destination. As a friend of mine recently commented, do not get too fixated on chasing your dream job, your dream city, your dream house, whilst life passes you by. Yes, it is paramount to look for stability and get settled as soon as you can once you arrive. But at the same time, it is equally important that you take some time off to enjoy the very aspects of Australia that made you apply for the visa in the first place. Pick up a new skill, go camping, explore the Outback, have a day out at the beach, join a local cycling group, volunteer at the library, travel and experience the beauty and diversity this country has to offer. Live the good life!

In my interaction with migrants of various ethnicities, cultures and economic background during the making of this book, I have identified two distinct groups in terms of attitude and general outlook on life.

**The Go-Getters** – These are people who are excited to start their lives in a new country, who look forward to the challenges that come with it and who have made themselves aware of the ground reality. They have their heads down on the task at hand and yet, at the same time, their chin up, ready to face any challenge. These are the kind of people who take the effort to learn the 'Australian Way', are grateful for the opportunity given to them and eventually are able to achieve the levels of success that they had dreamed of when they left home shores. These people, more often than not, get their 'lucky' break sooner than most other migrants. After all, luck, as it is often said, is what happens when preparation meets opportunity.

**The Whiners** – The people in this category will always find the grass greener on the other side. These are the people who feel they have been short-changed when things do not go their way during the initial period when they first arrive in Australia. They will focus on all negative aspects of the Australian economy – The unemployment rate, the perceived bias towards migrants, the tax structure, the cost of living and even the weather!

Here is what Australia has to offer and why so many people flock here seeking a better lifestyle:

Australia has over 500 national parks and more than 2,700 conservation areas, ranging from wildlife sanctuaries to Aboriginal reserves. There are also seventeen UNESCO World

Heritage sites – more than any other country – including the Great Barrier Reef, Kakadu National Park, Lord Howe Island Group, Tasmanian Wilderness, Fraser Island and the Sydney Opera House. Apart from the well-known fact that Australia is a beautiful country offering a variety of experiences for tourists from around the world, it also has world-class infrastructure, with five of the top 40 cities with the best infrastructure in the world. Melbourne and Adelaide are constantly on the leader board as the most liveable cities in the world. Australia places a lot of emphasis on family life and work life balance. With all these wonderful attributes around Australia, Australians have good reasons to be happy. So much so, Australia was recently ranked as the fourth happiest country in the world, only behind Norway, Denmark and Sweden.

In contrast, Australia, like any other country, also has its own set of challenges. Australia's population continues to grow strongly. The population has risen by an estimated 400,000 people since 2013, increasing the total population of the country to over 23.5 million. Australians are predominately urban-dwelling people. As cities continue to grow and age, there will be significant challenges, including infrastructure and transport planning, for all levels of government.

In addition, Australia's population is ageing. Over the past half-century, there has been a steady increase in the number and proportion of older people in Australia. This will lead to future challenges, including increased costs to governments for health and aged care. Future projected population growth, including new migrants, and changing demographics of an ageing population will also offer challenges.

Most of the leading world economies today are in recession. In Australia, the unemployment rate is at an all-time high and the country is facing a range of ongoing socio-economic challenges. That does not mean that opportunities do not exist. Neither does it imply that Australia does not need migrants anymore. On the contrary, Australia's successful migration policy is one of the factors that is acknowledged as being a contributory factor to its overall positive growth (Some people may have a conflicting opinion on this topic).

Difficult times or fresh new possibilities? Go-Getter or Whiner? What's your outlook going to be as you embark on your own journey in your newly adopted country?

Remember one thing, though. You and I, as migrants and new entrants to this country, are the ones who will shape the future of this nation. Much like single drops of water that make an entire ocean, every person and every migrant become a part of the nations fabric. Our choices and decisions today will have a long-lasting impact on future generations. Let's make sure they are the right ones.

So smarten up that tie, spit-shine your shoes, straighten your hemline, put your best foot forward and go get that dream job.

I wish you all the best with your job hunt and many great Australian adventures!

A Fellow Migrant,
Jason Rebello

# 17. Acknowledgements

I would like to thank all my friends and fellow migrants who helped me with the research that went into making this book. Most of them have preferred to remain anonymous and they derive satisfaction from the fact that the future stream of migrants may benefit from their experiences and feedback.

Thanks to Wanda Hayes, for writing the Foreword for this book. Wanda is presently the National Vice President of the Career Development Association of Australia (CDAA) which has been a major contributor to developments in the profession, and to research, government policy and national and international forums. The Association currently has more than 1,300 members in every state and territory and across all sectors of the profession.

Wanda's experience as a career development practitioner spans all ages and a wide range of settings. From 2000-2016, she 1was a business owner and private consultant, specialising in providing individual career counselling and coaching, She was also an occasional guest presenter on ABC Radio in Brisbane and on the Sunshine Coast during that period, providing information and advice to listeners on career-related issues.

Her Linkedin Profile - Wanda Hayes.

A special mention of Judith Leeson AM, for all the help and insight provided by her throughout the making of this book. There is a Q&A by Judith which is covered in Chapter 14 of this book. Brian Leeson has also provided a most invaluable contribution of a sample resume and cover letter (with explanatory notes) (Sections 15.2 and 15.5)

Judith is one of the first persons I contacted when this book was still just a budding idea in my head. Ever since I first contacted her, she has generously given of her time and expertise and connected me with all the right people. Judith's titles and accolades are far more than can be easily accommodated in one paragraph. She is a Fellow and Life Member of the Career Development Association of Australia, having served five consecutive terms as National President and was the inaugural President of the National peak body (CICA). Judith is also an accredited Myers-Briggs facilitator and has been appointed as a Member of the Order of Australia (AM) for her services to the community, particularly to people seeking support for life-long learning and career development, and was recognised as a "South Australian Great" for her work in the community.

**I would also like to acknowledge the contributors to this book:**

Thanks to Terry O'Reilly for contributing to the entire chapter on - 'The Selection Process' as well as certain other sections. Terry not only helped me with the content of this book but also provided me with a lot of support and advice despite his busy schedule.

Terry is the founder and owner of OBP Australia and has interviewed and advised over 3,000 overseas born professionals in the past 10 years, assisting in their transition to employment in Australia. Through his 25 years of experience as an 'English as an Additional Language' (EAL) teacher and industry liaison, he has developed a deep understanding of the systemic barriers & cross-cultural issues facing newly arrived skilled migrants.

His company, OBP Australia, provides services to overseas born professionals trying to secure their first job in Australia or develop their careers once they've become established

Terry's Contact Details:

OBP Australia

Address: 829A High Street Thornbury VIC Australia

Phone: +61 409 330 727

terry@obpaustralia.com.au

www.obpaustralia.com.au

Big thanks to Samantha Saw for helping me with the chapter on Resume Writing, the Rules for Job Hunting and Interview Preparation. Samantha is an Australian business professional working in Asia. She is the CEO of Successful Resumes Australia and the Founder and Director of Successful Resumes Hong Kong. With a passion and enthusiasm for helping people navigate a journey to success, Samantha has worked across corporate, not-for-profit and government sectors to create better outcomes by improving processes, systems and structures. With expertise in management, finance, business development and the arts, Samantha uses her experience having read thousands of selection criteria and resumes as an employer, to help clients articulate their value proposition.

Samantha specialises in working across the APAC region to support senior managers identify their next opportunity or transition to Board placements.

Her Linkedin Profile – Samantha Saw

Thanks also to James "The Jobs Guru" Innes and his highly motivated team at The Resume Centre. Founded in 1998, the Resume Centre has since written over 150,000 Resumes. Employing over 200 skilled writers and interview coaches helping everyone daily get the job they deserve.

Their Contact Details:

Website: www.resumecentre.com.au

Email: customerservices@resumecentre.com.au

Address: Levels 4, 5 & 12, 95 Pitt Street, Sydney, NSW 2000, Australia

Phone: +61 (02) 5507 9000

Thank you, Pria, for the invaluable insights on the topic on improving employability in Australia. Pria is presently an Indigenous Education Officer at the prestigious Ryan Catholic College in Townsville. She is also the Principal Consultant of STRYD Consulting which provides services like Training, Career Guidance, Employment workshops, Interview preparation and business solutions to corporate, government, not-for-profit, private enterprise and individuals. A migrant herself she has been providing career counselling for the last eight years now.

Pria's Contact Details:

Pria D'Souza, Principal Consultant

STRYD (**S**triving **T**owards **R**eaching **Y**our **D**reams) Consulting

Tel: +61(0)0403 557 972

email: 2priadsouza@gmail.com

Finally, my sincere gratitude to the University of Tasmania's Student Leadership, Career Development and Employment team who gave me access and permission to use their material on writing resumes and cover letters, as well as the topic on addressing Selection Criteria and Interview Skills. I had the good fortune to attend one of their free seminars whilst attending a maritime course in Launceston, Tasmania. Although their main focus is on empowering college graduates and university students, their content is just as relevant and invaluable to new migrant job seekers.

# 18. About the Author

A Sailor by profession, Jason's career at sea spans over two decades. During his last few years before he quit active sailing and migrated to Australia, he was employed as a Captain on board modern container ships for a reputed German company. An avid traveller, blogger, adventure seeker and a marathoner, he thrives on anything remotely related to travel or the great outdoors and it was this passion that provided the impetus for moving to Australia.

Having migrated to Australia in August 2014 with his wife, they went on to break the mould of an ideal migrant by backpacking extensively in Australia for two months. They travelled to some amazing places like the Mossman Gorge, Atherton Tablelands and Whitsundays Islands in North Queensland, the 12 Apostles and Great Ocean Road in Victoria, Blue Mountains and Jenolan Caves in NSW and also visited Sydney, Canberra, Cairns, Brisbane and Melbourne apart from some other charming regional towns. This exposure helped them pick up a little bit of red dust from the continent and a lot of invaluable insight about living in various states, cities and regional cities. For those interested, Jason has shared his travel stories on his travel blog www.theevolvingbackpacker.com

Later on, they established themselves in Brisbane and faced all the challenges a newly arrived migrant would. In due course of time, a job offer came along and the couple had to relocate to Townsville, a regional town in North Queensland where they lived for over two years until Jason's job pulled them back to

Brisbane. Jason speaks from his own personal experiences as well as all the research done during the entire settling-in phase and his interaction with fellow migrants, migration experts and other industry leaders.

His website www.aussie-migrant.com.au provides a platform where he shares information related to settling down in Australia.

Other Books in the series – **Aussie Migrant: Money** (Available on Amazon as Kindle version and also as a PDF download directly on his website).

**Contact Jason:**

**Email –** info@aussie-migrant.com.au, theaussiemigrant@gmail.com

**Twitter -** @migrantninja

**Facebook –** www.facebook.com/AussieMigrantNinja

# 19. Appendix

*NOTE: This appendix is for the readers who have purchased the physical copy of this book. In it you will find all the links which are mentioned in the book and are arranged chapter-wise just as they appear in the book for ease of reference.*

*In case some of the website links do not work (due to updated links or various other reasons) you can get the latest updated links on my web page - www.aussie-migrant.com.au/aussie-migrant-jobs-links/*

## 3. The Basics

www.border.gov.au

**General Skilled Migrant (GSM) Stream**

SkillSelect - https://www.border.gov.au/Busi/Empl/skillselect

Expression Of Interest (EOI). - http://bit.ly/2jLu1D9

**Different Visas for Living and Working In Australia**

DIBP Information on Temporary visa (subclass 457) - http://bit.ly/2jLlNuW

Subclass 457 – A Quick Guide - http://bit.ly/2j7HO59

DIBP info on ENS visa (subclass 186) - https://www.border.gov.au/Trav/Visa-1/186-

DIBP info on RSMS visa (subclass 187) - https://www.border.gov.au/Trav/Visa-1/187-

### 3.1.2 Tested Skilled Migration

Skilled occupation list. - http://bit.ly/2jqZObP

DIBP Information on visa subclass 189 -
https://www.border.gov.au/Trav/Visa-1/189-

Citizenship web page. - https://www.border.gov.au/Trav/Citi

Consolidated skilled occupation list- http://bit.ly/1N7O64E

DIBP Information on visa subclass 190 -
https://www.border.gov.au/Trav/Visa-1/190-

DIBP Information on Skilled - Regional (Provisional) visa (subclass 489), Sponsored - https://www.border.gov.au/Trav/Visa-1/489-

Links for specific states if you're interested in applying for a 489 visa:

VICTORIA - http://bit.ly/2jL93Er

QUEENSLAND - http://bit.ly/1sbp5uc

NEW SOUTH WALES - http://bit.ly/2jKQgta

WESTERN AUSTRALIA - http://bit.ly/2bu0Bnx

NORTHERN TERRITORY - http://bit.ly/1TFqjqD

TASMANIA - http://bit.ly/2iXXP2n

SOUTH AUSTRALIA - http://bit.ly/2jqKxYd

AUSTRALIAN CAPITAL TERRITORY https://goo.gl/sFguh3

### 3.2 Visa Specific Conditions and Restrictions

DIBP Information on Subclass 417 Visa -
https://www.border.gov.au/Trav/Visa-1/417-

DIBP Information on Subclass 462 Visa  - http://bit.ly/1NIjeRd

Get further information on the 457 visa through this guide. -

https://goo.gl/PQTFdm

Net overseas migration (NOM) - https://goo.gl/l7sJNQ

VEVO - https://goo.gl/xHUphV

### 3.3 Averages Wages in Australia

Industry Averages - Weekly Salary for 2016 (Source ABS) - www.abs.gov.au

PAYSCALE - http://www.payscale.com/research/AU/Country=Australia/Salary

### 3.4 Statistical Data

Australian job occupation matrix - https://goo.gl/FMKmJF

Starting-your-career in regional-rural-options  - https://goo.gl/6qVN4x

Occupation Matrix  - https://goo.gl/Er1uSO

Profile.id/Australia - http://profile.id.com.au/australia

### 4. Getting Started

Department of Immigration and Border Protection - http://www.border.gov.au/

Assessing authorities  - https://goo.gl/w6v3sr

National Office of Overseas Skills Recognition (NOOSR)  - https://goo.gl/Dd2Cdf

Skills Assessment by  VETASSESS - https://www.vetassess.com.au/skills-assessment

Following are the statewide websites Links for Overseas Qualifications Unit (OQU)

MAIN WEBSITE - Department of Education and Training / Qualification Recognition - http://bit.ly/2jqDiQi

Western Australia - http://bit.ly/1GBtmql

Australian Capital Territory - http://bit.ly/2jSasv0

Queensland - http://bit.ly/2klrAX0

South Australia - http://bit.ly/2kligXi

Victoria - http://bit.ly/2jqQi8k

Northern Territory - http://bit.ly/2jL50rU

New South Wales - https://www.training.nsw.gov.au/

Tasmania - No website. Email: enquiries@tqa.tas.gov.au

Recognition of Prior Learning (RPL)

AQF(Australian Qualifications Framework) - http://www.aqf.edu.au/

Following are the statewide RPL website Links:

Western Australia - http://bit.ly/dtwd_training_providers

Australian Capital Territory - http://bit.ly/ACT_SKILLS

Queensland - http://bit.ly/qld_Recognition

South Australia - http://bit.ly/2j7okO5

Victoria - http://bit.ly/VIC_Recognition

Northern Territory - http://bit.ly/2jqNMit

New South Wales - http://bit.ly/2jShXlC

Tasmania - http://bit.ly/2klkeXG

Training.gov.au - http://training.gov.au/

Australian Skills Quality Authority / About RTO's - http://bit.ly/1tr69Aq

VET Sector Websites - http://training.gov.au/Link

**4.4 Contacting Prospective Employers**

ExpatForum  - http://www.expatforum.com/

Australia Forum  - http://www.australiaforum.com/

Some of the top job sites:

www.careerone.com.au

www.seek.com.au

www.careerjet.com.au

www.jobs.com.au

www.jobisjob.com.au

www.mycareer.com.au

## 5. Resumes, Cover Letters and Selection Criteria

## 5.2 Preparing a Winning Resume

www.careerone.com.au (click on 'Resume' or 'Career Advice')

www.seek.com.au (click on 'Salary, Advice & Tips')

www.dummies.com (click on Business & Careers then Careers)

## 6. The Selection Process – By Terry O'Reilly, OBP Australia

## 6.8 Negotiating Salary

HAYS Salary Guide - https://www.hays.com.au/salary-guide/

## 7. Australian Job Market – An Introduction

## 7.3 Types of Employment

 Fairwork/employee-entitlements/types-of-employees/casual-part-time-and-full-time  - http://bit.ly/fairwork-employee-types

## 7.3.2 Part Time Jobs

Fairwork.gov.au/employee-entitlements/casual-part-time-and-full-time/part-time-employees - http://bit.ly/fairwork-part-time-employees

## 7.4 Voluntary Jobs

Employment.gov.au/Resources for young job seekers - http://bit.ly/government-resources

Volunteering organisations:

Go Volunteer - https://govolunteer.com.au/

Volunteering Australia - http://www.volunteeringaustralia.org/
Good Company - https://www.goodcompany.com.au/

Pro Bono Volunteer Match - http://www.probonoaustralia.com.au/volunteer

State and territory offering volunteering centres:

Volunteering WA - http://www.volunteeringwa.org.au/

Volunteering ACT - http://www.volunteeract.org.au/

Volunteering SA & NT - http://www.volunteeringsa.org.au/

Volunteering Tasmania - http://www.volunteeringtas.org.au/

Volunteering Victoria - http://volunteeringvictoria.org.au/

Volunteering Queensland - http://www.volunteeringqld.org.au/

The Centre for Volunteering (Volunteering NSW) - http://www.volunteering.com.au/

SEEK, - https://www.volunteer.com.au/

CAREERONE - http://www.careerone.com.au/

Unpaid Work Experience and Volunteer Work - http://bit.ly/employment-unpaid-work

## 7.5 Trades

Services Seeking - https://www.serviceseeking.com.au/

Trades Recognition Australia (TRA)  -
http://www.tradesrecognitionaustralia.gov.au/

TRA/Programs  -
http://www.tradesrecognitionaustralia.gov.au/Programs

TRA offers a number of different programs:

Job Ready Program - http://bit.ly/Jobready

457 Skills Assessment Program - http://bit.ly/Skills-assessment

Offshore Skills Assessment Program  - http://bit.ly/offshore-skills-assessment

Migration Skills Assessment - http://bit.ly/migration-skills-assessment

Migration Points Advice - http://bit.ly/Migration-Points-Advice

Optional Skills Assessment Service -  http://bit.ly/optional-skills-assessment

Trades Recognition Service - http://bit.ly/Trades-Recognition-Service

## 8. Getting Ready for the Workplace

### 8.1 English Speaking Skills

Adult Migrant English Program (AMEP) - http://bit.ly/AMEP-Australia

AMEP webpage. - http://www.education.gov.au/amep

 TAFE – http://bit.ly/TAFE-AMEP

Education.gov.au/AMEP-service-providers  - http://bit.ly/Government-service-providors

SEE ( Skills for Education and Employment) -
https://www.education.gov.au/see-providers

DHS  - https://www.humanservices.gov.au/

jobactive provider.- http://www.employment.gov.au/jobactive

Remote Jobs and Communities Programme. - http://bit.ly/Remote-jobs

## 8.4 Trade Unions

Australian Council of Trade Unions (ACTU)  - http://www.actu.org.au/

Affiliates and Trade and Labour Councils (TLCs) Of The ACTU

TLC's: Trade and Labour Councils in Australia:

Queensland Council of Unions - http://www.qcu.asn.au/

Victorian Trades Hall Council - http://www.vthc.org.au/

Unions NT - http://www.unionsnt.com.au/

Unions ACT - http://www.unionsact.org.au/

Newcastle Trades Hall Council - http://www.newtradeshall.com/

Unions WA - http://www.unionswa.com.au/

SA Unions - http://www.saunions.org.au/

Unions New South Wales - http://www.unionsnsw.org.au/

Unions Tasmania - http://www.unionstas.com.au/

ACTU/about-the-actu/affiliates-and-tlcs – http://bit.ly/ACTU-about

Some other important related links:

Australian Unions  - http://www.australianunions.org.au/

ACTU Worksite  - http://worksite.actu.org.au/

## 8.5 Workplace Health And Safety (WHS)

 Business//workplace-health-and-safety-in-your-state-or-territory - http://bit.ly/Business-whs

## 8.6 Rights as an Employee

Fariwork.gov.au - http://bit.ly/fairwork-protection-from-discrimination

WH&S Laws- SafeWork Australia -
http://www.safeworkaustralia.gov.au/

Fair Work - http://www.fairwork.gov.au/

457Visas Holder - Working Rights. - http://bit.ly/457-work-rights

Fair Work Act 2009 webpage - http://bit.ly/fairwork-act

## 8.8 Work Cards

White Cards In Construction

National Register for the Vocational Education and Training -
http://training.gov.au/

'White Card' training - http://bit.ly/White-card

Blue Cards (For Working with Children in Queensland)

Blue Card-Volunteer - http://bit.ly/blue-card-system

Education provider http://bit.ly/blue-card-education-providor

Blue Card Trainee students - http://bit.ly/2jjQ6dk

Refer to the information below if you are based in another state in Australia:

Victoria Working with Children Check website -
http://www.workingwithchildren.vic.gov.au/

Western Australia Working with Children Check website -
http://bit.ly/2jSnjxe

New South Wales Working with Children Check website -
https://goo.gl/rRgX5I

ACT Working with Vulnerable People website - http://bit.ly/2klsW8s

South Australia Screening and Background Checks website - http://bit.ly/2jqSXyX

NT Working with Children website - http://www.workingwithchildren.nt.gov.au/

Tasmania Working with Children Check website. - http://bit.ly/2kb6bRb

Other Occupations Requiring Work / Accreditation Cards

'Driver Authorisation Card' = http://bit.ly/2kb4rYa

Application forms for driver authorization in

Queensland - http://bit.ly/2kb6nzT

New South Wales - http://www.transport.nsw.gov.au/professional-drivers/licences

Victoria is available here.- http://bit.ly/2klMfdo

Driver accreditation for South Australia is available here. - http://bit.ly/2klz24n

## 8.10 Employee Entitlements

National Employment Standards (NES). - http://bit.ly/2jjRnRS

Employee entitlements page - http://bit.ly/fairwork-protection-from-discrimination

## 8.11 Work Flexibility

Flexible Working Arrangements - http://bit.ly/2jL1pKn

## 8.12 Protection from Adverse Action

Unfair dismissal - https://www.fwc.gov.au/termination-of-employment/unfair-dismissal

**8.13 Protection from Coercion**

Fairwork-Coercion - http://bit.ly/2jVVMLR

**8.14 Resolving Disputes at the Workplace**

Fairwork – Resolving Disputes http://bit.ly/2jqKaNu

Fairwork –Forms - https://www.fwc.gov.au/resources/forms

**9. Your First Job**

**9.1 Employment Contract**

Employment contract  - http://bit.ly/2jjUdpX

Fairwork/Employment Contracts.  - http://bit.ly/2jjUdpX

**9.2 Wages**

National minimum wage in Australia - http://bit.ly/2jjO9hg

 Fair Work Ombudsman.  - https://www.fairwork.gov.au/

**9.3 Superannuation**

Low Income Super Contribution (LISC) - http://bit.ly/2jjYkCz

ASICs - Moneysmart - https://www.moneysmart.gov.au/

**9.4 Taxation**

Tax for Individuals - Moving to Australia  - http://bit.ly/2kbeM6u

MyTax online  http://bit.ly/2kbbWyf

Tax Early lodgment.  - http://bit.ly/2jL6Ad7

 Deductions you can claim.  - http://bit.ly/2klC88P

Individual Income Tax Rates -
https://www.ato.gov.au/rates/individual-income-tax-rates/

**9.6 Leave Entitlements**

Leave entitlements - https://www.fairwork.gov.au/leave

Annual leave - http://bit.ly/2j7G8Zb

Parental leave - https://www.fairwork.gov.au/leave/maternity-and-parental-leave

Long service leave - https://www.fairwork.gov.au/leave/long-service-leave

WorkSafe ACT - http://www.worksafe.act.gov.au/

Commerce WA - http://www.commerce.wa.gov.au/labour-relations

NT Government - https://ocpe.nt.gov.au/

SafeWork SA - http://bit.ly/SA-leave

Business Victoria - http://bit.ly/2kbbG2j

NSW Industrial Relations - http://www.industrialrelations.nsw.gov.au/

Queensland Industrial Relations - http://bit.ly/2kbbMqw

WorkSafe Tasmania - http://bit.ly/2jLaqmP

Fairwork - Fact sheet - http://bit.ly/2iYcnyP

Sick and carer's leave - https://www.fairwork.gov.au/leave/sick-and-carers-leave

Fairwork – Sick and Carers Paid Leave - http://bit.ly/2jqWOvT

Fairwork – Sick and Carers Unpaid Leave - http://bit.ly/2jjYp95

Other leaves

Public holidays - https://www.fairwork.gov.au/leave/public-holidays

Compassionate and bereavement leave - http://bit.ly/2jL5MoG

Community service leave -

https://www.fairwork.gov.au/leave/community-service-leave

Worker's compensation leave - https://www.fairwork.gov.au/leave/workers-compensation

Fairwork - Help web page  - http://bit.ly/2j7GLSx

## 9.7 Salary Slip + PAYG Summary

PAYG summary - http://bit.ly/2jjVPAd

ATO – PAYG Summary. - http://bit.ly/2klloT7

## Salary Slip Templates

www.fairwork.gov.au

Pay-Slip - https://www.fairwork.gov.au/pay/pay-slips-and-record-keeping/pay-slips

Creative Commons Australia website - http://bit.ly/2jqIsfa

## 10. Job Seeker Support

## 10.1 Career Advice and Counselling

Australian Job Search - https://jobsearch.gov.au/

Community Development Programmes  - http://bit.ly/2kb8Z0F

## 10.2 Support for Job Seekers / Unemployed

Centrelink - https://www.humanservices.gov.au/customer/dhs/centrelink

DHS – Human Services - http://bit.ly/2iY7WEa

DHS – Sickness Allowance - http://bit.ly/2j7G4ZD

Human services – Youth Allowances - http://bit.ly/2jjU6dQ

Payments to help you Study – Austudy - https://www.humanservices.gov.au/customer/services/centrelink/aus

tudy

## 10.3 State Government Support

Western Australia - http://bit.ly/2iYbpCX

Victoria - http://bit.ly/2jqYmpI

Queensland - https://training.qld.gov.au/

Tasmania - http://www.skills.tas.gov.au/funding

Northern Territory - http://bit.ly/2klhhX8

South Australia - http://bit.ly/2jjV3TK

Job Services Australia (JSA)

Australian Job Search - http://bit.ly/2jr7L0n

Job Services-Australia  - http://bit.ly/2jqSQ6m

## 10.4 Local Council Support

QLD councils - http://www.dilgp.qld.gov.au/local-government-directory/

NSW councils - http://www.dilgp.qld.gov.au/local-government-directory/

WA councils   https://mycouncil.wa.gov.au/

SA councils - http://www.lga.sa.gov.au/councils

NT councils  - http://bit.ly/2jLeVh2

TAS councils - http://bit.ly/2klD2ll

ACT councils - http://bit.ly/2jLcsD7

VIC councils  - http://bit.ly/2jVOlo6

## 10.5 Support for Families

### 10.5.1 Family Tax Benefit

FTB Part A  http://bit.ly/2kbaImM

Newborn Upfront Payment and Newborn Supplement - http://bit.ly/2jLbEOX

Immunising your children - http://bit.ly/2klJOYl

 Income test for FTB Part A - http://bit.ly/2jSAVZg

Income test for FTB Part B - http://bit.ly/2klzTCa

Learn more about taxable income - http://bit.ly/2jL05ah

Living in Australia  - http://bit.ly/2jVTUTm

Temporary Protection visa - http://bit.ly/2jLhy2B

Partner Provisional Visa - http://bit.ly/2j7HeEp

Human Services – Grandparent Carer - http://bit.ly/2iYa92x

### 10.5.2 Child Care

Mychild   - http://www.mychild.gov.au/

Childcare rebates Work, Training, Study test - http://bit.ly/2klusai

Child Care Rebate - http://bit.ly/2jLlK2a

Human Services – Child Care Benefits - http://bit.ly/2jSC4A2

### 10.5.3 Parental Payments

Income & Asset Test  - http://bit.ly/2jjWhhw

Australian resident - http://bit.ly/2kbq5vd

 Social security agreement - http://bit.ly/2kbgmFh

Human Services – Waiting Periods  - http://bit.ly/2kb4Vxk

### 10.5.4 Single Income Family Supplement

Centrelink Rate estimator - http://bit.ly/2jVTRaf

### 10.5.5 Energy Supplement

Human Services – Energy Supplement - http://bit.ly/2jqYUvD

Human Services – Essential Medical Equipment  - http://bit.ly/2jqQkNI

### 10.5.6 Low Income Supplement

Low-Income Supplement - http://bit.ly/2j7MEzd

Low-Income Family Supplement - http://bit.ly/2jSAVZg

### 10.5.7 Family Assistance Payments

Balancing your family assistance payments - http://bit.ly/2jSAVZg

Service Finder - https://www.humanservices.gov.au/customer/service-finder

Human Services – Payment Finder  - http://bit.ly/2kbgqF9

### 11. Website Links and Resources

### 11.1 Job Portals

Seek  - http://www.seek.com.au/

Career One   - http://www.careerone.com.au/

Indeed - http://www.indeed.com.au/

Jobjobsjobs  - http://www.jobsjobsjobs.com.au/

Adzuna - https://www.adzuna.com.au/

LinkMe  - http://www.linkme.com.au/

LiveHire - http://www.livehire.me/

Jora - https://au.jora.com/

Glassdoor - http://www.glassdoor.com.au/Job/jobs.htm

Apply Direct  - http://www.applydirect.com.au/

Mitula - http://jobs.mitula.com.au/

Careerjet  - http://www.careerjet.com.au/

Aussie Employment - http://www.aussieemployment.com.au/

Australia.recruit.net  - http://australia.recruit.net/

Simplyhired - http://www.simplyhired.com.au/

Oneshift  - https://oneshift.com.au/

Working in Australia  - http://www.workingin-australia.com/

Jobserve  - http://www.jobserve.com/

Casual Staffing - http://www.casuals.com.au/

Neuvoo  - http://au.neuvoo.com/

Any Work Any Where  - http://www.anyworkanywhere.com/

SpotJobs - https://www.spotjobs.com/

**11.2 Recruitment Agencies**

RCSA - http://bit.ly/2kloBll

Australianrecruiting - http://www.australianrecruiting.com/

Ignite - http://www.igniteservices.com/

Rpb Consulting - http://www.rpbconsulting.com.au/

Chandlermacleod - https://www.chandlermacleod.com/

Greythorn (IT Recruitment) - https://www.greythorn.com.au/

Clicks (IT Recruitment) - http://clicks.com.au/

Michael Page - http://www.michaelpage.com.au/

Morgan Consulting - http://www.morganconsulting.com.au/

Hays - https://www.hays.com.au/

Hudson - http://au.hudson.com/

Randstad- https://www.randstad.com.au/

Nspire Recruitment - http://nspirerecruitment.com.au/

Six Degrees Executive - http://www.sixdegreesexecutive.com.au/

SHK (For Senior Management Roles) - https://www.shk.com.au/

Carmichael Fisher (For Senior Management Roles) - http://www.carmichaelfisher.com/

Devlin Alliance - http://www.devlinalliance.com/

Charterhouse - http://www.charterhouse.com.au/

Robert Half -  https://www.roberthalf.com.au/

Xpand (Digital, Technology, Media, Sales and Marketing) - http://www.xpand.com.au/

Command Recruitment - https://www.command.com.au/

## 11.3 Industry Specific Job sites

Jobs in Mining  - http://www.entrylevelminingjob.com.au/

Environmental Jobs  - http://environmentaljobs.com.au/jobs

Salon Staff - http://www.salonstaff.com.au/

Bluecollar - http://bluecollar.com.au/

Health Job Search - http://www.healthjobsearch.com.au/

Health Care, Nursing - http://bit.ly/working_in_OZ_nursing

Care Careers - https://www.carecareers.com.au/job/search

Jobnet - http://www.jobnet.com.au/

Webjobz - http://www.webjobz.com.au/

Jobswiregurus- http://jobswiregurus.com.au/

Mining Australia - http://www.australia-mining.com/

## 11.4 Career Guidance, Coaching, Psychometric Testing & Career Expos

Career Guidance and Coaching

The Career Development Association of Australia (CDAA) - https://www.cdaa.org.au/

## Psychometric, Personality and Aptitude Tests

Psychometric Institute (Offers free tests) - https://www.psychometricinstitute.com.au/

Practice Psychometric Tests Online - http://bit.ly/2klpaM9

Hudson - Psychometric Testing Examples - http://bit.ly/2jVTFYo

JobTestPrep - https://www.jobtestprep.com/

## 11.5 Government Support and Job Websites

My Skills - http://www.myskills.gov.au/

Job Outlook - http://www.joboutlook.gov.au/

Australian Job Search - http://www.jobsearch.gov.au/

Job Search - http://jobsearch.gov.au/jobs/default.aspx

Myfuture.edu.au - http://www.myfuture.edu.au/

National Centre for Vocational Education Research - http://www.ncver.edu.au/

# AUSSIE MIGRANT: JOBS

Jobactive - https://jobactive.gov.au/

Help for Job Seekers   - http://www.employment.gov.au/jobactive-help-job-seekers

 Labour Market Information Portal  - http://lmip.gov.au/

Training.gov.au  - http://training.gov.au/

Jobs and Workplace – States and Territories  http://bit.ly/2kblcT2

State Government advice and information to help local job seekers consider their vocational education and training options:

ACT Skilled Capital - http://www.skills.act.gov.au/

NSW Smart and Skilled - http://www.smartandskilled.nsw.gov.au/

Victorian Skills Gateway -
http://www.education.vic.gov.au/victorianskillsgateway

Queensland Skills Gateway -
http://www.skillsgateway.training.qld.gov.au/

SA Work Ready  - http://www.skills.sa.gov.au/

Tasmania Skills Tasmania - http://www.skills.tas.gov.au/

WA Future Skills WA - http://www.futureskillswa.wa.gov.au/

VET NT - http://www.vet.nt.gov.au/

Australian Jobs   - https://australianjobs.employment.gov.au/

Australian Public Service (APS) Jobs  - https://www.apsjobs.gov.au/

State and Territory APS government jobs  - http://bit.ly/2kba2xq

LG Assist  - http://www.lgassist.com.au/

National, State and Territory Governments Job Websites  -
http://bit.ly/2iYn0Su

Harvest Trail  - https://jobsearch.gov.au/harvest

Harvest jobs - https://jobsearch.gov.au/harvest/towns-and-crops

## 11.6 State and Territory Links

### Australian Capital Territory

### Job Sites

Careers with ACT Government –  - http://www.jobs.act.gov.au/

ACT –Looking for Jobs: Government Website
http://www.jobs.act.gov.au/find-a-job

### Information

ACT- Looking for Jobs  - http://www.jobs.act.gov.au/find-a-job

Moving to ACT: Government Information Portal  -
http://www.canberrayourfuture.com.au/

ACT - Government Information Portal for Employment  - -
http://bit.ly/2klsC9u

### New South Wales

### Job Sites

Careers with NSW Government  - http://iworkfor.nsw.gov.au/

### Information

Living and Working in NSW - http://www.industry.nsw.gov.au/live-and-work-in-nsw

Moving to NSW: Government Information Portal  -
https://www.nsw.gov.au/

Multicultural NSW – Information for New Arrivals - http://bit.ly/2jLljVx

### Northern Territory

## Job Sites

Careers with NT Government  - http://bit.ly/2jLfhUJ

NT – Looking for Jobs: Government Website  - http://bit.ly/2jqYWnp

## Information

NT – Looking for Jobs - http://bit.ly/2jVVAfz

Living and working in NT - https://nt.gov.au/employ/for-employees-in-nt

Moving to NT: Government Information Portal - http://bit.ly/2jLlznt

## Queensland

## Job Sites

Careers with Queensland Government  - https://smartjobs.qld.gov.au/

Queensland- Looking for Jobs: Government Website - http://bit.ly/2klgC7V

## Information

Queensland – Looking for Jobs  - https://www.qld.gov.au/jobs/

Moving to Queensland: Government Information Portal - http://bit.ly/2jrOZrG

## South Australia

Job Sites

Careers with South Australian Government https://apply.sa.gov.au/Jobs/Pages/

South Australia – Choosing Your Career – Search Careers & Industries - http://bit.ly/2klDy2P

## Information

South Australia – Support for Migrant Job Seekers -
http://bit.ly/2jVXGfu

Moving to South Australia: Government Information Portal -
https://www.sa.gov.au/

**Tasmania**

**Job Sites**

Careers with Tasmanian Government –  - http://www.jobs.tas.gov.au/

Tasmania – Looking for Jobs: Government Website -
http://bit.ly/2klqgaJ

**Information**

Tasmania – Resources for Job Seekers - http://bit.ly/2jSuCoI

Moving to Tasmania: Government Information Portal -
https://www.tas.gov.au/

**Victoria**

**Job Sites**

Careers with the Victorian Government - http://careers.vic.gov.au/

Victoria – Looking for Jobs: Government Website -
http://bit.ly/2j7JefW

**Information**

Victoria and Melbourne – Looking for Jobs - http://bit.ly/2jLdkaW

Moving to Victoria - Government Information Portal -
http://bit.ly/2jr5qTl

**Western Australia**

**Job Sites**

Careers with WA Government - https://jobs.wa.gov.au/

Western Australia – Looking for Jobs - http://bit.ly/2kbhA3x

**Information**

WA – Looking for Jobs - http://bit.ly/2jr4HRQ

Moving To Western Australia - https://www.wa.gov.au/

Office of Multicultural Interests - http://www.omi.wa.gov.au/

**11.7 General Research and Handy Information Websites**

Payscale  - http://www.payscale.com/index/AU/Industry

DSS – Settling in Australia Guide  - http://bit.ly/2kbemNi

Centrelink  - https://www.humanservices.gov.au/customer/dhs/centrelink

Australian Tax Office - http://www.ato.gov.au/

Border.gov.au - http://www.border.gov.au/

Australian Government: Career Information and Services - http://bit.ly/2jqWNYK

Employment Research and Statistic - http://bit.ly/2klMpSp

Fairwork Ombudsman - https://www.fairwork.gov.au/

Best Practice Guide  - http://bit.ly/2klzCiy

Employment.gov.au  - https://www.employment.gov.au/

Australia.gov.au - http://bit.ly/2iYn0Su

Jobs and Workplace – State and Territories - http://bit.ly/2kblcT2

 Finder.com.au  - https://www.finder.com.au/

SBS settlement guide  - http://www.sbs.com.au/radio/settlement-guide

Australian Demographics - http://www.about-australia.com/australia-demographics/

Carsales - http://www.carsales.com.au/

Choice - http://www.choice.com.au/

Dial an Angel - http://www.dialanangel.com/

My School - http://www.myschool.edu.au/

Realestate - https://www.realestate.com.au/

## Resumes & Interviews

How to Write a Resume - http://how-to-write-a-resume.org/

Tribuslingua/Skilled-migrants that need Australian CV Resume - http://bit.ly/2kInFhc

Expat Arrivals - http://www.expatarrivals.com/

40 Interview questions you should be prepared to ask answer - http://bit.ly/2jk35Me

Resumes and Cover Letters – UTAS Fact Sheets - http://bit.ly/2iYpccu

Interview Question Tips –Hays - http://bit.ly/2jk18PW

## Local Newspapers

Online Newspapers - http://bit.ly/2iYp7Wc
The Australian - http://www.theaustralian.com.au/careers

## Australian Capital Territory

Australian Capital Territory Newspapers – A Comprehensive List - http://www.newspapers.com.au/ACT/

Canberra Times - http://www.canberratimes.com.au/   Wednesday and Saturday editions

The Advocate - http://www.theadvocate.com.au/classifieds/

# AUSSIE MIGRANT: JOBS

The Examiner - http://www.examiner.com.au/jobs/

## New South Wales

New South Wales Newspapers – A Comprehensive List - http://www.newspapers.com.au/NSW/

Daily Telegraph - http://www.dailytelegraph.com.au/classifieds

Herald (New Castle)- http://www.theherald.com.au/jobs/

## Northern Territory

NT Newspapers: Comprehensive List - http://www.newspapers.com.au/NT/

NT News - http://www.ntnews.com.au/

Katherine Times - http://www.katherinetimes.com.au/

## Queensland

Queensland Newspapers: Comprehensive List - http://www.newspapers.com.au/QLD/

Brisbane Times - http://www.brisbanetimes.com.au/

## South Australia

South Australia Newspapers – A Comprehensive List - http://www.newspapers.com.au/SA/

The Advertiser - http://www.adelaidenow.com.au/

## Tasmania

Tasmania Newspapers: A Comprehensive List - http://www.newspapers.com.au/TAS/

The Mercury (Southern Tasmania) - http://www.themercury.com.au/

The Examiner (northern Tasmania) - http://www.examiner.com.au/

The Advocate (north-western Tasmania) - http://www.theadvocate.com.au/

## Victoria

Victoria Newspapers: Comprehensive List - http://www.newspapers.com.au/VIC/

Herald Sun - http://www.heraldsun.com.au/
The Age - http://www.theage.com.au/

The Weekly Times - http://www.weeklytimesnow.com.au/  - Regional Jobs in Victoria

## Western Australia

WA Newspapers: Comprehensive List - http://www.newspapers.com.au/WA/
The West Classifieds - https://www.thewestclassifieds.com.au/

The Courier - http://www.thecourier.com.au/

## 12. Additional Training

### 12.1 Upgrading Skills

Seek Learning-TAFE. - https://www.seeklearning.com.au/study-types/tafe

TAFE Institutes in Australia

TAFE Institute List  http://bit.ly/2klBfNk

TAFE institutes:

NSW: TAFE NSW - http://bit.ly/2j7GPlC

ACT:  - http://bit.ly/2jqXpgU

TAS: TAFE Tasmania and Tasmanian Academy - http://bit.ly/2jr242t

QLD: TAFE Queensland - http://bit.ly/2jSo4X4

VIC: Victorian Skills Gateway - http://bit.ly/2klshUj

NT: CDU VET - http://bit.ly/2klIDZa

WA: Training WA - http://bit.ly/2jk0tOi

SA: TAFE SA - http://bit.ly/2klx1ta

TafeCourses.com.au  - https://www.tafecourses.com.au/

Training.com.au  - https://www.training.com.au/

More information about TAFE institutes in Australia -
http://bit.ly/2jLj5p1

My Skills - https://www.myskills.gov.au/

National Centre for Vocational Education Research (NCVER) -
http://www.ncver.edu.au/

## 12.2 Additional Courses for Developing Soft Skills

Toastmasters International - http://www.toastmasters.org.au/

## 12.3 Apprenticeship

Australian Apprenticeship - http://bit.ly/2iYq3do

List of websites for apprenticeship training programs:

AMA Apprenticeship & Traineeship Services WA -
http://www.amaats.com.au/jobs/

Year 13 - https://year13.com.au/category/apprenticeships/

Group Training Australia  - http://www.grouptraining.com.au/

MAS Jobs National. - http://www.masjobs.com.au/

ApprenticeshipCentral - http://www.apprenticeshipcentral.com.au/

MRAEL QLD - http://bit.ly/2klvjIp

Skillsroad jobs board - http://www.skillsroad.com.au/job-seekers/jobs-board

MEGT Apprenticeship jobs - http://www.megt.com.au/jobs/

Skill 360 Far North QLD  https://www.skill360.com.au/jobs/

Trade apprentices QLD   - http://www.tradeapprentices.com.au/

Apprenticeships in minerals & energy sectors - https://nationalapprenticeships.com.au/

Apprentice Match  - http://www.apprenticematch.com.au/jobs/

Need an Apprentice (NSW & VIC)  - http://needanapprentice.com.au/

Steps to becoming an Apprentice - http://bit.ly/2j7FXNJ

**12.4 Additional Australian Government Initiatives**

Training.gov.au - http://training.gov.au/Link

Australian Skills Quality Authority  - http://bit.ly/2jW3oOB

Australian Qualifications Framework  - http://www.aqf.edu.au/aqf/about/what-is-the-aqf/

**13. Alternate Professions**

**Taxi Driver**

Taxi Driver - Average salary - http://bit.ly/Taxi_Driver_Average_Salary

For licensing visit:

Western Australia - http://bit.ly/2klNSbn

New South Wales - http://bit.ly/2j7NcVU

South Australia - http://bit.ly/2jk3bDD

Queensland - http://bit.ly/2kbkmFQ

Victoria - http://taxi.vic.gov.au/drivers

Tasmania  - http://bit.ly/2kbiddj

Northern Territory  - https://nt.gov.au/driving/industry/driving-a-taxi-or-CPV

Australian Capital Territory  - http://bit.ly/2jk42UK

**Photographer**

Seek Learning – Photographer - http://bit.ly/2jqU6q3

**Farming**

How to get farm jobs  - http://www.jobaroo.com/farming-jobs-in-Australia

Farmer - Average pay - http://bit.ly/2kbd3Ow

For Jobs visit:

Rural enterprise  - http://www.ruralenterprises.com.au/

Queensland Farmers Enterprise - http://www.qff.org.au/projects/rural-jobs-skills-alliance/

Seek – Farm Jobs - https://www.seek.com.au/jobs-in-farming-animals-conservation/farm-labour

Jobsearch – Harvest - https://jobsearch.gov.au/harvest

**Private Tutor**

How to become a tutor - https://accreditedtutor.org/how-to-become-a-tutor/

 Australian Tutoring Association  - https://ata.edu.au/

Landscape Gardener -http://bit.ly/2jLmPHo

**Retail Jobs**

Seek – Jobs in Retail Industry - http://bit.ly/Seek_Retail_Jobs

Spotjobs - https://www.spotjobs.com/

**Franchising**

Franchising - http://www.franchise.org.au/what-is-franchising-.html

Startupsmart.com.au- Franchise advice - http://bit.ly/2klLpxB

**Online Jobs**

UBER/Australia  - http://love.uber.com/australia/

Airtasker - https://www.airtasker.com/